RIVER GANSEYS

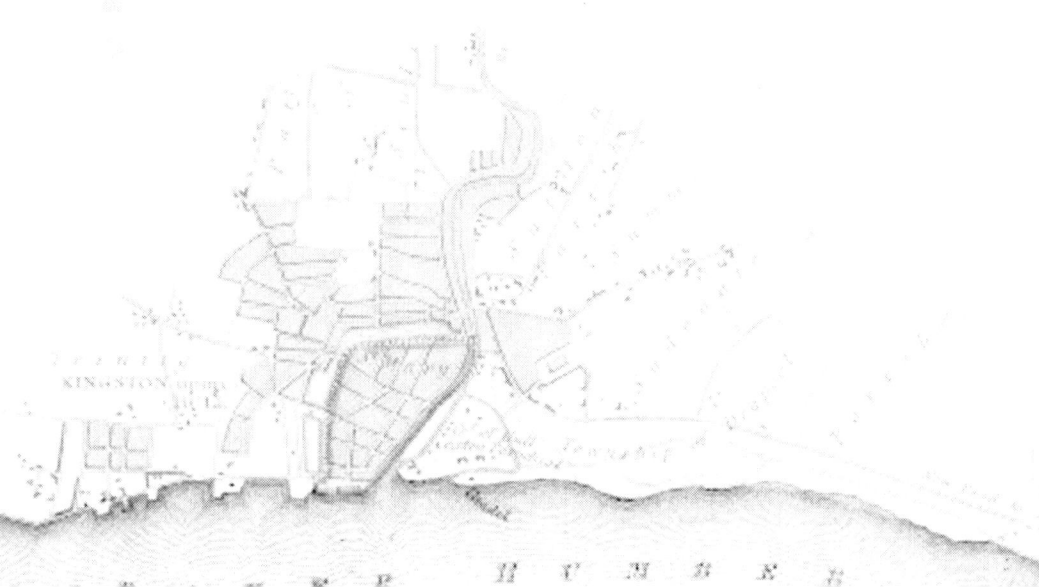

RIVER GANSEYS

*Strikin' t'loop, Swaving, and
Other Yorkshire Knitting Curiosities
Revived from the Archives*

Penelope Lister Hemingway
The Knitting Genealogist

COOPERATIVE PRESS
Cleveland, Ohio

Library of Congress Control Number: 2011921220
ISBN 13: 978-1-937513-40-5
First Edition
Published by Cooperative Press
www.cooperativepress.com

Text and patterns© 2015, Penelope Lister Hemingway
Pattern photography © 2015, Nick Murway
Additional photography © 2015, Shannon Okey
Models: Derek Grubaugh, Leslie McCombs Grubaugh, Jaala Spiro, Ben Szporluk
All rights reserved.
Charts made with Knit Visualizer (knitfoundry.com).

Every effort has been made to ensure that all the information in this book is accurate at the time of publication. Cooperative Press neither endorses nor guarantees the content of external links referenced in this book. All business names, trademarks and product names used within the text are the property of their respective owners. If you have questions or comments about this book, or need information about licensing, custom editions, special sales, or academic/corporate purchases, please contact Cooperative Press: info@cooperativepress.com or 13000 Athens Ave C288, Lakewood, OH 44107 USA

No part of this book may be reproduced in any form, except brief excerpts for the purpose of review, without prior written permission of the publisher. Thank you for respecting our copyright.

COOPERATIVE PRESS

Senior Editor: Shannon Okey
Art Director / Assistant Editor: Elizabeth Green Musselman
Technical Editor: Andi Smith
Copy Editor: Rebecca Campbell

For my boys
David, Will, Nathaniel, Alex, Tommy, and Alfi

Herring Girls at Blyth, 9th July, 1910. Image courtesy of Dr Alec Gill, MBE.

Contents

FOREWORD 9
The particulars of a childhood spent on the River Ouse, among other tales.

INTRODUCTION: YORKSHIRE KNITTING HISTORY 15
Ms. Hemingway begs to inform her Friends, concerning particulars of intrepid ladies; also some remarks concerning the lifting of the Parish Chest lid.

GANSEY ORIGINS & MYTHS 25
In which we introduce to you TARDIS-like peregrinations and picaresque adventures through time and place. The Author begs to introduce to you exploding Sacred Cows; smouldering victims, CSI York, and the wreck of The General Carleton…

KNITTING IN SCHOOLS, PRISONS, & HOMES 51
In which we encounter nine "miserable girls" knitting upon the town, deranged teachers, and knitting as hard labour.

INLAND WATERWAYS GANSEYS 73
Tales of horse marines, gunslingers, gamblers, and Blue Coat boys.

MOTIFS: SUPERSTITION, FOLKLORE, & INLAND GANSEYS 89
In which we whistle up the wind, visit the Stalberg Ghost and Suicide Sid, and learn why one must never wear the Forbidden Colour.

PIONEER YORKSHIRE KNITTERS IN THE NEW WORLD 99
In which we learn it may not be prudent to leave one's belongings in sea chests by Lake Erie.

GANSEY KNITTING 101 113
Early and correct information and skills to complete a knitted gansey.

HAND SPINNING FOR TRADITIONAL KNITTING 129
In which the reader may learn to spin a satisfactory, lustrous and strong gansey yarn.

GANSEY PATTERNS 149
Seven modern gansey patterns for the whole family, inspired by traditional techniques – plus alphabets to personalize your garment.

ABBREVIATIONS, BIBLIOGRAPHY, ABOUT THE AUTHOR 215

Foreword

The particulars of a childhood spent on the River Ouse, among other tales.

"From Hull and Halifax and Hell, the good Lord deliver me."
—Frederic William Moorman, *Dalesman's Litany*

ONE WINTER'S DAY IN THE LATE 1960S, SNOW THICK IN THE AIR and on the ground, I walked across Leeds Bridge, the famous bridge across the River Aire, with my parents. I was nine years old. Without warning, my dad let go of my hand and crossed the road to the other side where he stood talking with a man for some time, both men dark shapes against the snow. I couldn't even see the man's face, though I was certain I'd never seen him before. I asked my mom who the man was.

"That's your grandfather. Dad's dad," she said.

I was pole-axed. No one had ever mentioned a living grandparent, and I knew my mother's parents were buried in the churchyard a few yards from our house. There was another grave in Leeds that my dad took us to visit sometimes. I'd grown up thinking I didn't have one of those mythical beings – a grandparent. Some of my friends had grandparents, and to me they were always fascinating, exotic creatures like unicorns or zebras. I'd been sure I never had one. But there he was. My grandfather.

Dad didn't introduce us to him that day but soon after took us to his house in Leeds. The chance meeting on Leeds Bridge mended their long-fractured relationship. I found my grandad, Billie, intriguing. He was seventy years old but wiry and strong as a man in his twenties and immensely charismatic. He'd been a sergeant in the West Yorkshire Regiment in both World Wars. He'd run away from home in Holbeck, Leeds, to be a soldier at the age of fifteen. His first action was the notorious first Day of the Somme.

My grandfather's house was fascinating. Billie could play the violin, viola, and piano. Dad told me Billie could hear a movement of a piano concerto just once on the radio and walk to the piano, sit down, and play it note for note perfectly from

FACING PAGE: RIVER OUSE, ACASTER SELBY. CREDIT: DAVID HUNT.

memory. He had a cuckoo clock. I'd never seen one before. And apparently, he also had a boat.

He spent half the year living and shark fishing in Western Ireland. This hinted at my grandad's glamour and mystery. The rest of the time he spent in Yorkshire, either rattling around his large, empty house in Leeds or on his boat, *Solaria*. She was moored on the River Ouse, strangely only a dozen or so miles from our house. We'd never known she was there.

After that first Friday evening visit, we spent most weekends on the river on *Solaria*. I grew to love the river. My brother would fish while I wandered along the riverbank or played in the garden of a derelict eighteenth-century pub near our mooring. Billie's boat was moored next to fancy modern ocean-going vessels, all white and chrome, and also ancient canal boats used as houseboats. One neighbouring boat was a narrow former navy vessel, still painted grey. My other grandad had been a recluse, I was told, but this one was immensely popular and sociable. Everyone would pop in and chat with him or wave at him as they went past. In the 1960s, the Ouse was full of small yachts and dinghies. Now they are all gone. It was colourful as well as beautiful – a pastoral idyll. Occasionally, Billie would take us all upriver to York where we'd pass under York Bridge. I'd always remember that day in the snow on Leeds Bridge when we first saw dad talking to the man I didn't know at the time was my grandfather.

Grandad often spoke with regret of a boat he nearly bought, *Three Brothers*, then moored in Bridlington harbour. He'd wanted a boat to keep on the Ouse that was also seaworthy, and only *Solaria* and *Three Brothers* had fit the bill. Fast forward forty years and *Solaria* is long gone, but *Three Brothers* remains the only sailing coble in Bridlington harbour. It's one of the town's major tourist attractions as the oldest surviving boat in the harbour, built in 1912. I often think with regret of the coble that might have been mine.

My grandfather only lived another eighteen months or so after we met him, but after that day on Leeds Bridge, all our holidays and weekends were spent on the river Ouse. I grew up with a love for the river. One night, while my grandfather slept on *Solaria*, which was an Edwardian built wooden vessel, a modern steel-hulled boat crashed into her side and she sank in her moorings. Grandad got out in one piece and *Solaria* was shipped to the local boatyard. When he was working on her, grandad fell from a ladder and was sent to hospital. That's when the doctors found he had cancer. My parents brought him home after he discharged himself, refusing to die in a hospital bed.

While grandad was ill and *Solaria* still only half-fixed in the boatyard, my mom started knitting us navy blue guernseys that we could wear on the boat when things got better. In hindsight, the knitting was probably done more as a distraction to herself. She started with mine. Grandad died in July of 1971, and the guernsey must have been put aside in the flurry of funeral arrangements and clearing the Leeds house. Only four months later, my mom died suddenly and unexpectedly in the night. Dad stuffed her half-finished knitting into a laundry bin that had been

THE HOUSE IN LEEDS MY DALES-BORN GREAT GRANDAD HAD BUILT, PHOTO FROM AROUND 1938. OUTSIDE, DAD AND DOG.

grandad's, and that was it. Not long after, my aunties came around when dad was at work, and, thinking they were doing him a kindness, disposed of all mom's possessions by piling them into a big heap and burning them. Stuffed in the old laundry basket, the guernsey survived.

Months later, I retrieved the half-finished guernsey. My mom had taught me to knit when I was five, but I was a tomboy and never really had the patience for it. Now I wanted to finish something she'd started with such love, but when I picked it up, it started unravelling. Thinking I was somehow making sense of it if I unravelled a little more. I kept going until there was nothing left. I'd forgotten how to cast on, and with no mom to show me, that was it. Dad probably found the unravelled knitting and threw it away, knowing it would never be completed.

Something drew me back to ganseys and knitting much later when I was in my twenties. I think a part of me longed for that navy blue, half-finished gansey that was lost forever. As I couldn't pick up my mom's long-gone stitches, I learned all over again how to make my own. Only I realized, from other people's comments, that I knitted strangely. I knitted how I remembered being taught, as it had come back to me, like riding a bike. Just as I managed to re-access and retrieve my knowledge of how to knit and resurrected first one navy blue gansey then many different ones, I also wanted to resurrect the lost knowledge for others to use.

The *Daleman's Litany* tells of the experience of many nineteenth-century Dalesfolk. They had to leave the land and find jobs in the industrial cities. Most of Yorkshire's industry was textile-related. There was an even older, and well less-documented, branch of the textile industry – hand-knitting. Hand-knitting retreated to the

Dales, even as the heavy industry spread over the West Riding. Dales knitters were by no means the only Northern hand-knitters, but they are the best documented. So I will turn first to them.

Like many Leeds folk, my grandad Billie had Dales ancestors. His grandfather, whose name he bore, William Stephenson, was from Barnoldswick in the Dales. His family before him were Ravenstonedale sheep farmers. Whenever I think of the *Dalesman's Litany*, I think of my ancestor, William Stephenson. Compelled to leave the Dales for industrial Holbeck, then Shipley, his story was the story of many Yorkshirefolk of the nineteenth century. The story was nearly lost to us but for the researches of two indefatigable Yorkshire women, the writers of *The Old Hand-Knitters of the Dales*, Marie Hartley and Joan Ingilby. These ladies worked hard to preserve the culture of the Yorkshire Dales that people like my great-grandad lost when they moved to the cities in search of work.

Foreword—13

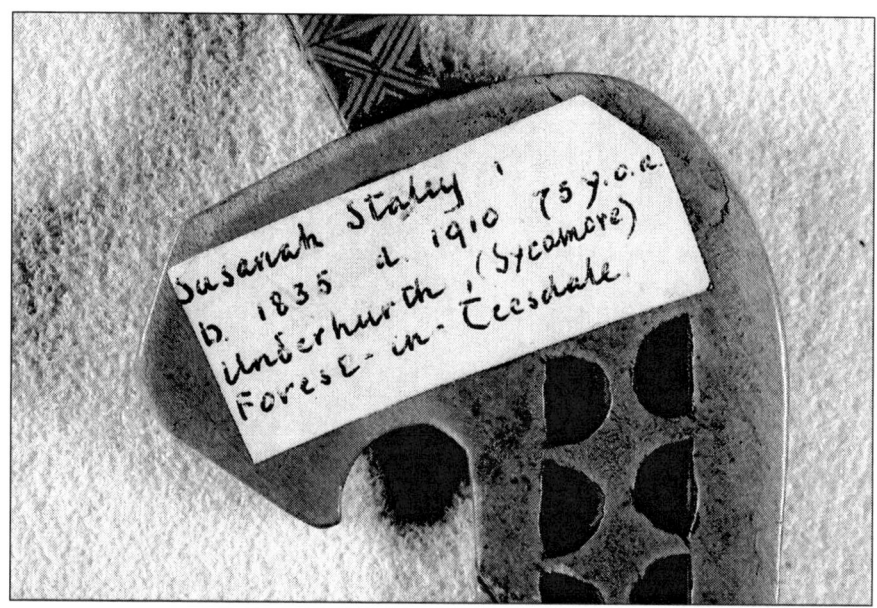

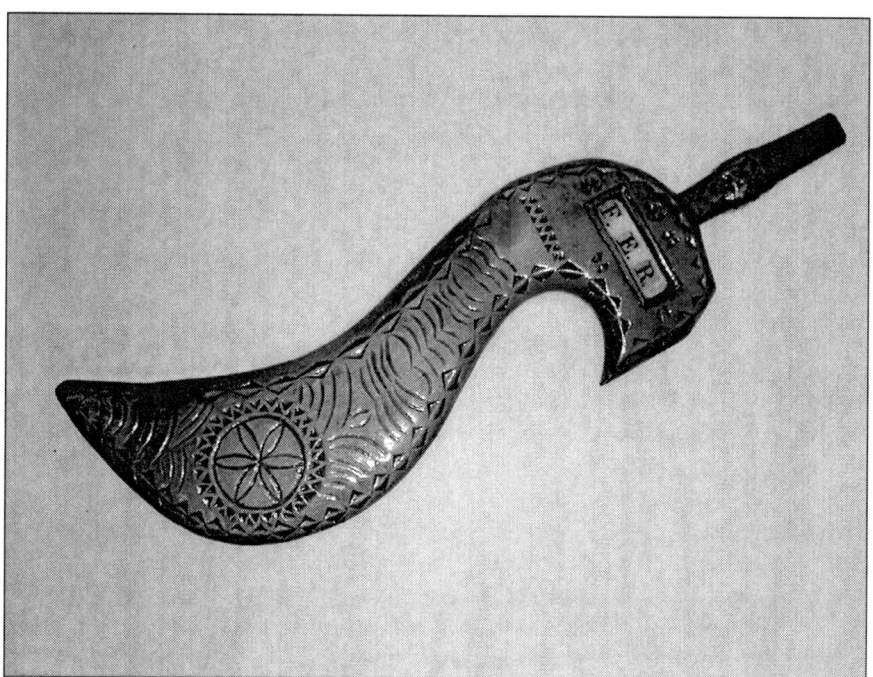

KNITTING STICKS. IMAGES COURTESY YORK CASTLE MUSEUM.

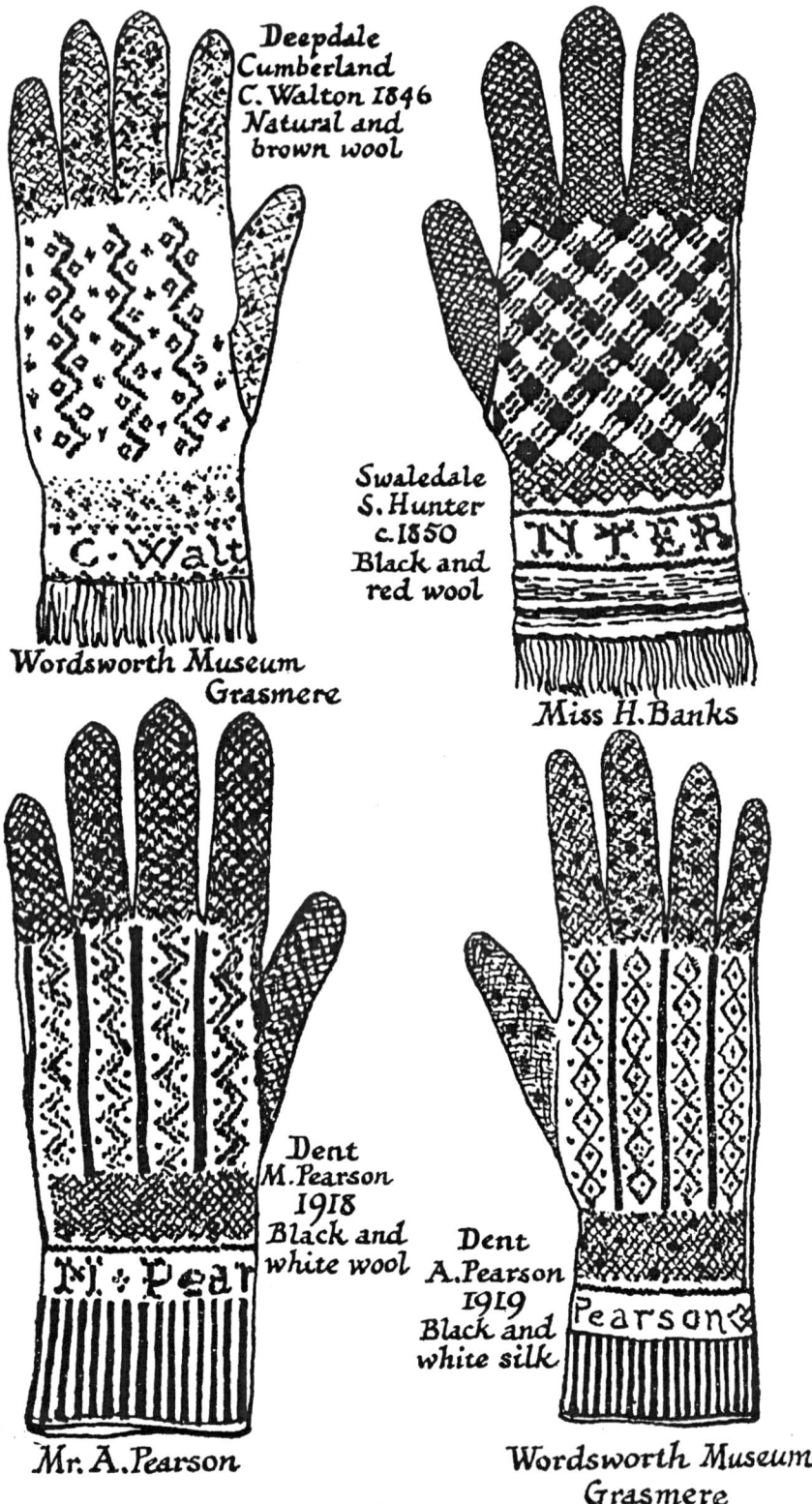

Introduction: Yorkshire Knitting History

Ms. Hemingway begs to inform her Friends, concerning particulars of intrepid ladies; also some remarks concerning the lifting of the Parish Chest lid.

> Writing [*The Old Hand-Knitters of the Dales*] in the late 1940s we glimpsed a way of life which in spite of the Industrial Revolution, had remained unchanged for centuries. Since then the picture has faded rapidly; and as the years pass, by the round of any oral tradition, becomes faint, soon perhaps to cease altogether.
>
> —Marie Hartley and Joan Ingilby, "Quest for the Hand-Knitters," *Dalesman* (August 1970), pp. 424–26.

Knitting is a deep, old part of Yorkshire history. The oldest surviving knitting needles in England, the first written evidence of a professional knitter, and the earliest known knitting stick in the United Kingdom were all found in Yorkshire.

Yorkshire has been described as the eighteenth and nineteenth centre of the wool universe. Bradford's nickname was Worstedopolis. Doncaster, as well as the Yorkshire Dales and Westmorland, were the centres of the English hand-knitted stocking trade.

Books on knitting history often concentrate on the oral history. Since the 1950s, writers have visited knitters working in the old way. This was valuable and wonderful but had its limitations. Sometimes, this emphasis has skewed the way we see knitting traditions. This book is different. Rather like a medium, I hope to speak to the dead, rather than the living.

Facing Page: Engraving by Marie Hartley from *The Old Hand-Knitters of the Dales* (1949).

I have gone in search of the history of Yorkshire knitting in the archives, first-hand, from original documents and images, wherever possible. I made the decision early on not to look for contemporary knitters but focus on the primary sources. And this was no easy task: those primary sources are elusive! Unpublished photos were blurry or indistinct. Gansey designer and historian, Dr. Elizabeth Lovick, asked me if I'd heard of Lovick's Law: The quality of a photograph is inversely proportional to the interest of the stitch pattern. I discovered on my travels that Lovick's Law is a fact. Ganseys and stockings by their very nature do not survive. Accounts of knitters and knitting had to be garnered by thinking laterally.

In his definitive and exhaustive book, *The Yorkshire Woollen and Worsted Industries*, Herbert Heaton barely touched on the history of hand-knitting in Yorkshire. Like most histories, it concentrated on woven cloth. Most of what we know about the history of hand knitting in the county comes from *The Old Hand-Knitters of the Dales*, published in 1951. It is valuable, for it teaches tools and techniques used not only in the Dales but across the United Kingdom.

In their autobiography, Marie Hartley and Joan Ingilby remarked, "In 1948 we found that very little work had been done on either knitting in general or knitting as a branch of the textile industry in the Dales and elsewhere. It was inclined to be thought of as a hobby entirely for women." Knitting had been done by male and female alike once, but as it slipped into being perceived as women's work, so its importance seemed to diminish for the historians. Anyone who follows in their footsteps and tries to write a history of Yorkshire knitting is indebted to Marie Hartley and Joan Ingilby.

When I first read of *The Old Hand-Knitters of the Dales* in the early 1980s, it was out of print. I longed to find a copy but had to wait some time. Years passed. At last, on a day trip to Haworth on the Yorkshire Moors, I found it in a tourist trap bookshop. The book didn't disappoint.

The world that Marie Hartley and Joan Ingilby documented in the late 1940s is no more. There have been sporadic attempts to revive the hand-knitting industry. But it is close to impossible to pay knitters enough for their work. In the early 1980s, Michael Pearson managed to find a handful of knitters in Yorkshire trying to revive the Humberside mariners' knitting traditions. Yet in 2011, the Humber Keel and Sloop Preservation Society told me there was no one, thirty-odd years later, knitting the old keelmen ganseys. I hope my book helps clarify this issue. Time and again, people referred me to the handful of well known, existing commercial gansey knitters at Flamborough and Whitby. No one knew of anyone else, from the tradition, active in the tradition.

When I saw the excellent and interesting DVD, *Women's Voices*, about the Scarborough gansey knitters, it was clear that the gansey myth had clouded even the last pockets of surviving tradition. Contemporary knitters eagerly perpetuated the florid tales of initials identifying drowned mariners, etc. I wanted to strip it back and take a long, hard look at the truth beneath the myths, which I do in Chapter 3.

Introduction: Yorkshire Knitting History—17

STILLINGFLEET VILLAGE SCHOOL REGULATIONS: "... THEIR OWN WORK OR KNITTING FROM HOME MAY BE BROUGHT, BUT NO KIND OF FANCY WORK CAN BE ALLOWED..." COURTESY STILLINGFLEET PARISH CHURCH.

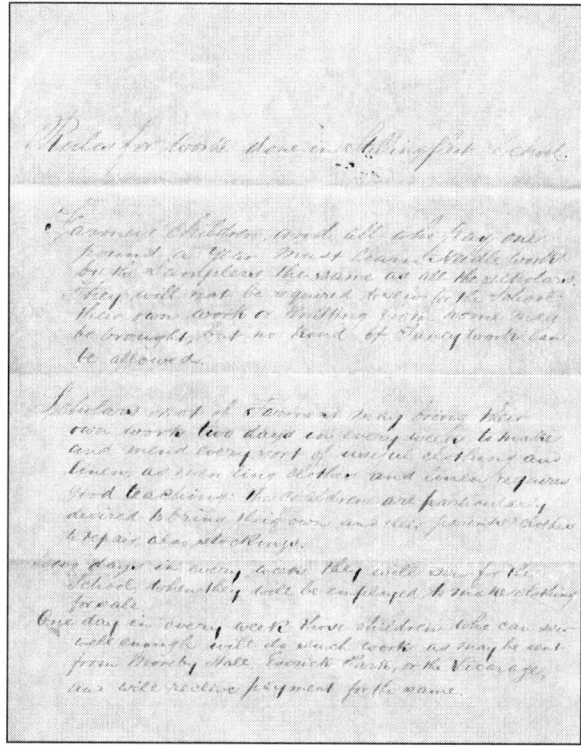

Discussing the writing of *The Old Hand-Knitters of the Dales*, Hartley and Ingilby describe their favourite day during research for their book:

> Possibly a walk to Hebblethwaite Hall, two miles North East of Sedbergh, gave us our greatest thrill. We had been lent a ledger from this mill. One letter, written in February 1822, reported, "It is only a few of the old knitters that can now manage all sorts of caps and these are not good to meet with." Even then the traditional skills were disappearing. Mr. and Mrs. Betham have since died, and we have been unable to trace the present whereabouts of the fascinating ledger.

A former neighbour and friend of the ladies for many years told me that the women did not keep track of all their sources, or always reference them well, but Marie Hartley remarked to her friend J.B. Priestley that they saw themselves as topographers more than historians. It is apparent how fleeting some sources are, and how evasive the facts are for us. I have searched, but the 1822 ledger does not appear to have been deposited in the National Archives. All we have now is this brief account, and the quotes the women transcribed from their notes that day that made it into the book. Hartley and Ingilby said in *Yorkshire Life* they "wish they had recorded on cinefilm some of the local traditions and pastimes, for example the old hand knitting." As Beth Brown-Reinsel remarked, "In most of the literature about gansey knitting, the pattern motifs have been categorized by place of origin. While this system has great merit historically, it is frustrating from a designer's point of view" (Morgan-Rees, "Heritage of Patience").

The drive to classify motifs geographically came about with earlier researchers into gansey history working in a travelogue style, probably at their publisher's behest. They travelled from village to village, collecting patterns, chatting to knitters and fishermen, and collecting photos from local museums. Apparently, while researching her *Guernsey and Jersey Patterns* in the 1950s, Gladys Thompson worked for a day as a toilet attendant so she could watch a fisherman wearing a certain pattern! Without Thompson's careful collection of gansey motifs, we'd all be the poorer. But it's problematic, too. Academic and designer Kate Davis puts this very well in *The Knitter*, "Thompson was a middle class landlubber, and, perhaps, inevitably, she thought and wrote like one, determined to fix each style of gansey and stitch pattern to a place." Thompson often ignored the fact that there was a rich fusion of gansey tradition along the coast and even far inland between Scotland, Norfolk, Yorkshire, and, latterly, the Netherlands. This gentlewoman collector approach made for a coherent travelogue, but from a knitting history point of view it may have done us a disservice. It has left us with ideas that are misleading.

I wanted to bring a fresh perspective to the history of knitting. Using standard genealogical techniques puts the history of our craft under a microscope and yields new information, verifies some, and questions other sacred cows. Amazingly, my several years in archives and museum libraries gave me the names of some 1790s knitters. My goal then became to put names, if not faces, to some of our knitting ancestors.

We can find our knitting ancestors by looking in the pages of censuses, reading trade directories, searching millions of eighteenth- and nineteenth-century newspapers online. The latter are great because they yield so much from small ads to articles, letters, discussions, and, most of all, news stories that feature ganseys and other knitted items. Then there's evidence to be found in archives, parish records, parish chests, churchwardens' records, welfare records, and the records of charity schools and jails from the eighteenth and nineteenth centuries.

Further back in time, there are wills and probates. Yorkshire and Westmorland have the most complete eighteenth-century probate inventories in the United Kingdom. In the sixteenth and seventeenth centuries in the United Kingdom, people of all social classes had their goods inventoried on death. All these are standard sources genealogists study, but earlier knitting historians haven't always had access to this information. As clothes, cloth, yarn, spinning wheels, and sheep represented considerable investments, they were often inventoried.

The more I searched the more I realized that ganseys were worn by a much wider population than previously thought, and knitting caps and stockings were universal. Much of that knitting got done in cottage doorways, but far more was carried out on an industrial level or by children as young as seven in charity schools or was considered hard labour for women in prisons.

I found accounts of the debtors in prison knitting to make a small income to supply their needs. Then I discovered the inmates of the Quaker asylum in York who frequently bought yarn and wool to knit stockings. Some of them spun wool almost

RECORDS OF ASYLUM PATIENTS'
SPINNING AND KNITTING.
COURTESY THE BORTHWICK
INSTITUTE, UNIVERSITY OF YORK
CREDIT: NATHANIEL HUNT

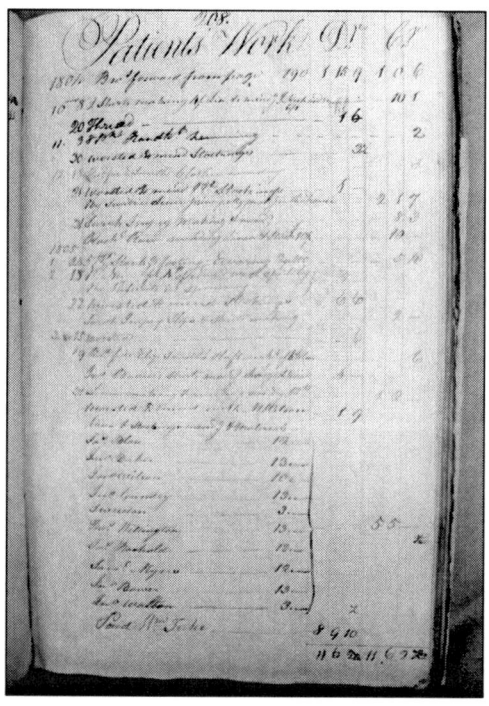

as therapy. In these contexts, knitting leaves a paper trail. Sometimes it's fragmentary. But always it's informative – if you know where to look. Looking at some of this previously neglected material might yield more clues about what was knit and why. This research might also help us reconstruct how some of these garments looked. The more I researched, the more the old knitting history shibboleths were challenged. Ganseys were worn by more than just mariners, the usual suspects. As I looked into the history of Yorkshire knitting, tales of both saints and sinners, from the highest in the land to the lowest, were unravelled.

One great aspect of applying genealogy to knitting history is the fact that we can rescue some of these anonymous but incredible people from obscurity. We can even use genealogy to name specific knitters depicted in photographs or art. I set myself the challenge of using genealogy techniques to pinpoint a knitter mentioned casually in George Walker's seminal 1814 work *Costumes of Yorkshire*.

Walker described "a woman of the name of Slinger who lived in Cotterdale, was accustomed regularly to walk to the market at Hawes, a distance of three miles, with the weekly knitting of herself and family packed in a bag upon her head, knitting all the way. She continued her knitting while she staid at Hawes purchasing worsted for the work of the ensuing week; all of which she placed upon her head, returning occupied with the needles as before." Mrs. Slinger could turn out a pair of men's stockings in a day. I wondered if a bit of sleuthing could track her down. A bit of a challenge as 1814 is well before the first census and before births, marriages, and deaths were certified.

Kit and Betty Metcalfe of Gayle, famous Dales knitters. Image courtesy of Beamish Museum

I managed to find a John Slinger, son of John and Mary Slinger, who was baptised in nearby Hardraw in 1784. There was a John Slinger who married Margaret Whitfield in Hardraw in 1806. Mary was baptised at Hardraw also in 1784. Margaret is possibly our knitter. She would have been thirty in 1814 when George Walker turned up in Hawes to research his book. I found John Slinger, an elderly widower, on the 1841 census. He had a daughter called Margaret.

I live in the same parish where my sixth great grandfather was parish clerk in the 1750s. Our parish chest has not been deposited at a temperature-, moisture-, and light-controlled facility in the vaults of the local archive. It remains in someone's living room in the village. Had I not been a local, I would have had no way to know that. Sometimes it pays to research a folk art from within its culture, and an accident of birth gave me the passport to do just that!

From time immemorial, the parish churches were the repository of all records. Civil registration of births, marriages, and deaths only came along in 1837. If you want to know about the hatches, matches, and dispatches prior to 1837, you have to look at things like parish records, maybe churchwardens' accounts, and the contents of the parish chest where they survive. Other useful records are those of charity schools, elementary schools that emerged in the eighteenth century to educate children of the poor, and prisons. The charity schools are especially relevant to knitting and spinning history as they tended to employ the children in spinning and knitting.

In our parish chest, I found some 1870s instructions about the village school's curriculum, which included knitting.

> Farmers' children … their own work or knitting from home may be brought. Scholars not of Farmers may bring their own work two days in every week and are particularly desired to bring their own and their parents' clothes to repair; also stockings.

Records are patchy. Some were destroyed by enemy action in WW2. Some were destroyed by 1950s clerks who decided the old stacks of dusty paperwork were so much clutter. Many a prison record book has been rescued from a dumpster! At York Archive, I was told a certain nineteenth-century York coroner took it upon himself to destroy all the coroners' reports for most of the entire century. Unbelievable when you think how important these records were.

My own roots are almost entirely in Yorkshire with a tiny bit of the bordering counties Westmorland and Lincolnshire. My family was precisely the old farming family Marie Hartley and Joan Ingilby would have interviewed for their work as well as the farmers' children mentioned in the school curriculum. Some of my paternal ancestors came from Ravenstonedale in Westmorland, a famous bastion of hand knitting. Others farmed close to Hawes in the Dales, although most came from the lowland, Vale of York. My knitting heritage includes upland Westmorland and Yorkshire Dales sheep farmers, hand spinners, and sea-level Vale of York yeoman farmers. Among my mother's ancestors, there was also a sprinkling of Humber and Ouse fishermen and their wives, Humber vessel owners and haulers, and their horse marines. No knitting sticks or knitting lore came down directly in my family, but I do knit using a strange technique that likely did not came from them. In a small way, I come to the history from the inside and hope to give that perspective. Although in my case, it was not an unbroken tradition. During the course of my research, two well-known knitwear designers contacted me with their stories, too. One designer descends from Cornish fishing families; the other, from Leeds-Liverpool canal river boatmen.

Knitting historians might have overlooked some of the primary sources explored here, but they're the first place a genealogist will look. Lift the parish chest lid with me. A part of me belongs on the river – Billie's lass – and indeed I live just yards from the river now. Researching this book has become my way to regain that lost world that I was once, briefly, a part of. The clues lead home. Meander along the rivers with me awhile for to know the history of Yorkshire knitting is to know the history of English knitting.

GANSEY HISTORY

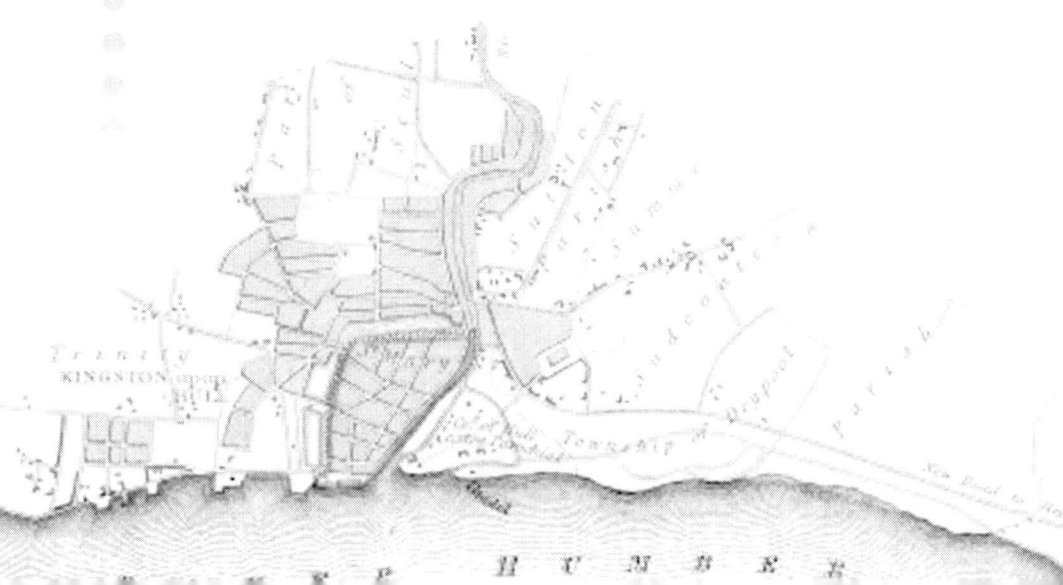

Gansey Origins and Myths

In which we introduce to you TARDIS-like peregrinations and picaresque adventures through time and place. The Author begs to introduce to you exploding Sacred Cows; smouldering victims, CSI York, and the wreck of The General Carleton...

> Gansey: A thick, knitted, closely-fitting vest or shirt, usually made of blue wool, worn by seamen.
> —*The Shorter Oxford Dictionary*, 1851

THE WORD GANSEY HAS LONG BEEN INTERCHANGEABLE WITH guernsey, leading to some confusion around its origins. The word appears to be a less formal, colloquial word for guernsey as gansey was usually used in inverted commas in nineteenth-century sources. 1851 is the first known usage of the word. There are references to ganseys from around 1820 onward, but whether they were mentions of knitted pullovers or the older sewn garment, Guernsey frocks, which were made from canvas and worn by fishermen and farmers as a sort of work overall, was sometimes unclear.

I suspect the word gansey might come from older roots, and the similarity to guernsey is purely coincidental. The Yorkshire dialect I grew up speaking has a swathe of Viking words from the Old Norse. The modern word yarn comes from the Old Norse *garn* (Old English *gearn*). That initial *g* in Old English was actually pronounced more like a cross between an *h* and a *y*. So the *gan-sey* could just be a

FACING PAGE: SUSPICIOUSLY LATVIAN-LOOKING GLOVES FROM THE WRECK OF THE *GENERAL CARLETON*. AS SHIPS OUT OF WHITBY AND HULL FREQUENTLY TRADED IN THE BALTIC, THEY MAY WELL BE YORKSHIRE KNIT WITH EXOTIC INFLUENCES! COURTESY POLISH MARITIME MUSEUM, GDANSK.

corruption of yarn. That is, thing made from yarn. In the Yorkshire Dales, thick bump yarn was called bump garn in dialect well into the twentieth century.

The whole guernsey complication came later and has confused endless historians who aren't philologists. As the island of Guernsey happened to become a centre of excellence in hand-spinning, people assumed gansey was a corruption of guernsey and that the two were interchangeable.

Origins

So how did the garment we now call a gansey come about?

In the Museum of London, is the knitted silk shirt of Charles I, the king we so rudely interrupted with a beheading in 1649. The shirt only survives due to the status of its owner. Charles' shirt has all the same structural elements as a gansey: underarm gussets; knit in the round; reliant on plain-and-purl relief for its visual interest. It is not unlike the Scandinavian *nattrojer*, and some extant pieces of seventeenth-century knitting are indeed reputed to be Scandinavian imports. The United Kingdom (particularly northern England) and Scandinavia have always had close ties.

Men's shirts and women's shifts remained mostly unchanged from medieval times to the nineteenth century. Both were usually cut from 30-inch-wide linen, and the whole width of the fabric was used selvedge to selvedge. If cut with economy, the underarm gussets could be made from leftover fabric from where the neck hole was cut. And so the shape of shirts remained unchanged for centuries as they were cut with regard to economy, from a single length of linen, folded at the shoulder seam. This gave them the characteristic tubular shape, with dropped sleeves and underarm gussets. Precisely like the gansey.

It's likely the gansey slowly evolved from a piece of high-status seventeenth-century underwear to a piece of lower-status outerwear by the late eighteenth century. The gansey as we understand it did not really exist at all until the late eighteenth century or turn of the nineteenth century. There is no evidence whatsoever for ganseys prior to the nineteenth century no matter which sources we look at – archaeological, art, literature, and Tudor and seventeenth-century wills and probate inventories.

Although ganseys shifted from under to outerwear at some point in the late-eighteenth century, they were still making this transition in people's minds during the nineteenth century. This advertisement from *The Hampshire Advertiser* in January 1854 shows that transition:

- The seamless knitted worsted vest may be worn either by itself, or (by Gentlemen of
- delicate constitutions), as a wrapper or over-vest, highly recommended for winter wear
- by R.D.ELYETT, 185 High Street, the sole agent for Southampton.

IMAGE COURTESY FILEY MUSEUM.

A Walter Fisher photograph of a Filey fisherwoman is a staged studio portrait, but you can see white knitted jersey peeping out from under her bodice. She also wore a knitted montag and socks. (A montag was a simple shawl, usually triangular in shape, and worn with the pointed edges crossed at or above the waist. Sometimes the edges were tucked into a skirt or apron waistband.) Arthur Munby's diary entry for 1865 supports the evidence of Fisher's picture. Munby described Scarborough bait-gatherers as, "all women, who wore white jerseys with long sleeves, short skirts, tarpaulin coats and strong boots." The undyed white jerseys were worn close to the skin; their long sleeves were visible under the women's bodices. Throughout history, shifts were regarded as underwear and even showing the arms of them was thought risqué. Women at work – like laundresses, or the female brick maker illustrated by William Pyne in *The Costume of Great Britain* – may well show a bit of shift, like Munby's bait gatherers.

Munby met a girl called Sarah Ann who wore, "a handkerchief tied over her bonnet [and] round her face [an] old shawl tied close round body, white jersey sleeves, a striped linsey kirtle to the calf, blue wool stockings and stout highlows." These plain white jerseys worn by Yorkshire fisher lasses are never mentioned in dispatches in knitting histories. Yet we can clearly see something transitioning from underwear to outerwear.

The plain white undergarments knit in fine wool (most likely 4-ply or finer) resemble nothing so much as the sporting ganseys worn by Victorian gentleman gymnasts and early professional athletes – ancestor of the modern (machine knit) football or rugby shirt.

28—*River Ganseys*

There is a paucity of evidence for ganseys in the eighteenth century. In 1995, a team of Polish archaeologists excavated an eighteenth-century ship wrecked off Gdansk. At the time the vessel was called, rather boringly, *W-32*, but it turned out to be the wreck of *The General Carleton*, a ship out of Whitby in Yorkshire, which had sunk in 1785. Incredibly, 775 artifacts, including many knitted items that had belonged to the 1785 crew, were recovered. By some phenomenal chance, the ship had a cargo of pine tar on deck when it sank. This formed a matrix with the cold Baltic water. Although the sailors' slop chests rotted away, the clothes inside remained intact, still eerily folded and left as they had been the last time the Yorkshire mariners stored them away the day the ship sank. Among the numerous knitted items were stockings, hats, gloves, and mittens. There was no gansey or trace of anything like a gansey.

Yet by the 1850s, we have photographic evidence of some sophisticated gansey patterns – patterns so fine, in fact, they can't possibly have come out of the blue, fully formed but must have evolved somehow. It looks like they developed from around the turn of the eighteenth to nineteenth century to the middle of the nineteenth century. This is feasible. Knitters are, of course, ingenious!

The fact that the early origins of ganseys are hazy has created the opportunity for numerous myths to attach themselves to the garments like so many burrs. I think the romance of these myths is attractive – but, also, myths are for exploding; especially when they get in the way of exploring the truth of a subject.

The Knitted Initials Myth

Perhaps the most popular myth attached to the gansey is that knitters purled initials above the welt to identify their loved one if he drowned – a fairy tale. Like all fairy tales, there is a kernel of truth in there. There is no doubt that many knitters outlined the wearer's initials in purl stitches, just above the welt, before starting the gansey's pattern. It has been suggested this was to aid identification of drowned mariners. In *Cornish Guernseys and Knit-Frocks*, Mary Wright offers a more prosaic reason for so doing. Mr. Jim Honey told her the story of the time a gansey his grandmother knitted, went missing:

> Twelve months after, Granny saw a man wearing Uncle Willie's jersey and called a policeman to arrest him. "How do you know this is your boy's jersey," the policeman asked. "You make'n lift up his arms," said Granny. "You'll see I knitted a *W* under one arm and an *S* under the other and my boy's name is Willie Steer. What's his?"

Running a search of several million nineteenth-century newspapers online, I found remarkably few references to the initials knitted above ganseys' welts actually being used to identify a corpse. Out of millions of newspapers, I found only two direct mentions, in fact.

GANSEY INITIALS
CREDIT:
NATHANIEL HUNT

First comes this quote from an 1843 article, "Loss of the Conqueror East Indiaman," from *The Morning Chronicle*:

> Among the bodies cast on shore on Sunday, was that of the sail maker drowned in the Reliance. The remains were frightfully mutilated, and the head altogether gone. His identity was proved by the name worked on his Guernsey frock.

Note that the article says *name* not *initials*. At this date, sailors often had the full name of their ship embroidered in large letters across the chest of the canvas Guernsey frocks. So we can't even establish if this is a reference to knitted initials.

The only other reference I found comes from an 1851 Coroner's inquest, reported in *The Royal Cornwall Gazette, Falmouth Packet, and General Advertiser*:

> At Monday last, on Gerrans, on the body of a man supposed to be a sailor was dressed in a light-colored oil-skin coat and trousers, with a blue linen trousers inside, and a pair of drawers, a plaid waistcoat, grey Guernsey frock, marked FM, a blue woollen shirt and a check cotton one, grey worsted stockings, and sea-boots. Before it was removed, it was identified by the master and supercargo of the French sloop Ernest who stated the deceased was one of their crew.

Even this does not necessarily support the gansey-initials-as-identifier theory, as the article refers to a French mariner, not an English one.

Looking at parish records from here in Yorkshire, along the banks of the Ouse and the Humber, I found that when an unidentified body washed up, between the seventeenth and nineteenth century, very little effort was made to identify it at all. Usually the body was buried that same day, at the expense of the parish, in a pauper's grave. For example, here is a typical laconic parish record burial entry for a stranger's body found in the river, found in the Stillingfleet parish records: "A Man Unknown. Found drowned. April 21, 1812. Buried April 22nd 1812." In the eighteenth- and early-nineteenth-century, villages had leet courts, appointed constables, a magistrate, etc., but there was no national, organized police force until

THE BLACKNELL FAMILY, HULL. IMAGE COURTESY HUMBER KEEL & SLOOP SOCIETY.

the 1840s. There was no central place to record the missing or lost or to store items taken from a body pulled from the river so that the lost one might be identified at a later date. In other words, our ancestors were more pragmatic about the dead – getting them buried within hours, sometimes, and not enquiring beyond the parish if the body washed up was not immediately recognizable to someone.

There are thousands of references to drowned mariners in nineteenth-century newspapers. These are a rich source of information for the knitting historian, as clothes, including ganseys, are sometimes described in an attempt to identify the dead. The reason there are so many notices about drowned sailors was that most mariners at this date could not swim. They were superstitious and many thought by learning to swim, you were tempting fate. The poet Shelley (who was also to drown, in 1821, when sailing), said in *Julian and Maddalo*, "If you can't swim, beware of providence." Cawood parish registers record the burial of one of my own mariner ancestors, Captain Abraham Wood. He was buried in 1817 and cause of death was simply recorded as "drowned." He probably fell in the water at the dockside. The river is tidal and has some treacherous reaches that defeat even strong swimmers. No doubt someone saw him go in, and Abraham was pulled straight out so he was identifiable.

Even a tight-fitting garment, like a gansey, could be peeled off a body by the elements by the time it washed up. As Alec Gill pointed out in his book about superstitions of Hull mariners, tattoos were used to identify drowned sailors. He wrote of the Williams brothers, fishermen from a 1950s Hull trawler who were washed up in the Soviet Union some time later. They were identified by their tattoos. Tattoos for mariners were a way of wearing your good luck symbol. Some of those lucky symbols and motifs from tattoos found their way onto ganseys as motifs as stars and anchors, for example.

The Hull mariners of Hessle Road were famously superstitious. Alec Gill was told of most mariners' refusal to have a corpse on board vessels. Within living memory, sometimes a dead colleague was left in the sea rather than brought home, so averse were they to having a corpse on board at all. There was, as ever, a pragmatic side to this. Gill remarked, "If the trawled-up body was long-decayed, the corpse was quickly tossed back into the sea to avoid getting involved with red-tape ashore."

It seems Rae Compton was on the money when she wrote in *The Complete Book of Traditional Guernsey and Jersey Knitting*, "In Caithness today it is still believed by some that guernseys were patterned for recognition in cases of drowning, particularly 'if they were drooned wi' their heid aff.' No knitter has ever confirmed that a pattern was designed for this purpose, although all knitters would recognize their own handiwork under any circumstance." We would all recognize our own work, but if a mariner drowned at sea or inland of tidal waters there's no saying that he'd wash up at a place where he was recognized or where a knitter was waiting to verify, "Yes, that's one of mine!"

Gansey Origin Myths

There are also many fanciful myths surrounding the gansey's origins. Sacred cows are for exploding. Let's do some more. First of all, there is a far-fetched claim that the gansey existed from medieval times in the form we know it now. This is simply not the case. There is scant evidence for knitting at all in England prior to 1460. We can look at the entire period of history right up to the fifteenth century to say we can't prove knitting was even here in these islands, let alone a full-blown gansey knitting tradition. After that date, knitting was done here but only specific items of clothing at first, such as caps, hose, scoggers (sleeves), and at the high end, ecclesiastical adornments like fancy silk and metal thread cushions. No jumpers. We can venture, Dr. Who style, so far back in time as a thousand years to prove that fragments of textile can and do survive in the Yorkshire mud. It has been said they would be as rare as finding a Rolls Royce in the mud. The truth is, if woven textiles can survive in the soil, why not knitted textiles? And woven textiles that are a couple of thousand years old, such as Roman sprang work, have been found in York.

Penelope Walton Rogers's *Craft, Industry, and Everyday Life: Finds From Medieval York* has a very useful summary of the hard evidence for the introduction of knitting to England. Why? Because among the finds were three copper alloy rods, two of 2.6 mm and one of 1.9 mm diameter. They have been designated knitting needles, but no one's entirely sure what they are. The two larger ones were found in the floor of 2, Aldwark, a street in York. The other, which is thought to be post-medieval, was found at the Foundry site. The earliest samples of knitting in England are of a similar date – late fourteenth-century London and early fifteenth-century Newcastle. Rogers points out that both are port towns and, for this kind of date,

32—*River Ganseys*

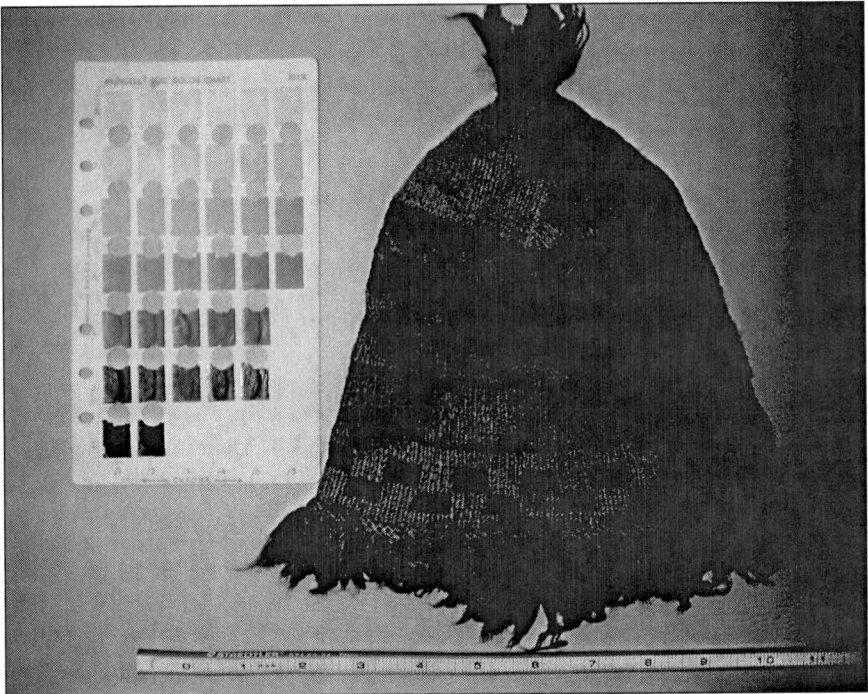

The General Carleton hat. Yorkshire knitting from the early 1780s.
Sea chests full of Yorkshire knitting but not a gansey in sight!
Courtesy Polish Maritime Museum, Gdansk.

"there are records of knitted garments being imported in Italian galleys." The river Ouse bisects York, and York is also a port. So maybe it is no surprise that imported knitted items found their way into the county town of Yorkshire from the earliest dates, leading to a desire to learn this new craft.

York might boast the oldest knitting needles in England because it was a huge, ecclesiastical centre, famously having a parish church on every major street (or two!), York Minster, and being the city where Constantine, the first Christian emperor of Rome, was made emperor. Early knitting was ecclesiastical – cushions and caps. Nary a gansey in sight.

The City of Ripon Chapter Acts give us the first hard evidence of an English knitter – one Marjory Clayton of Ripon in Yorkshire, referred to as cappeknitter in 1465. Until that date, there is no hard documentary evidence for knitting. No doubt it existed. But the earliest evidence we have comes from 1465 and that is for a cap knitter – which is in line with everything else we know about the history of knitting in England: caps, hose, and ecclesiastical fol-de-rols came first. Ganseys, as the wreck of the 1780's Whitby ship *The General Carleton* suggests, came later. Much later.

Apparently, one reason put forward to suggest that ganseys have great antiquity, maybe even go back as far as medieval times, is the discussion of the negative evidence. The argument is that we have no earlier evidence of mariner ganseys because slop chests, even of abandoned ships, were plundered. Clothes were valuable. Plus, of course, the conditions on a sunken vessel are not conducive to textile preservation, archaeologically speaking. That all sounds logical until you've heard of *The General Carleton*.

In 2010, the Captain Cook Memorial Museum in Whitby held a temporary exhibition. In that exhibition were some knitted artefacts from a vessel, *The General Carleton* of Whitby, which sank in the port at Gdansk, Poland, in 1785. *The General Carleton* artefacts can normally be found at the Polish Maritime Museum in Gdansk. The items on display included a wool serge jacket, called in the crew records a Fearnought, and smaller woollen items. Several of the knitted artefacts (excavated in 1995 and previously only on display in Gdansk) were on loan to the Captain Cook Memorial Museum. These included stockings, mittens, gloves, and, most glorious of all, a colorwork thrummed cap. The story of *The General Carleton* and the rescue archaeology that brought the Yorkshire ship's artefacts to the Polish Maritime Museum is told in *The Yorkshire Mary Rose*, by Yorkshire born and bred writer, Stephen Baines. Mr. Baines's ancestors were Whitby mariners in the eighteenth and nineteenth centuries at precisely the same time my ancestors were Humber and Ouse fishermen and inland waterways haulers.

The General Carleton's contents (around 775 artefacts) were saved by a weird and wonderful chance. The day it sank, *The General Carleton* had a cargo of pine tar, which mixed with the Baltic seawater and sand, formed a matrix which acted as a protective barrier, preserving even the contents of maybe nine or ten slop chests. Aboard the vessel were the captain, William Hustler; John Pearson, carpenter; John Swan, second mate; six new seamen – Nicholas Theaker, George Taylor, John Purvis, Andrew Gibson, Andrew Noble and Thomas Edes – and the apprentices, James Hart, John Thompson, John Noble, John Fraiser, Richard Neale, John Johnson, and Richard Trueman. Only Hustler and Theaker perished during the storm. Local tradition has it that the other mariners made it to shore. Among the retrieved body of artefacts were gloves, mittens, stockings, waistcoats, sailors' serge jackets, shoes – basically almost the entire and intact contents of the crew's slop chests. Some of the items look to have been traded, most obviously some very Latvian-style mittens, which were two-coloured and thrummed on the gauntlets. Others, notably the stockings and the beautiful Shetland patterned hat with a thrummed border, looked to be Yorkshire knit. The hat is a natural white, with orange and brownish green forming the patterns. I suspect it was locally knit because I have found an image of whalebone scrapers in George Walker's *Costumes of Yorkshire* that are almost identical – white knitted caps, patterned with bright orange and green. The orange could be from madder or something like marigolds or coreopsis. Green would be buckthorn or, more likely, woad or indigo over-dyed with weld.

The reproduction pattern has a tension of 20 stitches over 4 inches. When I observed the hat, it was in a glass display case, but the gauge of the knitting seemed to be around 3 stitches per centimetre. Baines's book, *The Yorkshire Mary Rose*, includes the pattern already worked out for a reproduction of the hat. By way of contrast, the stockings, which had a very high likelihood of being Yorkshire-knit, had a gauge of around 6.5 stitches per centimetre and were clearly a fine piece of knitting. They were blue (woad) and cream (natural wool) with russet toes. This bears out the practice of sorting wool for stockings into leggings and feetings: The coarser, stronger, more hard-wearing fiber was reserved to spin separately for the feet, as mentioned in *The Old Hand-Knitters of the Dales*. The stockings appeared to have a square heel. Another pair had a cast on of around 140 stitches. The ribbing at the top was oddly irregular, alternating knit and purl stitches in a random way: columns of knit stitch that were 5 stitches wide but columns of purl varying from 3 to 8 stitches wide. These are rare, almost unique examples of eighteenth-century knitting, and we have to recall that, at these dates, stockings had probably recently transitioned from having garter-stitch rows at the top to the more modern and elastic ribbing. (They do seem, otherwise, an expert piece of work, so maybe the need we now feel for regular ribbing is a fairly modern thing?)

A photo in Stephen Baines's book shows some of the clothing as it was excavated, still neatly folded with a felt hat on top exactly as it was left in the slop chest, which must have rotted away around it. Mr. Baines wrote:

> A sailor's most valuable possessions were his clothes, which might include a jacket or two, a waistcoat or two, three shirts, a pair of trousers and a pair of breeches, two pairs of drawers, two or three pairs of stockings, two pairs of shoes, a couple of handkerchiefs, a pair of mittens, a hat, and a cap. The surviving clothes were all from the stern section of the ship, and so are likely to have comprised the contents of the sea chests of the master, mate, and the servants, possibly the carpenter, of all nine or ten people.

The sailors were of course, wearing clothes when the ship went down. Most, but not all, hands survived. So, given the fairly liberal amounts of clothing found on the wreck, we can imagine the crew were pretty well provided with clothing. Given the abundance of clothing on board, it is noteworthy that there is not a shred or trace of a gansey or anything that could be a fragment of one, and I doubt pine tar discriminates. The woven wool dreadnought jacket is in a remarkable state of preservation, as are the knitted items.

So there we have it. A perfect time capsule of a Yorkshire vessel with a named crew, the original muster rolls for every voyage survived, out of a Yorkshire port in the 1780s. But no ganseys. This in itself is valuable information.

Paintings and cartoons depicting Georgian sailors also bear out that ganseys were not worn at that time. In 1774, Gabriel Bray set sail as second lieutenant on HMS *Pallas* during a voyage to the coast of West Africa and the West Indies. During his time on board *Pallas* he did many watercolours of life on board ship. Sailors can be seen wearing shirts or shirts and jackets. No knitted garments. In 1811, Thomas Rowlandson's cartoon of the sailors ashore, *Portsmouth Point*, shows many sailors but no ganseys. Further evidence can be found in William Pyne's *The Costume of Great Britain*. One engraving shows fishermen. There are no ganseys, just shirts and jackets.

I have long suspected that ganseys are instead a product of the machine age. England was the first industrialized nation on the face of the earth. Spinning jennies in factories could provide predictable yarn which, when five-plied, had a nice circular cross section that was suitable for relief-pattern knitting. Purl stitches pop when knit from worsted rather than woollen-spun yarn. Mr. Baines remarks that less than half of the extant stockings were machine-knitted. Looking at Whitby businesses of the time, and extant clothiers' records, he concluded the mariners' clothing was probably a complex mix of shop-bought, commercially made clothing and homemade. Experienced sailors would buy their clothing from specialist slop-shops that could be found near docks in most ports. Young mentions that in 1816 Whitby had six slop-shops, and there would certainly be some in 1777, with the proprietors of such establishments appearing in the parish records as shop keepers.

I stumbled on an exhibition of the textile items from the wreck of the Whitby ship, General Carleton, at the Captain Cook Memorial Museum in Whitby the very week I'd been at the York Reference Library, researching the York charity schools, a hotbed of stocking knitting in the 1780s. So very odd to have held Catharine Cappe's 1799 book in my hands and then, within days, see some actual 1780s Yorkshire stockings! The hat was probably the star exhibit. And while some of the mittens look Latvian (or at least are Latvian in influence), the stockings and caps are likely to be Yorkshire made. Looking at them, we can understand more of our ancestor's techniques and sophistication. Two-colour knitting is something not exclusive to, but largely associated with, the nineteenth century and Shetland and the Fair Isles. Yet here it is, in eighteenth-century Yorkshire.

The hand-coloured images of the Whalebone Scrapers (men working at Whitby, no less!) in George Walker's *Costumes of Yorkshire* is interesting as the hats conform in colour and style to the one found in the wreck of *The General Carleton*. The hat, a natural white with orange and green patterns, was knit at a tension of around 3 stitches per centimetre. It was thrummed around the base and topped off with a pompom. After the thrummed border was a two-round garter stitch edging followed by two rounds of plain knitting, then two stacked checker motifs, each four rows high. Then came four rounds of plain knitting followed by one row of dark. Ten rounds of pattern, one round dark, four rounds white, diamonds five rounds high, three rounds white, six rounds dark, followed by three bands of checkers 2×2, plain knit then up to the top, decreasing on what looks like every alternate round.

The fact that we have this one extant cap and also an illustration showing several men wearing identical ones, from the 1780s and from 1814, suggests the Georgian Yorkshire mariner might have commonly worn this kind of thrummed hat in these three colours. It is a fascinating idea that ganseys may have existed before the

THE WHALEBONE SCRAPERS, FROM *COSTUMES OF YORKSHIRE*, GEORGE WALKER, 1814.

Industrial Revolution, but there is no evidence to support it. There are also extant Navy list records that outline precisely what was worn at sea. In the Captain Cook Memorial Museum, there is a letter that does exactly this. A letter from Captain Phipps dated 10 May 1773 listed the clothing requested for a crew of a similar ship to *The General Carleton*. Again, there was mention of knitted items but no mention of a gansey or anything we could interpret as such. In 1773, *Racehorse* attempted an expedition to the North Pole, so this is detailing clothing from the most extreme conditions imaginable. Captain Phipps took both *Racehorse* and *Carcass* to explore the North West Passage in 1773. Horatio Nelson was midshipman on the *Carcass*, and it was on this expedition he had his famous brawl with a polar bear. From the Mulgrave Archives, this letter, loaned to the exhibition by Lord Normandy, read:

> Navy Office
> 10th May, 1773
>
> Sir,
>
> Having received Directions for the Right Honble [sic] the Lords Commissioners of the Admiralty to furnish the under mentioned Extra Necessaries for the crews of His Majesty's sloops *Racehorse* and *Carcass*:
>
> Flannel jackets two for each Man
> Cotton shirts
> Cotton Handkerchiefs
> Fearnought Jackets, lined: Two
> Kersey Inside Waistcoats, lined: Two
> Milled Yarn Caps: Two
> Boots: One Pair
> Boot Stockings: Two Pair
> Fearnought Trousers: Two Pair

Mittings [sic]: One Dozen Pair each Man

We desire you will please to let us know what Numbers of Men are to be furnished therewith

And are

Your Humble Servants,
H. Palliser Williams [sic]
Geo. Marsh
Hon'ble Captain Phipps
Racehorse at Deptford

Nelson's famous cry, "I see no ships," during the Battle of Copenhagen could be paraphrased as, "I see no ganseys!" No ganseys maybe, but it gives us a strong sense of what was knitted in eighteenth-century Yorkshire: hats and stockings, mainly. The skills acquired while knitting these would be easily transferable to the knitting of a more ambitious gansey. There are extant records for some of the county's charity schools, and none of them ever mention the word gansey or any garment analogous to it.

The "Superhero of Garments" Myth

Let's briefly examine the myth that ganseys were some sort of super heroic garment, capable of turning the very sea. Those knitters interviewed by earlier researchers stated that ganseys were made from unoiled worsted. They were generally knit at a tension of around 7 stitches per inch, usually with 2.5mm or 2.75mm needles (US size 1 or 2). But the gauge could go up to double that. This makes for a firm fabric but not a waterproof one. In fact, there are numerous references to, and photographs of, oilskins, canvas overalls, and sailors' brooks (a sort of waterproof coverall), and no one would be reliant on a gansey alone to keep out the elements. Although if you believe some modern pundits, you might be forgiven for thinking so.

A related myth is that the gansey's elaborate patterns were designed to make the fabric thicker and keep out the cold. When researching his book, *Traditional Knitting*, Michael Pearson was able to speak to Staithes knitters who told him, "The men now prefer more elaborate designs than their fathers who wanted their ganseys plain, with only a little decoration on the shoulder." There is a paucity of evidence, maybe a handful of photographs, of ganseys from the inland waterways. Along the rivers, ganseys were fairly plain or only the upper body is ornamented, which negates the often promulgated idea that ganseys were always heavily patterned to double the fabric. It is easy to overstate the idea that somehow knitting an elaborate pattern increases the thickness of the garment. There is some truth in this. But not a lot. Scandinavian double knitting technique, or stranded Fair Isle, would trap a layer of air far more effectively than a relief pattern in just one yarn.

Myths about Pattern Motifs and Geographical Variation

Yet another myth that's grown up, and is even repeated by traditional knitters themselves, is the idea that each village had its own distinctive pattern. Ganseys can be broadly characteristic of an area or even place, but their distinctiveness, and different patterns' exclusivity to certain towns, even families, is exaggerated.

At Beverley Museum, we went in search of images of inland mariners. We found a lovely photo of a Humber mariner called Mr. Pockley sitting on his front doorstep. The photo was donated by family, but we had no clue as to Mr. Pockley's given name. What jumped out at me instantly was that his gansey did not look like an inland one. It looked more Flamborough or Scarborough. Armed with just the name Mr. Pockley, I went in search of him and found a Richard Pockley, aged 60 in the 1891 census, who I'd found on earlier censuses as a "fisherman" but was now a "grocer" in Sutton, with Stoneferry near Hull. The family had no memory of coming from anywhere but Humberside. His wife Eliza was 50 and from Scarborough. Tellingly in the 1871 census, Richard Pockley was still a fisherman in Flamborough, and his lodger was a Beverley man.

His elaborate gansey breaks all the stereotypes about the stark simplicity of the Ouse/Humber men, with alternating vertical patterns centring on either moss stitch masks (diamonds) or hearts, divided with purl stitch lines. There are no ropes. But the pattern is an advanced one. Welts are the usual 2×2 rib, and the neck is the older, upstanding type. Frustratingly, the photo is not crisp enough to make out every detail, but it's clear Mr. Pockley's gansey would stand comparison with the finer coastal ones. This indicates that there is a blurring between coastal and inland styles. Mr. Pockley ended his days on Humberside but started them at Flamborough with a Scarborough wife to knit his ganseys. Just as men from the inland towns and villages worked the boats on the river, some of which ended up in Hull, the Humber fishermen sometimes came inland to find work along the river. This shows graphically the interchange between coastal and inland. Gansey motifs, just as the trade, must have gone both up and down the river.

It has also become a commonplace thing to suggest that drowned mariners' home might also be recognized from the pattern configuration on their ganseys. Again, this is not likely. There are broad characteristics sometimes. A Filey gansey, for example, may have a lot of ropes; a Scarborough, more moss stitch. But those are really broad generalizations. Sometimes, as with Mr. Pockley, they help identify the motif's origins. Sometimes, they do not. Most patterns became universal too quickly for us to say which was from where. We only started talking in terms of Whitby or Filey or wherever patterns after the first books on gansey history started being published.

As a genealogist and local historian, I turned to the recorded words of knitters themselves to find the truth. And knitters said patterns were made up on the spot. Dentdale knitter Clara Sedgwick said, "Patterns were knitted 'out of the head.'

LEFT: HUMBER MARINER RICHARD POCKLEY. COURTESY OF BEVERLEY MUSEUM.
RIGHT: AN UNKNOWN FAMILY GROUP. COURTESY FILEY MUSEUM.

They were not written down because, of course, many people in the early days could not write or wouldn't know how to describe patterns in writing" (Kinder, "Knitting in the Dales Way"). Inland mariner Harry Fletcher said of his mother's ganseys, "She never used a pattern. No one did. They all made it up as they went along, ropes and cables and knots and diamonds, all kinds of patterns" (Fletcher, *Life on the Humber*).

This also suggests the diversity of patterns. The photographic evidence does not support the romantic idea of family patterns. If you examine Lewis Harding's famous Polperro portraits of 1860s fishermen, you can see immediately that within a single family group (for example, the Jolliffs, photographed at various times) there may be several wildly different patterns going on. We can sometimes use genealogical techniques to trace those named in photos and confirm their family relationships. And then, when you go back to the photos you can see, quite starkly, that there was no such thing as a family pattern of motifs.

This might seem obvious, but you never see it documented that even the same mariner may have two entirely different patterned ganseys. Most gansey histories have reproduced the famous Frank Meadows Sutcliffe photo of Whitby lifeboatman, Harry Freeman, wearing a gansey that alternates horizontal bands of 2×2 moss stitch with three rounds of garter stitch. There is a less well known photo of him, which looks to be around the same time, also taken by Sutcliffe, where he is wearing a gansey with long, lazy cables alternating with vertical bars of garter stitch.

These examples dispel yet another myth. Again, a unique pattern would make no difference in identifying a dead mariner. As we have seen, tattoos did that. Mariners may have had more than one gansey with different patterns, too. Any knitter would instantly be able to identify a jumper they'd spent more than 100 hours on in any case! There is no reason to assume knitters from 150 years ago were that much different than us. Patterns evolve with experience, too. In my own knitting, the closed hearts from Bridlington and inland patterns evolved over time into alternation open with closed hearts. I am in love with one pattern, then halfway through knitting it, spot the next one I want to knit, which may be very different.

Then there were intermarriages, which meant patterns shifted geographically. There is a famous Lewis Harding photograph showing two little girls knitting (see previous page). The little girls were Mary Jane Langmaid and Ann Elizabeth Jolliff. Lewis Harding was working in Cornwall. You couldn't physically get further from Yorkshire than Cornwall and still be in England. According to censuses, almost everyone in the fishing village of Polperro, Cornwall, in the mid-nineteenth century was born in Polperro. Except one woman. I was able to find both girls in the famous photo on the 1871 census. Mary Jane was on Lansallos Street, aged 8, and living with her parents Joseph (fisherman) and Ellen. Ellen was born in Grimsby, at that date a Yorkshire fishing port, which would have influenced Mary Jane's knitting and given her different patterns to the Cornish ones. Ellen Langmaid was born Ellen Forward, a Cornish girl. Her father was a gunner for the customs service and in the late 1830s must have been posted to the Humber area. In 1845, he was gunner on the *Lapwing*, according to an advertisement in the *Hull Packet*. In 1856, he was summonsed for assaulting two women, but the charges were dropped. In the 1861 census, Samuel Forward is listed as "Superannuated from the Revenue and Fisherman." Mary Jane's mother, Ellen, would have been familiar with the inland river patterns of the Humber, having spent some time there. This is highly suggestive of cross pollination from one fishing community to another. Gansey historians have mentioned this many times, but, using genealogy, we can prove they were correct.

Patterns famously moved around the coast with the herring and the well-documented herring girls. Liz Lovick's research has documented this wonderfully. Here in Yorkshire, Alec Gill interviewed Louisa "Cissie" Ashley of Gillett Street, Hull. Scots herring girls are well documented, but little has been written of the herring girls of Hull. The Yorkshire lasses worked alongside the Scottish girls, gutting the herring and sometimes also helped with the kippering process. Gill remarked, "Unfortunately, the herring girls were looked down on by outsiders, and some considered their filthy work as 'the lowest of the low.'" Work was seasonal. The girls worked until the herring fleet left. Cissie became a travelling girl based at Scarborough. They would travel the coast, sometimes as far as Scotland, where they lived rent-free in huts. This fusion of the Scottish with Yorkshire patterns is probably one of the most interesting cross-pollinations in the gansey tradition. Ellen Langmaid would have taken her own Cornish patterns up to Yorkshire and

Gansey Origins and Myths—41

MARY JANE LANGMAID AND ANN ELIZABETH JOLLIFF. COURTESY POLPERRO PRESS.

returned from the north with some of the Humber. Back in Cornwall, Ellen's neighbours and friends would have seen her patterns and maybe copied them.

Scarborough was famous for its tunny until they were all fished out by Icelandic fishermen in the mid-twentieth century. The hugely popular Scarborough Tunny Club brought in tourists from all over England. Again, some of them would have brought new patterns with them on their backs. Tourism had been a phenomenon in England since the time of the Romantic poets, whose work attracted people to the Lake District. The coming of the railroads of the 1830s meant tourism expanded exponentially. So old spa resorts like Scarborough and more refined tourist venues like Filey had a steady stream of visitors from outside the county, bringing with them, their own ganseys and influences.

I wouldn't be the first knitting historian to observe that we sometimes see traditional motifs through the prism of those early knitting historians, and what has been handed down to us is how they were first collected and recorded rather than the pattern's actual geographical origins. A simple, or even complex, pattern might be thought of simultaneously in several places. But as we only have a photo of it in, say, Cornwall, we assume it is a Cornish pattern. Because Gladys Thompson first collected it in Whitby, a pattern becomes the Whitby pattern. Yet, as we have seen, people were mobile in the eighteenth century and nineteenth century. Maybe not the general population, but mariners were unusually mobile. When you start looking dispassionately at nineteenth-century photos of ganseys you can find, say, a flag motif in Scotland but also in Yorkshire and in Cornwall. Again, we can talk only of broad influences. And I think if we accept there is a huge cross fertilization between Scottish, Norfolk, and Yorkshire patterns then the inland ganseys would have to be influenced by those of the Netherlands. When we think of motifs, remember that none might have actually originated where they were first recorded or collected. What we call a Scarborough pattern is more likely just a pattern.

Here on the river, the salmon trade was ridiculously lucrative but also very seasonal. The rest of the year some fishermen would work as day labourers on the farms, maybe moving further inland, going where the work was. Along the river, fishermen often married the daughters of farm labourers and these women might not even be familiar with family or area distinct designs. Before commercial patterns were in print, and literacy was almost universal, the average farmer's daughter who married the average river fisherman would have not even known how to knit a gansey. When she learned, she might well have been learning from someone from a different area than her husband. As Harry Fletcher pointed out, many keelmen and their families were not literate. Patterns had to be carried in the head (Fletcher, *Life on the Humber*). Applying genealogy methods to studying knitting history has allowed me to locate concrete examples of that migration that knitting histories only vaguely talk about.

One of my ancestors is the Humber/Ouse fisherman, William Richardson. He was born in Keyingham, Yorkshire, in 1797. William married along the river, at Ottringham. His wife, Mary Ablett, had relatives in Wistow, on the Ouse. By the 1841 census, he was living in Wistow, listed as "ag lab" (agricultural labourer) on the Ouse. In the next census he is once more listed, as at his wedding, as "fisherman." William would have alternated fishing and labouring on the farms, as many fishermen did. Born near the coast, his movement inland along the Humber, and later the Ouse, would have brought Hull and Humber estuary patterns along the river as far as Wistow. That is, thirty miles inland. That is a concrete example of the migration of fishing folk, and, with them, their knowledge that some knitting historians mention.

In the context of the time, this was an unusual amount of mobility. In England there were settlement laws. Parishes didn't want to be saddled with paying out dole money for another parish's indigent poor, orphans, or illegitimate children who the parish would be liable to support if no father came forward. As a rule, if the average "ag lab" wanted to move villages he had to obtain a settlement order. This meant that the new parish was liable for him. Parishes were constantly fighting settlement orders and trying to compel unwanted poor folk back to their birth village as a result. The average working-class English family had to stay where they were born, in other words. Fishermen had a good income (sometimes) and also the physical means (their own vessels) to move from parish to parish or even county to county. The Abletts of Ottringham married for two successive generations into my own Wistow families. Both Ablett women were from fishing families and would have brought their store of Humber gansey patterns with them when they moved to the Vale of York and intermarried with the landlubbers.

One of the former fishermen who volunteers at the Scarborough Maritime Heritage Museum, a Scarborough man, told me that his ancestors came from Norfolk in the eighteenth century. When tracing the huge, internecine fishing family, the Jenkinsons of Filey, I discovered they also turned up from Norfolk in the eighteenth century. Fishermen were literally more mobile, from region to region, at a time when the rest of the UK population was absolutely static. With William Richardson I saw the same thing on my family tree. Six-hundred years' worth of farmers stayed in the same handful of Vale of York villages, but my only fishermen ancestors, William Richardson and Robert Guy Nattriss, had moved 30–50 miles from their birthplaces.

No reason to doubt, then, that little Mary Jane Langmaid down in Cornwall would have known the same Humber patterns my Abletts, Durhams, and Richardsons would be familiar with. Our patterns migrated, and probably morphed, as they influenced each other. Every time I look at the famous Harding photos now, I'm aware that a Humber-born child was among the folk knitting those Cornish ganseys. It is this same cross fertilization of patterns that defeats the old myth that ganseys were so distinct to one place or even family.

Seafaring folk's mobility makes them hard to find in local censuses. I searched for the fisherman wearing my favourite gansey pattern in the Lewis Harding photos, one Richard Searle. By the 1861 census, Richard was listed as married, 29, a sailor in the Merchant Service, living on Lansallos Street in Polperro. Sometimes, coastal mariners went to work for masters on merchant vessels or even the Royal Navy. They might be on board ship on census night but in a port five counties away. Crews might have been signed on from various places, encouraging still further the cross pollination of patterns. Censuses show us men shifting from fisherman to mariner to merchant seaman or sailor, Royal Navy, and back to fisherman across censuses. A crew could also come from many different counties. Patterns thus changed, evolved, and were subject to new influences. Women would admire each other's handiwork and have plenty of time to commit to memory new and interesting patterns, while at church or chapel.

Every year, on Robin Hood's Bay, Debbie Gillander holds the Propagansey event. Numerous ganseys: many from Robin Hood's Bay itself, also Whitby and other places along the Yorkshire coast, are displayed at the eerie, windswept, utterly beautiful location of Old St. Stephen's Church. I'll admit to keeping the old stealing-a-pattern-in-church tradition alive, by memorizing the most gorgeous gansey patterns, some of which might well surface later as part of a gansey design! We continue to influence and learn from each other. I doubt if 100 years ago a knitter would spot a pattern she fell in love with but continue to knit another simply because it was from "my village" or "my family." Knitters might have had favourite elements. I often incorporate a heart design, alternating open and moss-stitch filled hearts in a vertical pattern, down a gansey. As my father was dying, I distracted myself with my knitting and adapted an existing Bridlington pattern. My father's family always made a beeline to Brid, as the locals call it, on their rare days off work. Now I often knit heart motifs as a sort of memorial. I think all gansey knitters take, and transform, the old patterns, and often ganseys reflected what was going on in a knitter's daily life.

Motifs' Names

Part of the romance of ganseys are what Rae Compton called the patterns' "lyrical" names. What's not to love about names like Betty Martin, Eye of God, flag, ropes, steps, Humber star, Mary Ann's stitch, lattice, bird's eye, marriage lines, lightning, and so on? The same stitch might have different names in different counties. There was probably more geographical variation in the names than the actual stitches! I suspect colourful names were made up more as a form of mnemonic notation. If you found yourself sitting behind a particularly good gansey in church, it would be easier to memorize the pattern if you consigned it to memory as panels of Betty Martin, mask, heart, or rope.

The Myth That Ganseys Were Just for Mariners

Conventional knitting histories imply that only mariners wore ganseys. When we think of ganseys we think of mariners. In fact, even in the early days of ganseys, they were worn by many different professions, as a trawl of the British Library Online's collection of nineteenth-century newspapers reveals. Sometimes, the devil is in the detail – or the small ads! This ad for frame-knit ganseys, from the *Leicester Chronicle*, in 1840, gives us some idea of the wider population of gansey-wearers.

> A very superior Guernsey frock, which for elasticity, neatness, show, durability, etc., cannot fail to take with those by whom such articles are most worn, viz: labourers on rail-roads. They will also become an article of request abroad, particularly in Canada and the United States of America.

Leicester, in the Midlands, was one of the hubs of the frame-knitting industry. Yorkshire soldiered on throughout the century with hand-knitting on an industrial scale, making ganseys more widely available. Even trendsetting royals could be found sporting the gansey. As early as 1847, Queen Victoria and her family are described in *The Standard* arriving at Douglas, Scotland, on the royal yacht. "The

Prince of Wales ran about the deck of the Royal yacht, dressed in a Guernsey frock, and duck trowsers and having the further insignia of the daring trade of a Jack Tar in a knife slung to a piece of lanyard." From society's elite to the lowest brigand, a knitted body garment was seen as vital to the image. An anonymous man describes in *Lloyd's Weekly Newspaper* his theatrical costume when he was playing a brigand, "My dress was a sky-blue knitted vest, opening down the front, with a wide embroidered border of yellow and scarlet, clasped with a filigree brooch."

Nineteenth-century England had an almost scary specificity when it came to occupational costume. Given how cold Yorkshire can be, it's a mystery why no farmers are to be found wearing jumpers in nineteenth-century photographs – ever! Ganseys seem to have been the preserve of a certain band of folk – not just mariners as people now assume, but others, too. I scoured the nineteenth-century newspapers for references to ganseys, and most seemed to belong to mariners, of course, but there was also a lively sub-category of house-breakers and burglars described wearing a gansey. For example, this from *The Star, St. Peter Point*, a witness describing a house-breaker: "When the man left the garden, she took particular notice of him. He wore a knitted frock and a brown cap." Also convicts on the prison hulks (rotting ships moored on the Thames and at Portsmouth where convicts awaited transportation to Australia), were sometimes supplied with a gansey for winter wear. According to the *Morning Post*, a national newspaper, reported an inquest into the deaths of convicts on September 18, 1846.

> An erroneous impression having gone abroad that such unhappy creatures are nearly starved and worked to death, the following official return of food and clothing, issued from the Secretary of State's office, will tend to remove such doubts. Annual clothing, 2 jackets, 3 pair of trousers, 3 shirts, 4 pair of stockings, 3 pair of shoes, 2 hats, 2 handkerchiefs, 1 waistcoat, 1 blanket, and 1 Guernsey frock. Dr. Bossey said he had the power to order any luxury or indulgence during sickness to the convicts.

When we see Guernsey frock, we should exercise a little caution, as it can refer to a canvas smock and seems to have been used interchangeably for both this and a knitted frock. In the case of the convicts, it does seem likely the garment was knitted as references are sometimes made to its warmth. Also, they could have been easily made by female convicts who often had to knit for their hard labour. And most sentences involved hard labour in the nineteenth century! Ganseys are also useful for the commission of crimes. Occasionally nineteenth-century police or gamekeepers chasing poachers grumbled that the suspect got away because he was wearing a gansey. That is, he had greater freedom of movement!

There are countless mentions of ganseys in the context of sailors committing, or being victims of, crime, in the nineteenth-century newspapers. In the *Champion and Weekly Herald* on Sunday, December 11, 1836, a gansey featured in an act of chivalry, when a captain charges a prostitute with stealing. A sovereign is found in her bed, but, "An old man, who said he was a ship's carpenter, stepped forward. He said he had slept in the same bed on the previous evening alone and lost a half-sovereign out of his pocket. He also left a guernsey frock behind him." Ganseys are stolen from shop windows, which again tells us many weren't lovingly knit by

Image courtesy of Beamish Museum.

relatives but made by contract knitters to be sold. Ganseys were stolen from washing lines. Ganseys were found on suicides and mariners drowned at sea.

Real life convicts were issued Guernsey frocks in winter – though here we should show a bit of caution, as Guernsey frock can refer to a woven, heavy-duty sort of smock, as well as a knitted garment. Discussing the treatment of convicts in January, 1844, *Lloyd's Weekly Newspaper* gave the guidelines for convicts' clothing: "1 suit of clothes, 2 shirts, 2 handkerchiefs, 1 hat, Guernsey frock (in winter), 2 pair of stockings, 1 pair of shoes (without even laces)." Guernseys even come up in debates about convicts being neglected or maltreated. There were frequent assurances that convicts were adequately dressed, and mentions of guernseys or Guernsey frocks provided as evidence to that effect.

Prisoners weren't just wearing knitting but also producing it. Men committed to hard labour at York's House of Correction were doing things like stone-breaking. But according to the *York Herald* of July 10, 1858, "The female prisoners committed for hard labour had been employed in knitting, sewing, and washing for the other prisoners." So much for knitting being a sedate hobby for delicate Victorian ladies. It was perceived as hard labour for convicts and a female equivalent to stone-breaking! This tells us something about the vast quantities of knitting churned out, the sheer brutal pace of knitting stocking after stocking, year in, year out.

Arctic explorers, too, in the age before polar fleece and high-tech fabrics, relied on the warmth of wool. During the inquiry into the ill-fated Franklin Expedition of 1851, *The Morning Post* reported the clothing provided to expedition crew:

> The men should start in the following dress: 1 flannel shirt or Guernsey frock, 1 pair of drawers, 1 pair of blue serge or knitted frock, 1 pair of breeches, waist belt, 1 pair of worsted stockings, 1 pair cloth boots, comforter, Welsh wig, Southwester, mitts, veil, jacket or sealskin jumper, the latter is much preferable, being longer, less bulky and cumbrous (Anon., "Sir J. Franklin").

A serge frock was a heavy-duty woven woollen cover-all a bit like an agricultural laborer's smock. Welsh wig was a Monmouth cap, a simple, knitted hat.

This notice from the *Caledonian Mercury*, describing a suicide, hints at yet another section of society to be found wearing ganseys: "He was dressed in an old black coat and vest; moleskin trowsers, a blue Glengarry bonnet, and had a Guernsey frock over his clothes. The deceased had the appearance of a mechanic." The *Manchester Times* for December 13, 1845, gave an inkling that coal miners also might wear ganseys when one coal miner stole from another "a black jacket, white linen shirt, Guernsey frock and a silk handkerchief."

Crime reports are a feast for the average genealogist, and they prove to be rich pickings for the knitting historian, as well. I found numerous reports of ganseys stolen from clothes lines and shops as well as literally hundreds of descriptions of unknown suicides and witness descriptions of criminals at crime scenes. A Cornish newspaper, *Trewman's Exeter Flying Post*, described a burglar killed mid-spree when shot by a householder. "He was dressed in a blue Guernsey frock, striped." Then, at inquest, two days later, the newspaper reported, "The man who was shot is now for certain identified as Abraham Green, a well-known gypsy desperado."

Knitting even played its part in some early forensics in a horrific Mirfield (South Yorkshire) murder case in 1847. Two victims were found with their throats cut. One of them, Caroline Ellis, had been wearing a knitted garter (band to keep the stockings from falling down, commonly tied just above or just below the knee). McCabe was the suspect. The *York Herald and General Advertiser* reported:

> The garter taken from the leg of Caroline Ellis, and the portion of garter found at McCabe's house, will be produced. At the last trial, a lady whom, I am told, is the mistress of the blind school in York, was accidentally in court, and she has since communicated to us her thoughts with respect to the garters. I need hardly tell you that the mistresses of such establishments are conversant with all kinds of knitting because that is the way the children who are placed under their care are employed, and her judgement is the garter taken from the leg of Caroline Ellis, and the portion of garter found at McCabe's house, have been knitted by the same hand. Miss Lambert, the witness I have alluded to, will also tell you that she thinks that the two garters had been worn for about the same time.

On the Vale of York, in Escrick, suspicions were raised when a murdered farmer's wife, Ellen Taylor, who was a compulsive knitter, according to witnesses, was found dead without knitting in hand. Ellen's body was found smouldering by the farmhouse fire, but the local doctor realized she had been strangled and the body placed by the fire to make it look like accidental death. Ellen had been knitting a stocking that morning, when last seen by her family. Yet her knitting was nowhere near the body. Ellen's knitting mysteriously turned up the following day, found by a neighbour, in Ellen's bedroom. Her daughter, Elizabeth quoted in the *York Herald*, said at the trial:

> My mother was in the habit of knitting a good deal. She was knitting when I last saw her. She kept the knitting in the house. We looked for it but could not find it that day. I know Jane Brabbs. She brought my mother's knitting to me on the Wednesday morning; it was raffled [sic]. It looked dirty and the "loops" down. I had never before then seen my mother's knitting in that state.

At trial, Jane Brabbs recalled finding the stocking, "partly knit. It was raffled and the needle was half out." Ellen's husband, Jonathan Taylor, was found guilty and sentenced to death. Knitting was such an ongoing task for Yorkshirewomen, long after frame-knit stockings were around. One village away from poor Ellen Taylor, my own farming and river-fishing ancestors would also have knit constantly, in between other, more pressing tasks.

South of Yorkshire, on a Birmingham message board there was an interesting thread about the word *gansey*. Older Brummies recalled a time when the word *jumper* was used instead and discussed whether this was a universal thing or a Birmingham peculiarity.

> I think you will find it originates from the Irish community from my school days in Selly Oak with so many Irish school pals. They all called their football jerseys ganseys. I'm going back to late 1940s.
>
> It was a woollen knitted garment, I believe, distributed to the poor by a police charity in Digbeth. As a rule of thumb, I think if you qualified for the Mail Boots, you qualified for a gansey.
>
> My dad always called his cardigan a gansey. Even a nice jumper I knitted him, he called a gansey.

What I found interesting about this is that Birmingham is as far inland as you can be in the United Kingdom. In every direction! Although it is also famous for having more miles of canal than Venice. And yet here, this far inland, was a culture of ganseys. And the word which had died out before living memory, in Yorkshire dialect, remained alive and well in the West Midlands, further south and with no maritime culture, although a thriving inland waterways one.

Sometimes, the very same primary sources I'd look at for my family history research yielded knitting clues. Wills and probates are useful references for the history of clothing and textiles. In the days when every single thing was hand-spun and hand-woven or hand-knit, clothes and fabrics were valued, prized, and recycled. Sometimes inventories of the deceased's house and its contents were detailed, including knitted items, fleece, and yarn. In 1526, John Hemyngwaye of Halifax, Yorkshire, left "four stone of wool" to one of his sons. In 1557, Jenet

Hemmyngway left "my best weddersheip" (ewe) to one of her sons, and a lamb each to four other people. Farm records and stock books also might still exist and be archived somewhere locally. These could be a rich future source of further information.

Color Variants

We now think of English ganseys being a standard blue (at earlier dates it was probably dyed with a mixture of indigo and woad as they believed woad was less fugitive a dye) or cream, natural off-white wool. Grey specimens are not uncommon in museum collections either. There was more variation though. In *The Old Hand-Knitters of the Dales*, Marie Hartley and Joan Ingilby described various kinds of contract knitting going on throughout the nineteenth century. The jerseys showed a fair amount of variation. They knitted "spotted frocks" (probably usually a white background with a spot of blue, again suggestive of a Danish influence – think of the Danish *luskofte*) and seaman's jerseys, which they called "popped uns" with thin stripes or bands of coloured knitting popping out from a plain background. I think I have found the earliest extant photograph of a popped un in Adamson and Hill's photograph, Mr. Laing (1843), showing a young man with tennis racket in hand, wearing a white-and-colour-striped, tight-fighting gansey. Also, there were undyed, simple white jumpers, with a V of purl stitches at the neckline.

Later, the Dales knitters diversified into knitting jumpers for cyclists, too. In the late nineteenth century cycling became hugely fashionable and there was an influx of pedal-pushing tourists into the Dales. These jumpers would probably have resembled the mariners' ganseys in structure. In my searches through the nineteenth-century newspapers, I found accounts that back up Marie Hartley's description of the popped uns and spotted frocks. Describing the wreck of *The Louisa*, the *Morning Post* on November 5, 1841 stated: "Sir G. Brema landed on the Praya Grande in a red Guernsey frock and drawers." And this, in *The Standard* on November 10, 1840, described the mystery body found in a ditch: "An inquest was held today upon the body of a well-dressed man, [witness deposed body was wearing]. His clothes appeared to be quite new. A red-striped cotton shirt, a specked guernsey frock over his shirt, and a blue jacket over all, and canvass trousers which appeared not to have been washed." I found numerous references to striped or spotted guernseys, usually suggesting a colour against a natural cream or grey background and colours included scarlet. In *Good Old Hessle Road*, Alec Gill wrote about the Hull-born herring girls, who followed the herring fishing fleets around the coast of Scotland and England, throughout the summer. Herring girls spent their time gutting, kippering and packing the herrings, and as a result adapted their own ganseys, to a more practical short-sleeved version. The herring lasses' ganseys were all kinds of pastel colours, including pink, turquoise, and lemon. This challenges the idea of a stereotypical navy blue gansey. Today, gansey yarns are currently available from Frangipani in 26 colours, which reflects the gansey's true palette.

Mrs Catherine Cappe.

Engraved by W. Bond from a Miniature.

Knitting in Schools, Prisons, and Homes

In which we encounter nine "miserable girls" knitting upon the town, deranged teachers, and knitting as hard labour.

> 'Alright ... You can leave him here, if he's a good boy we will give him plenty of pudding, and if he's obstreperous he shall have plenty of strap.' I went up at once to the school-room; it was a very large room, by about 80 yards long by about 15/16 yards wide, and very lofty. Half of this room was occupied with hand-looms and spinning wheels at which the boys were accustomed to make grey calico.
>
> —Ups and Downs of a Blue Coat Boy, by 'A.O.S', London, Houlston & Sons (no date, Victorian)

ANOTHER MYTH WAS THAT KNITTING WAS A GENTEEL occupation done at the cottage door and by the light of a peat fire. While this was true in some rural areas, it is not the whole picture. As Herbert Heaton wrote in *The Yorkshire Woollen and Worsted Industries*, "Around the spinning wheel has centerd the Arcadian conception of eighteenth-century bliss; but, like most popular opinions as to the charms of the 'good old times,' it must be taken with a great deal of caution." In our haste to view knitting through rose-coloured glasses, we can easily miss how it was really practiced two centuries ago.

Home-Schooling Knitters and Farm Knitting Schools

Some children were taught to knit at home. The vast majority of knitting must have consisted of stockings, with caps and gloves/mitts running second. In the decades leading up to the flowering of the gansey, knitters were honing their skills on the stocking, which had something in common with the ganseys in that they were knit in the round, and sometimes had clocks (relief patterns on the sides, in purl stitch).

FACING PAGE: CATHARINE CAPPE. IMAGE COURTESY OF LONG PRESTON HERITAGE GROUP.

As we have already seen in some parts of the county, informal knitting schools were set up in remote farm houses where children would learn to knit at a galloping pace. These children tended to be the children of farmers or labourers who could afford to pay something toward their children's education.

The most famous example is the story that Lake Poet Robert Southey retold in *The Doctor*. Wordsworth's sister-in-law, Sara Hutchinson, transcribed the story in dialect by the elderly Betty Yewdale of Rydal. Back in the 1760s, Betty and her sister Sally were sent to a farm near Dent to learn to knit. The girls weren't mistreated as such, although child was set against child to teach them to knit swiftly. The girls disliked the foreign food, and they weren't allowed to eat dinner if they didn't knit the allotted amount. The school employed all kinds of tricks to make the girls knit more quickly. One snowy evening, they decided to run away and find home. It took them three days, and eventually, cold and exhausted, they reached Langdale at 2 a.m.

In the Dales, Westmorland and Cumberland, as on the Vale of York, boys as well as girls learned to knit. The emphasis was on speed and ergonomics, and plain stockings were considered the most suitable project for young hands. Dale farmers wore blue stockings; poorer people wore natural grey or white and some prison inmates, yellow. Workmen, navvies, and miners as well as mariners wore grey boot hose. Just as the York charity children were expected to be able to knit a stocking in six days, the Dale children learned by knitting their own purple socks. Douglas-Kay wrote in *The Dalesman* magazine, "Mrs. Bell recalls seeing her grandmother knitting long, grey sea-boot stockings of bump. This was thicker than worsted and very greasy. Any bump left over was washed, dyed purple with logwood chips, and knit into children's socks." Clara Sedgwick learned to knit at preschool age. Clara's first project were simple garters. "Mrs. Sedgwick was taught to knit before she went to school. When Clara had made the grade with garters, she graduated to stocking knitting on four needles, " wrote Kathleen Kinder in *The Dalesman* magazine in 1981. These would be simple strips in garter stitch, meant to be tied just above or below the knee, to hold up stockings. Garters seem to have been a common product of charity schools.

In 1996, Maurice Colbeck interviewed Dent knitters Betty Hartley and Elizabeth Middleton (Colbeck, "Gran Taught Her to Knit"). Betty said, "My grandmother was one of the terrible knitters and she taught me." Colbeck added, "Betty was only three when she first plied the needles. Betty's own first piece of knitting was a little bit of a sock – not surprising, since a great proportion of Dent's output was socks, plus nightcaps, waistcoats, and fishermen's ganseys, at first made from wool produced in the Dale from their own Swaledale sheep." (To clarify, socks and stockings were knit from Swaledale wool.)

As late as 1800, a lot of hand-spinning was still going on in Northern England. In *The Dress of the People*, John Styles writes:

'Woman Spinning', Plate XXX, *Costume of Yorkshire*, George Walker, 1814.

> Northern plebeian families characteristically spun both linen and woollen yarn, had it woven and dyed, and then made it into garments. Criminal cases in the north of England repeatedly mention yarn spun by the women of a household being woven locally and then made up into garments for the household's use. Knitting stockings for household use from yarn spun by members of the family was commonplace enough for Joseph Eastwood, a clothier from Huddersfield accused of stealing several pounds of white wool in 1785, to claim in his defence that he took the wool to make stockings.

Almost every Daleswoman interviewed in the 1950s by Freda M. Douglas-Kay mentioned the fact that a grandparent had taught them to knit. Their grandparents could well have learned from someone who attended one of the last knitting schools. Colbeck pointed out that Cage Farm was the site of one of the famous old knitting schools. A Mrs. Cornthwaite of Sedbergh told Douglas-Kay that she "was taught to knit by her grandmother, Mrs. Dinsdale, who as a child attended a knitting school at Blandses Farm, Frostrow, now in ruins." I went in search of the knitting school at Blandses Farm through censuses and could only find the Blands family farming there. At a later date, the area had lead miners and labourers, and the farm became known as Blades, probably as the original family died out of local memory.

Several other farms with knitting schools are mentioned in *The Old Hand-Knitters of the Dales*. The most notorious knitting school was the one in Dentdale where little Betty and Sally Yewdale were sent, where "neet an' day ther was nought but this knitting!" It seems that catching them young was the secret to building up speed and dexterity.

Dame Schools and Charity Schools

Apart from the farmers' knitting schools, other schools also taught knitting. Betty Hartley remarked during her interview with Colbeck, "At one time everybody in Dent used to knit, even the children who learned it at the dame schools, along with the three Rs" (Colbeck, "Gran Taught Her to Knit").

Dame schools were the cheapest form of education. Many taught almost no reading, writing, and arithmetic at all but concentrated on the children learning more practical skills like knitting and sewing. In *No Idle Hands: The Social History of American Knitting*, Anne L. Macdonald noted that the United States also had dame schools where children were taught their letters with horn books and given rudimentary instruction in knitting and sewing.

A surprising amount of knitting went on in charity schools in towns and cities across the country. Many of these schools had their roots in the seventeenth century. Bridlington's knitting school was established straight after the English Civil War in 1648. Leeds Prison was set up in 1629, and, according to Heaton, poor children were "taught to mix wools and perform other parts of that manufacture." In Beverley's poorhouse, the poor were put to work spinning and knitting from the seventeenth century onward. Heaton calls these "Yorkshire factories prior to the Industrial Revolution." Prisons and charity schools were centres of manufacture right from the beginning.

In coastal areas, children often honed their skills by knitting the plainer sections of ganseys, such as the lower sleeves or the tedious ribbed welts, passing the knitting over to a parent to complete, like an early form of the production line. In Bridlington, known for its ganseys, you would expect a strong tradition of children learning to knit at their grandparents' knee, but, in fact, Bridlington had an old, established knitting school. On June 22, 1849, the *Hull Packet* announced the death of Mrs. Pickery, "many years the mistress of the knitting school." In April 1861, the *York Herald* announced her successor's death. "April 19, at Bridlington, aged 59, Ann, with Mr. Nathaniel Smith. Mrs. Smith had been many years mistress of the knitting school at that place." Two years later, in the same newspaper came this announcement: "Smith. On the 29th January at Bridlington, aged 77, Mr. Nathaniel Smith, for several years master of the Endowed Knitting School."

I followed the Smiths through the censuses. In 1841, already middle-aged, Nathaniel was a farmer in his native Osmotherly. Later, he was in Bridlington and described as "late saddler." It seems Ann Smith was knitting mistress for some time, and on her death, her husband, the elderly ex-farmer, succeeded her. This is another hint toward the fact that some farmers, and not just in the Dales, supplemented their earnings by teaching knitting. Even in coastal Bridlington, an ex-farming family were the repository of knitting knowledge! For some years after Nathaniel's death, the school went into abeyance and money generated from the charitable foundation was still clocking up interest. It took some time for the school to be re-established as local councillors formed a committee to work out how to revive the former knitting school and so use the funds accruing.

At some point the phoenix must have risen from the ashes as the Yorkshire Herald of May 1891 covered an inquest into the sudden death of "Jane Coulson, 76, formerly mistress of the knitting school." I found Jane, the unmarried daughter of a Bridlington shoemaker, on censuses. In 1861 she was a boot and shoe binder. But by 1871, she was living on Church Green by the knitting school and was a "knitting school mistress." The Bridlington school was funded by a charitable foundation, set up in the 1640s, which presumably is why it continued to be able to function long after hand-knitting was really a viable trade. I do wonder how many of the Bridlington ganseys were influenced by Ann and Nathaniel Smith or Jane Coulson. Again, genealogy puts some names into the hat and brings back these ordinary people to us from more than one hundred years' anonymity.

What, exactly, were charity schools? Education was not free in England, or even accessible to all, until the 1870 Education Act. Prior to that, your best chance of obtaining a free education was a charity school. Knitting was a part of the curriculum for younger boys and all girls wherever working class children were taught.

By the late eighteenth century, Quaker women in particular were becoming a force to be reckoned with in British education. The *York Herald* of March 7, 1801, reported:

> We feel great pleasure in announcing, a very excellent institution, established at Campsall, near Doncaster, under the immediate management of Miss Franks. A Female Friendly Society is formed for the education of the poor in that village. The children are taught to read and write as well as instructed in knitting, spinning, sewing, and other useful employments, training them in habits of industry.

Fifty years later, the *York Herald* for May 4, 1850 discussed the Annual Report of the York Ragged School. "The younger boys are engaged in oakum picking, netting, and knitting. The elder in tailoring, shoemaking, and cobbling. The girls are taught sewing, knitting." In *The Old Hand-Knitters of the Dales*, Marie Hartley recalled, "As a dalesman said, 'Knitting's like stone-breaking, you have to carry on to make owt.'" The York House of Correction allowed women to knit in preference to stone-breaking which the men did. This gives us a sense of how back-breaking and relentless the volume of knitting was! Quakers reformed prisons and tackled poverty at a grassroots level. Knitting was seen as a weapon in the war on want, and these women weren't afraid to use it.

One such woman was the remarkable Catharine Cappe. In 1800, she wrote a sort of memoir of how she set up the spinning and knitting schools in York. Her book was cleverly titled *An Account of Two Charity Schools for the Education of Girls: And of a Female Friendly Society in York; Interspersed with Reflections on Charity Schools and Friendly Societies in General*. The book cost three shillings, and proceeds went to the

'Weasel' or wool winder, Bankfield Museum, Halifax. Credit: Caro Heyworth.

schools. The book is a fascinating insight into spinning and knitting in eighteenth-century Yorkshire and is also highly significant.

Yorkshire charity schools churned out stockings in industrial, even heroic, quantities. Maybe the mariners of *The General Carleton* had some of its products aboard when it sank in 1785. The girls knitted the plain vanilla stockings: hardy, useful, well-made hosiery, nothing fancy. The 1780s stocking that I saw on loan from Gdansk to the Captain Cook Memorial Museum in Whitby was one such stocking. Just days after I held Catharine's 1800 book in my hand, I was in Whitby and couldn't believe my luck when I saw the temporary exhibition of knitted items from the wreck of *The General Carleton*. Here was your actual 1780s Yorkshire knitting!

The stocking on display in Whitby was probably precisely the kind that the charity school girls knitted from the 1780s to the 1820s. The stocking looked to be fairly small – possibly a boy's – and was blue and white with russet-coloured toes. The gauge was 6 to 7 stitches per centimetre. The knitter started the round at the side, above the ankle. The stocking had a square heel, and the leg was carefully shaped, involving two series of increases followed by decreases. The intriguing thing about it was the lack of uniformity in the ribbing: no neat 2×2 rib here. The ribbing that was visible to me through the display case consisted of 5K, 8P, 5K, 5P, 5K, 3P, 5K, 4P. I calculated the cast on to be around 140 stitches. This may be because the stocking was a learner's piece. But I think it is more likely the bizarre rib can be explained by the fact that ribbing to hold stockings up was still in its infancy. (Earlier stockings had a welt of plain stitches at the cuff.) Also, people still routinely knitted garters to hold their stockings up. Knitters were only just figuring out the elasticity of rib as compared to plain knitting. Maybe the whole concept of uniform ribbing is a modern one. This stocking had decreases at around 5 cm (2") from the cast on, decreases lasting for around 5 cm (2"), then an increase for 3 cm (1"), followed by decreases down to the ankle (10 cm or 4"). There are no clocks (ankle patterns in purl stitch commonly used to imitate the side gussets on earlier cloth hose). The foot measures 18–20 cm (7–8") long. The heel appears to be a straightforward square one, not unlike those from the earliest 1650 stockings.

This plain vanilla stocking would have been the staple product of Catharine's school, and it's possible they supplied mariners. The spinning school came before the knitting school and was thought up by Catharine Cappe and Mrs. Grey in 1782 after seeing the industrious but ignorant children of the York snickets and alleyways, working in a hemp factory. Catharine wrote, "Our first thought, was to have them taught to read, knit, and sew on an evening after they had finished their work at the manufactory." Catharine's books never mention the actual address of the school, but I was able to locate the spinning and knitting schools in St. Andrewgate, a short walk from York's famous Shambles.

In November 1782, twenty-two girls were taken at the start of the spinning school, and the ladies decided "to establish a school for the spinning of worsted" to protect the girls from the hemp factory's bad influences. Catharine noted that working-class mothers in York had to work as either char-women or washer-women, and so would leave the girls unattended all day. So even those girls that did not work themselves often got into bad company.

At the start, the Quaker Ladies decided upon a system of humane punishment, noting the girls were already brutalized at home and so were not responsive to physical chastisement. So they settled instead on humiliation as a form of behaviour management. "For instance, if a child spun thick, be idle or wasteful of wool, it may be useful for the mistress to turn her bed-gown or to pin some of the thick-spun wool to her shoulder, threatening if she be not more careful and more industrious, she shall be exhibited to her patroness, or other accidental visitors to the school." Later in the century, an anonymous writer in *Souvenir of the Bi-Centenary of the York Blue Coat Boys and the Grey Coat Girls' Schools* described less humane forms of punishment at the Grey Coat School. "Every girl who goes without leave shall have a jacket put on with a red R upon it for one day; those who wish to go out twice, have the jacket put on, and handcuffed for a day; those who go out three times, to be locked up in the garret three days, fed on bread and water, and handcuffed for fear of hurting themselves."

By the nineteenth century the Grey Coat School doled out not just punishments for bad behaviour, but also weekly incentives for high production. Knitters who produced three stockings per week received 1½ d; for four mittens the reward was 1½ d; while the top-producing knitter received a pair of mittens. When you consider that the average stocking might have a cast on of around 150 stitches and be at least knee-length and knit at a gauge of 6 or 7 stitches per centimetre, that is a lot of knitting to complete in one week. Essentially, it meant a stocking every two days, which sounds steep to us, yet it must have been a feasible goal for the faster knitters to attain.

The Grey Coat School had been set up in 1705 to provide a "better education" for poor girls; firstly, orphans, then if places remained, children of parents "in distress," to save them from the parish poor house or "the houses of indigent relatives." The school had started with twenty girls. The girls were boarders with one master and one mistress and were taught to "read, sew, knit, and spin worsted." They were also taught to wash and do housework so that when they left, they could be apprenticed to "any decent family who might be desirous of taking them" (Cappe, *Account of Two Charity Schools*). Later, the school expanded to take thirty girls.

Simply being poor did not make you a shoo-in for the schools. Children had to qualify and vie for places. "In the year 1786, a knitting school was added for children too young to spin worsted. From this the spinners are taken as vacancies happen in the spinning school, and as they become eligible by knitting a stocking in the course of a week." What this tells us is that in the eighteenth century, knitting was considered to be easier than spinning, and mastered by younger children. When you consider these kids were turning a heel before age seven, it puts our contemporary fears of advanced techniques into perspective.

The children benefited directly from all this spinning. "As soon as the children can spin four hanks of wool per day, they are decently clothed, and moreover they receive one-fourth of their earnings in money." Two children were taken out, in rotation, to sew the clothes. Catharine remarked that if they hadn't made their own clothes in school, the children would have been "sent in such a state as would render their very superintendence nearly impracticable." By 1798, the spinning school had £207 and three shillings in the bank, a long-term lease on a house "containing rooms for the spinners and knitters," and an apartment for the two mistresses. The spinning mistress's duties included, "To superintend the wool spinning; to see it weighed before and after it is spun; to correspond with the manufacturers."

Catharine noted that it was difficult to find the perfect spinning mistress for her new school, on the wages available. They wanted someone who was not only competent but also kind and caring. They tried out several disastrous mistresses before, in April 1785, they engaged a Halifax woman. She left in 1786 and was almost impossible to replace. Periodically, ads would appear in the local papers, like this one in the *York Herald* of 1804.

- WANTED! At the Grey Coat School in this City,
- A Mistress to teach Reading, Sewing, Knitting, and Line-spinning.
- She must be a single woman and a member of the established Church.

The school's superintendents of the wool were Mrs. Dr. Withers and Miss Barton as well as Catharine herself. The school was a day school, with children coming in from home. In 1797, concerned with the fact the children had often had no breakfast and were flagging, the ladies arranged for them to have milk for breakfast. Catharine had pioneered the spinning and knitting schools, but York already had a girls' charity school, the Grey Coat School. When Catharine was called in to reform it along the lines of her knitting and spinning schools, she found the girls were more likely to be found turning tricks than turning the spinning wheel!

In 1780, Catharine had visited York, only to hear that while the boys' school (Blue Coat) was fine, the girls' school turned out girls who were "sickly, remarkably low of stature, and unfavourable." The school's doctor remarked to Catharine that there were, to his knowledge, "nine miserable girls upon the town, the wretched victims of prostitution." Catharine decided to investigate. In 1785, the school was rebuilt and Catharine asked to visit. She found the girls "generally diseased in both body and mind; their appearance sickly and dejected; their ignorance extreme; and the description given to me by the new master and mistress of their moral depravity, truly deplorable." Catharine asked the committee to appoint two assistant teachers – one in the wool spinning room and the other to teach sewing, knitting, and line-spinning. In April 1785, Mrs .Lazenby, the mistress, became deranged and her husband, the school's master, put her in the lunatic asylum. (Probably The Retreat, York's ground-breaking, Quaker-run asylum, about which more later in this chapter.) The school's new strict regime was blamed for driving Mrs. Lazenby mad, and rumours were rife round the town about the school (Cappe, *Account of Two Charity Schools*).

Catharine pressed on with her reforms, appointing a new mistress and finally getting the school's committee to agree to abolishing the apprenticeships from October 17, 1786. Children were expected to work at everything in rotation: "wool-spinners, line-spinners, sewers, knitters, and house girls." The superintendent had "to superintend the wool-spinning; to see that it reaches the proper counts; that every pound is marked with the girl's name who spun it; that it is reeled right; that the mistress keeps her spinning closet in order, and spinning book with accuracy, to correspond with the manufacturer; keep all the accounts; receive the money earned by spinning; and to see every pound of yarn weighed before it is returned to the manufacturer" (Cappe, *Account of Two Charity Schools*).

Catharine undertook the role of spinning mistress at Grey Coats herself. She wrote a footnote in her book, describing the contents of the spinning mistress's closet.

> The wool spinning mistress has a closet divided like the clothes closet and reward box, with the name of each girl upon the partition appropriated for the reception of her particular hanks, as soon as they are spun. This closet the mistress examines every night, and she enters in a book what every girl has spun in the course of the day. This book is shown at the end of the week to the lady who pays the rewards; and each girl is separately commended or reproved, and her respective task raised or lowered accordingly as the circumstances may require. A book is likewise kept by the assistant mistress, with the particulars of the stockings knit, and line spun, in the course of the week. The same method is followed in the spinning school.

There are no extant records for the spinning and knitting schools, only Catharine's accounts of the project; but, according to the *York Herald* on April 30, 1859, the schools had been closed by the spring of 1859:

> LOT 3
> ALL THOSE 2 OTHER DWELLING-HOUSES adjoining each other, also situate in St. Andrewgate, one of which for many years past has been used and occupied as the spinning school, and contains two very large and commodious rooms, lately used as school rooms, and is now occupied by Mr. Peace, and the other is occupied by Mr. James Rymer, joiner. The above properties being held under the sub-chanter and vicars choral of York Cathedral, will be sold on very reasonable terms, on a forty years lease, renewable every fourteen years.

Elsewhere in Yorkshire, other schools also taught children to knit. In her 1805 book, Catharine remarked, "At Leeds, some ladies, friends of the author, have a school of the sort, where the girls attend only one-half of the day, the other half being employed in some branch of manufacture." The Howden poor of the nineteenth century were doled out "yellow stockings," according to the parish records and vestry meeting minutes. In the 1820s it was noted that stockings in the prison "are all in future to be dyed yellow." Yellow at this date would be most reliably gotten from weld. It was a cheap and user-friendly dye stuff. Presumably the paupers' yellow stockings would have marked them out on sight. Meanwhile, over in Ackworth, the school's committee noticed, "There were very few resources for an active-minded boy, besides play and mischief, is clear. So perplexing was the provision of sufficient employment in the school, that the committee resolved in 1792, to introduce knitting among the younger boys." Knitting as Ritalin, in other words! It wasn't long before the Ackworth school's women's committee was concerned the kids were spending too long on their knitting. According to Henry Thompson's *History of Ackworth School*, "It is believed it would be much better for children to be in the sewing School a part of every day and only knit an hour or two at a time instead of being kept in that school for two to three months together."

Knitting Schools in Prisons and Houses of Correction

If knitting and spinning were meant to keep working-class children productive and out of trouble, it was a logical extension in the Victorian mind to employ prisoners in the same tasks. At York House of Correction, "the female prisoners committed for hard labour had been employed in knitting, sewing, and washing for the other prisoners" (*York Herald*, July 10, 1858). Just over the Pennines in Manchester, civic dignitaries devised a cunning plan to avoid paying outdoor relief (welfare) to the children of the poor. They opened an industrial school for children living inside the workhouse. Workhouses were where the unemployed and indigent were sent. At the workhouse, families would be divided: men to the men's side, women to the women's and children kept apart from both. Inmates – including children – were assigned "work." But children also had to attend the school, where they'd be taught a trade and given three square meals a day but no money. The anonymous civic worthy boasted:

> Our school was opened in November, 1851. The little urchins are kept together from nine in the morning until six in the evening. They revel in three meals daily, and they are taught reading and writing, knitting, and sewing. On Thursday last we found in school nearly 80 children, from 2 or 3 years old to 8 or 10. There are two school rooms, and during the day the children pass a certain amount of time in each; one is presided over by a male pauper who teaches reading and writing; the other by a female pauper who teaches stocking knitting and shirt-making.
>
> —*Hull Packet*, February 11, 1848

The male pauper mentioned above was a former grammar schoolmaster who wistfully recalled that he had once been paid £120 a year to teach the classics. To put that in perspective, at a similar date, Anne Brontë was paid around £20 per year to be a governess. The pauper schoolmaster touchingly remarked that he couldn't do more for the prison children, if he was paid that much now. In a line worthy of Dickens, the civic official said, "We charitably assumed that his love of the classics did not lead him to think them a necessary ingredient in pauper education." Instead he was expected to teach the pauper children to read and write. The civic official said that this man's bad luck was the city's good luck as they didn't need to pay him to teach. They doubted they'd have got the scheme off the ground if they'd had a wages bill. Contrast this brutal Victorian attitude to the more enlightened eighteenth-century Quaker ladies.

In either case, however, the teaching of the schools was thought to impart valuable lessons to poor children:

> In the room presided over by the woman, some ten or twelve boys were devoting their attention to coarse blue stockings; while the girls' thoughts were intently fixed upon the shirts. "The boys I find, sir, knit better than the girls," said the mistress, and she added, "Here's a stocking, now done by a very little girl." It certainly was not equal in appearance to the product of a grandam, much less the work of a Nottingham stockinger and his loom, but it was a strong, warm-looking stocking and probably the mother of the very little girl who had knitted it never gave her child instruction half so valuable as had been imparted to her in the pauper school, before that coarse stocking was produced. All the stockings and shirts go into stock'(the tramp-house stock).

As this experiment was reported in the Hull newspapers, it looks likely that some Yorkshire civic worthies were entertaining similar ideas for industrial schools based inside their prisons. Heaton, in *The Yorkshire Woollen and Worsted Industries*, wrote, "The houses of correction in the West Riding were centres of woollen industry, and here the inhabitants were compelled to spend their time not in picking oakum or breaking stones, but in preparing yarn." I'd refine that a bit. Men and boys were set to picking oakum and stone-breaking. Knitting was seen as the female equivalent. In 1874, a staff reporter for London's *Daily News* described a visit to a female prison. The account mentioned one infamous inmate knitting stockings:

Stocking knitting is carried on extensively during the hours when the prisoners are allowed to sit in the corridors, each at her own cell door, in silence for one term, and freely chatting through the second. Passing a file of stocking-knitters on my way out of the prison, I noticed a woman of about thirty standing at the end of the row. She was full-featured, of sallow complexion, with dark eyes, and had her short, dark hair, pushed back under her cap. She was noticeable among the crowd because, while all the rest curtsied as the lady superintendent passed, and looked eagerly for the ever-ready smile of recognition, she, after casting one sharp, angry glance at the approaching visitors, stood sullenly regarding the floor. "Who is that," I asked Mrs. Gibson when we were out of sight and hearing. "That," said the lady superintendent, "is Constance Kent and a very hard subject she is to deal with. She is one of the few women in the prison whom I cannot 'get at.'"

—*Daily News* (London), December 30, 1874

Constance was the young girl at the centre of a notorious child murder in 1865, recently turned into a novel and TV film *The Suspicions of Mr. Whicher*.

Knitting at The Retreat, York's Quaker-Run Asylum

The Society of Friends had a beneficial influence on the treatment of the "insane," as well as the lives of the poor children who ended up in charity schools. The Retreat opened in the countryside outside York's city walls in 1796. It pioneered the humane and thoughtful treatment of the mentally ill and, like York's charity schools, became a model followed by enlightened social reformers all over the United Kingdom. The patients' disbursements' ledgers are a fascinating insight into the patients' personal expenditure: a series of meticulously kept account books detail the clothes, books, cloth to make clothing, sweets, tobacco, wine, magazines, and other little indulgences patients bought. It also lists their laundry bills and hair cuts. The disbursement books are large, dusty vellum volumes, with pages dedicated to individual patients. For many patients, their own page ends with a poignant list of funeral expenses. In among these detailed records, I trawled for any references to wool, knitting, and purchasing knitted items. From all I had read about The Retreat, I suspected the institution might have latched onto the idea of knitting or spinning as early occupational therapy. My suspicions proved correct: these records are a goldmine for any costume historian and proved to be fascinating for the knitting historian in particular.

In 1796, Ann Barrow spent one shilling and eight pence on a "Pr [pair of] stockings." That same year, shoe repair cost the same. "Spectacles" were more than double the cost of the stockings at three shillings. In 1797, Margaret Holt spent two shillings and five pence, on "1lb wool for her stockings and twining." (Twining probably meant plying.) One pound of wool would make three or four stockings, depending on the grist of the yarn spun. Also in 1797, Mary Pyle bought "1 Pr stockings ¾ silk for three shillings and 7 pence." Three-fourths silk clearly meant stockings that were three-fourths silk and one-fourth a fine yarn like merino; they were worth nearly three times the cost of ordinary woollen stockings. A year later, Mary was buying "worsted for stockings" at a shilling and eight pence, so

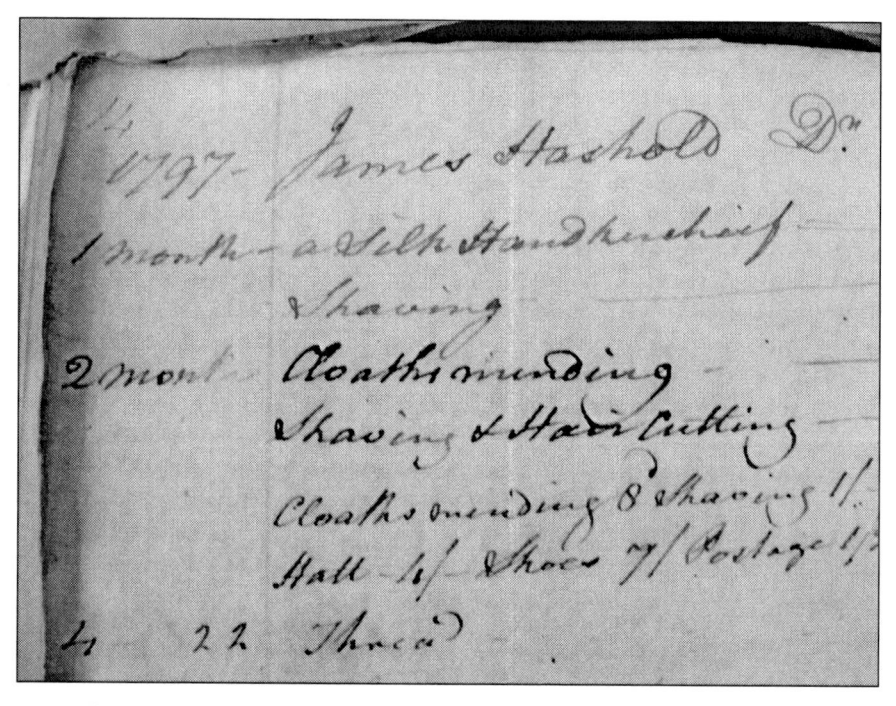

RECORDS FROM THE RETREAT ASYLUM, YORK. COURTESY BORTHWICK INSTITUTE.

presumably, the three-quarters silk were not an everyday thing. On July 12, 1799, Mary purchased "10 oz. of knitting yarn of cotton thread" for a mighty five shillings and one penny. Patients would have used cotton thread to knit either night caps or stockings, and ten ounces is a prodigious amount, clearly enough for a pair of stockings or two, again depending on how finely spun it was. At these dates, cotton or silk stockings with vertical stripes were highly fashionable, and maybe Mary chose to knit her own, as they would have been expensive to purchase, even if frame knitted. Frame-knitted, striped stockings were often worked flat then sewn up later. They tended to fray and yet were still a costly item. Knitting your own would be a practical solution.

Entries specifying knitting yarn continued consistently for decades. For example, Mary Kendall paid one shilling and eleven pence for "worsted for knitting" on August 28, 1805. At these dates, most worsted would end up being knitted into stockings. It was harder wearing than woollen-spun yarn (sometimes called fleecy in the earlier nineteenth century).

Patients were allowed out on day trips and even excursions lasting days or weeks; they were encouraged to take exercise both indoors and out, and so the need for stockings and stocking repair, as well as entries for shoes, and shoe repair, are very common. In May 1798, Hannah Ponsonby had "worsted for stockings paid H. Hull 3 shillings and 8d." Hull would either be another inmate spinning for income, or a local tradesperson. In 1811, Hannah spent five shillings on worsted for knitting. You could get two or three pairs of the cheapest quality woollen stockings for three shillings, and this is just the raw material, so I suspect the quantity would be enough to make more than a few pairs.

In 1799, long-term patient Hannah Forster had several items of haberdashery: "Silk 1½ crewel 3d knitting yarn," the lot totalling three shillings and seven pence. The silk and crewel may either have been to repair something or for embroidery, as most of the sum Hannah spent was on the knitting yarn. Just more than two weeks after Hannah bought the yarn, she needed just thruppence (three pence) worth of "stocking worsted," suggesting she needed just a little more to complete a project, or maybe to repair a different colour stocking! Hannah continued buying yarn regularly. For example, in 1807, she purchased "worsted last year. Silk. Cotton." In her second decade in the asylum, still knitting, her poignant entries remind us that at these dates there were no knitting manuals yet in print, and recipes for knitting were either carried in your head, passed on by a friend or relative, or possibly invented. As a young girl, the two Hannahs, Ponsonby and Forster, would have been taught to knit stockings, and that was so ingrained, they could continue even when shut away from the world for years on end, presumably knitting from memory.

These account book entries also tell us that some of the patients continued to knit while in The Retreat, sometimes to supplement their own stock of clothing, sometimes for something to do, and sometimes for other patients. The accounts' first mention of knitting needles comes in September 1799, when Judith Robertson had this entry: "10 Sept, Knitting needle 3d." In June 1800, Judith bought "patent knitting needles 3d pasteboard 4d–7d." Pasteboard was used to stiffen the brims of bonnets, and it is interesting that the patent knitting needles were actually cheaper than the pasteboard. Sadly, Judith's knitting career was brought to an abrupt end only months later, according to the entry for September, 1800: "shrowd: 7 shillings and 6d coffin 42 shillings." In 1807, Sarah Impey was to have a whopping "4 Pr knit stockings." A year later, we have an unusually detailed knitting reference, in Sarah's account, "Lambswool yarn for stockings' needles and fillet 3 shillings and 3d." A fillet was a lacy cap. It is not clear whether that was knitted or not but it is interesting Sarah had lambswool for stockings as that is rarely specified. Rennies' mills, in Scotland, were founded in 1798, and at the time of writing, they still produce a lambswool yarn that is remarkably sturdy and good for sock and stocking knitting, as many UK-based reenactors will attest. According to early knitting manuals, lambswool was a way of designating local, rather than imported, finely spun yarn. At later dates, it was thought to be a home-grown, and therefore cheaper, version of the imported Berlin wool. Sarah Impey's purchase was made during the Napoleonic Wars, when there were so many trade embargoes and restrictions across Europe that most, if not all, of the wool would have been grown in the UK anyway. After Napoleon was defeated, trade opened up and fancy German yarns became fashionable.

Knitting in Schools, Prisons, and Homes—65

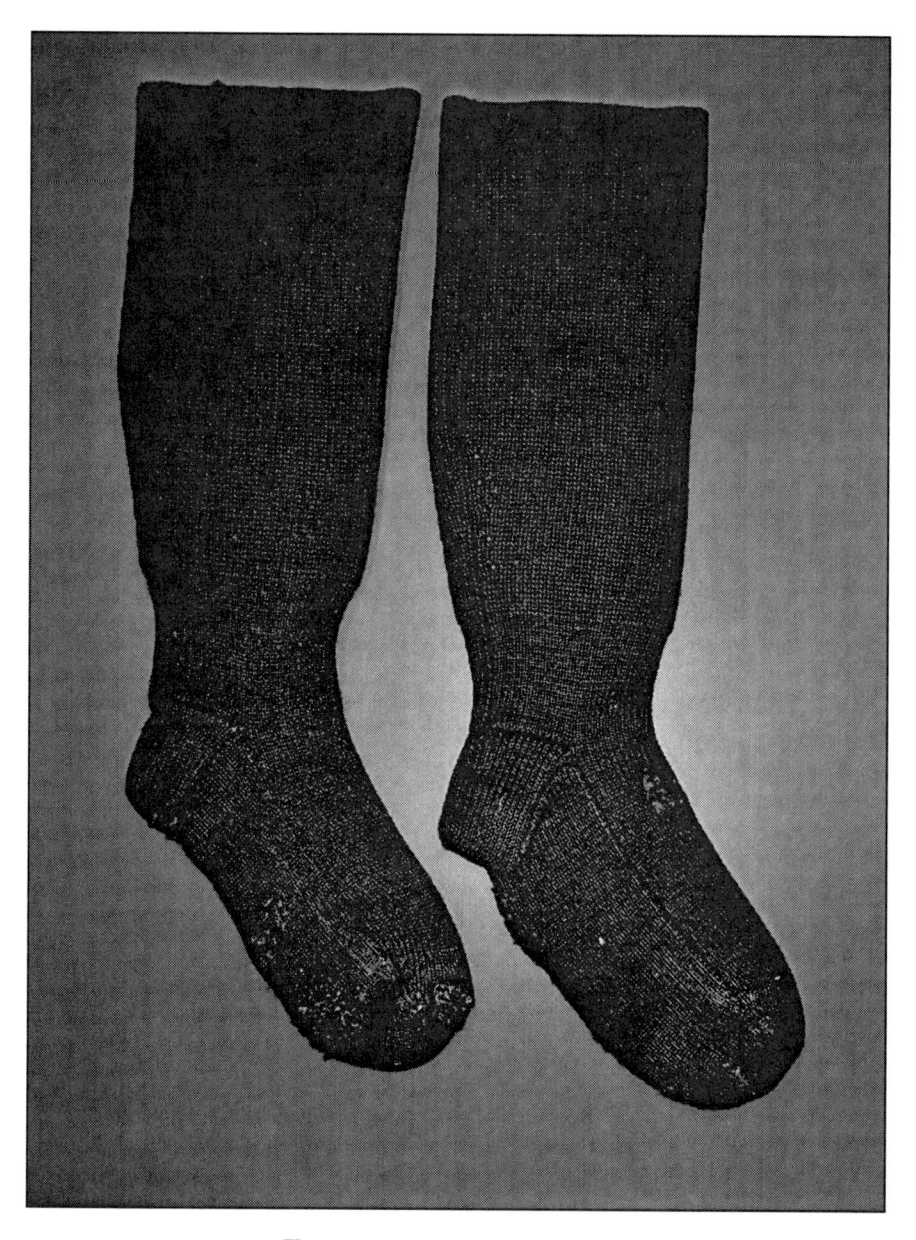

THESE STOCKINGS WERE KNITTED ON THE INLAND WATERWAYS.
COURTESY GOOLE MUSEUM.

In 1807, Ann Jepson paid just over three shillings for 15 oz. of stocking worsted. This would have been enough to make one pair of not too fine or coarse stockings. As the patients buying stockings are paying around this for the finished product, it seems that labour was the cheapest part of knitted goods at this time. A year later, Mary Smith paid two shillings and tuppence for "cotton yarn" and ten pence for needles. In 1809, there is this entry for Mary Boone, "Fleecy gloves 4 shillings." This could well mean they are made from fleecy wool, but it could also be an early reference to thrummed gloves. In the nineteenth century fleecy wool often was made from Blue-faced Leicester fleece.

Another interesting item is the 1812 entry for Thomas Atkinson, who ordered "yarn for muffatees ... 2 shillings and 9 pence." Muffatees were tubes, like fingerless mitts; sometimes with a slashed hole for the thumb. The fact that Thomas's muffattees needed more than two shillings' worth of yarn suggests they were rather lengthy, bearing in mind it cost between 1½ and 2½ shillings or so for enough yarn to knit a pair of stockings. Sometimes a knitter is named, as in Ruth Sheffield's account: "27 Jan 1809; worsted for stockings (knit by Ann Smith) 1 shilling and 9d." And this, from frequent flyer Sarah Impey's records, "4 August 1809 Prideaux for a Pr Stockings of her knitting 4/6."

It is almost unique for actual knitters to be named. For most of its history, knitting has been an anonymous art. As knitting historians, we see the famous extant pieces but have no clue who made them. To glimpse the real people behind the knitting is a privilege.

Increasingly, after the early 1800s, there are cryptic references to knitting worsted being supplied by "MW." Interspersed with the individual patients' accounts, at random intervals, entire pages are dedicated to recording the patients' work. From these accounts, it appears that patients both spun and knitted during the early years of The Retreat and interestingly, at the earlier dates, there are more male knitters and spinners than female. In 1797, there is a "Record of the Men Patients' Work: 17 Oct 1797 Rec'd for spinning one shilling and 2d. Knitting: two shilling and 5½ d." The accounts appear to record money raised by patients spinning and knitting for themselves or each other. Here, in 1797, the spinner is not named, but we know someone "rec'd for knitting Elizabeth Thompson 2 pair 2 shillings and 1d Received for knitting J. Reynolds 3 pair 3 shillings and 1d." In December of the same year, "Paid for 2lb 2 oz of dyed yarn (debit) 5 shillings and 3d." This means one pound of dyed yarn would cost around two and a half shillings. One pound of yarn would make maybe two pair of stockings. The same month one spinner received 11d for her spinning. In January 1798, we are told, "HK" had "received per pound of gray wool spinning and twining" 1 shilling and 3d. Twining probably means plying, so the spinner has been paid to spin and ply the yarn. Natural, undyed yarn like this would make the cheapest sort of stockings.

Here in these records we have proof of men still knitting and spinning, as well as women. It is in the male patients' work records we have entries like the one for May 5, 1798 that tell us "JW" had "Rec'd for knitting 1 shilling and 6d." Lucky "GS" received more than three shillings for "2 Pr of yarn stockings knitting" on the last day of 1798. It is possible these 1790s-1810s male knitters were from the Dales, and other hotbeds of commercial knitting, where men continued to ply the needles. The Retreat drew its patients from all over the United Kingdom, such was its fame, not just all over Yorkshire. At least one patient, according to case note records, Margaret Thwaite, a Quaker admitted with a "religious mania" came from Dent.

In 1800, the accounts record a payment of a shilling and a penny for one inmate's stocking repairs. "J Hasholds 2 Pr stocking footing." Seventeen years on, "James Hashold" was still being paid for knitting. From the 1808 patients' work record, we get the name of the recipient of the knitting, rather than the name of the knitter. "Jno Baker 2 Pr stockings & 2 night caps knitting. 4 shilling." On the May 18, 1808, we finally find out who the mysterious "MW," supplier of worsted, was. "Mary Wilson and J Cotton for Worsted 7 shillings and 11d."

The records of patients' work are patchy but those that exist for this period show there are patients consistently knitting stockings for certain other patients, and sometimes other items are knitted like cotton night caps. Taking November 1815 as an example, four pairs of stockings are knitted "in house." This might suggest anything from one to four regular stocking knitters, among the patients, knitting for other patients. One of the more prolific knitters was buying herself stockings from outside suppliers at the same time she was knitting them for other inmates, which suggests The Retreat had sensed the occupational therapy aspect of knitting. Additionally, there are the accounts of patients whose names do not appear on the pages except for the accounts of in-house knitting, who were buying yarn to knit, presumably, for pleasure. In 1808, one of the wealthier patients, Samuel Waring, paid a staggering eleven shillings for two pair of stockings. From this and his other expenditure, we can assume he was possibly buying silk stockings. In June, 1809, Benjamin Boynes had "a Pr of woollen gloves" for one shilling and 3d. Throughout the 1800s, 1810s, and 1820s, patients continued to knit with worsted, sometimes with cotton or silk or silk and wool blend. Knitting and spinning were almost the only pursuits where patients could profit and clearly were seen to have therapeutic benefits.

The End of Commercial Hand-Knitting in Yorkshire

By the middle of the nineteenth century, the annual report from the Wilberforce School for the Blind in York, bemoaned the fact that although the boys could find employment after their time at the school (they learned shoe-making and tailoring), the visually impaired young women fared much worse, with all of the female graduates remaining unemployed. They had been taught knitting. By the later nineteenth century, frame knitting was superseding hand-knitting. Frames became faster once they were steam-powered, but also they were improved to the point that they could knit fancier patterns, once the preserve of the hand-knitter. The Manchester prison guardian's comment that the little girl's hand-knitted stocking was not close to the quality of a Nottingham stockinger's, is rather telling. This same year it reported the Manchester experiment, the *Hull Packet* newspaper

EMILY STEPHENSON LISTER. IMAGE COURTESY SIMON LISTER.

reported this little snippet: "STOCKING KNITTING BY STEAM. A Norwich paper mentions that stockings are now knitted in Ipswich by machines, driven by steam, which perform this work with remarkable accuracy. One young person can attend three machines, and each machine can make a stocking in three hours." Norfolk's and the Midlands' gain was to prove Yorkshire's loss. At the same time, let's not forget that hand knitting and frame knitting had been in competition almost from the start as the first knitting frames dated back to Tudor times. There was a certain inevitability about what happened to the hand knitting trade.

Even so, as late as the 1890s, some women and children were still making a living by their needles. My only knitting ancestor is Lillian Stephenson, my great grandmother's cousin. Although cousins, the two little girls grew up together as Emily's father had died young, and Lillian was illegitimate. Both girls were cared for by their grandfather, leaving their mothers free to work. In the 1891 census, Lillian was living with her mother, grandfather, and my great grandmother, Emily, in industrial Shipley, in the West Riding of Yorkshire. Lillian was only thirteen and the only person for streets around to be described as a "stocking knitter." This tells me she probably was a hand knitter, not a frame knitter, as census enumerators usually made that distinction. Also, had she worked as a frame knitter, there would be others in the streets around. Frame knitters usually rented the machines they worked on and kept them in their own homes. They'd pay to rent the machines from the hosiery warehouse owner, and he'd buy from them the socks/stockings produced. So, although frame knitters tended to be spread out in censuses, a number of them often cropped up on one street or neighbouring streets. Emily was my father's favorite grandma, and he spent a lot of time with her, growing up in the 1920s and 1930s. He didn't recall her knitting, sadly. This does not mean she couldn't; for many it was a drudgery they were glad to leave behind.

By 1891, Lillian and Emily's grandmother was dead. Emily's father, Joseph Stephenson (a carpenter) had died, and her mother remarried so the little Yorkshire cousins lived with their grandfather, William Stephenson. My great grandma, Emily, was probably living there as Emily's mother had remarried. Emily clearly had a great love for the old carpenter, as she named one of her sons after him. "William Stephenson" were my grandfather's given names. Family legend had it we descended from Northumbrian father of the railways George Stephenson. In fact, William Stephenson descended from a long line of sheep farmers in neighbouring Westmorland. Cousin Lillian's unusual occupation may be explained by the fact that old William was from the Eden Valley in the uplands of Westmorland. His parents had married at Ravenstonedale, one of the areas discussed in *The Old Hand-Knitters of the Dales*.

Asked what were the highlights of writing *The Old Hand-Knitters of the Dales*, in 1970, Marie Hartley recalled, "Another walk led us to Ravenstonedale along a farm track three miles where we had heard there was a spinning gallery. Although we have never been since, no doubt it is still there." In the same interview, Marie Hartley said, "We regret that we did not meet Polly Stephenson who also used the 'swaving' action in knitting." I have no idea if Polly might be related to my Ravenstonedale Stephensons. I'm determined to think she was!

In 1801, Ravenstonedale folk knitted 1,000 pair of stockings a week. As the town's population was just more than 1,000 that's an average of one pair per person per week! Like the Vale of York families who alternated farming and being horse marines, the Ravenstonedale folk would earn up to six shillings a week from knitting, after the harvest was done. It could be that grandad William, master carpenter, or Lillian's late grandmother, had attended one of the upland knitting schools back in the 1830s, or were themselves taught by someone who had been there in the eighteenth century. Whatever the case, it is instructive that in the heart of industrial Shipley as late as 1891, one lone little girl who lived with a Westmorland grandfather was the only professional hand-knitter for streets around.

In the United Kingdom, education had been piecemeal and costly. Schooling ranged from the confusingly named "public" schools for the aristocracy, such as Eton and Harrow, down to the humbler town grammar schools where boys were taught the classics by Oxbridge dons, to board schools run by local churches, to the dame schools where boys and girls learned knitting, sewing, and a little reading and writing from a dame of the parish for a penny a week. Many people had no formal education at all. In 1870, the government passed the Education Act in a bid to make education universally available and free. The resulting board schools had a sort of national curriculum. Soon thereafter, in a pamphlet titled *A Standard Guide to Knitting According to the New Code*, an anonymous "Lady Manager" wrote of the different levels of knitting taught. Children started knitting a strip in garter stitch on two needles and progressed through to stockinette knitting, following a rigid, structured curriculum. After March 1879, knitting must be taught to girls but was only recommended for boys. The first and cardinal rule of knitting was, "The knitter should not talk while knitting."

Standardizing the way knitting was taught had long-reaching effects on knitting in Britain. The fact that it was mandatory for girls but only recommended for boys was probably a final nail in the coffin for knitting being non gender-specific. Also, board schools knitters tended to teach in the more "refined" style of parlour knitting with needles held like pencils. No mention was made of using knitting sticks. These factors together mitigated against knitting being fast or industrial. Knitting was also divided into categories of "plain" and "fancy," the latter only suitable for the middle classes. In our local parish chest, handwritten notes by the board school teachers state that farmers' and labourers' children should only be allowed to do plain work at school. The only fancy needlework permitted was if the children were mending items from the local lord of the manor's house.

The 1870 Education Act gentrified some knitting, and downgraded the rest. It must have led to a huge change in ordinary folks' attitude toward knitting. Isolated pockets of knitters remained unaffected. In my own farming family, women continued to knit "old style," holding needles under fists, and knitting "continental" rather than "British." This would have happened because children had already been taught to knit at home and were therefore unaffected by board school rules. I'd imagine many knitted school style and home style. My own mother, born in 1924, was left-handed but literally forced to write right-handed, in order to conform with board school ideals. It is unlikely that farmers' children were allowed to knit at school the way they did at home but no doubt as soon as they were away from the steely gaze of the teachers, they'd revert to knitting in a way they felt to be more comfortable.

In the nineteenth century, knitting became all kinds of things to all kinds of people. For some it was an industry. For others, a chore. For still other folk, it was occupational therapy, punishment, distraction or educational.

During the Napoleonic Wars (1803–15), international trade had been so disrupted that exports were badly affected. When the various trade embargos were lifted, British people discovered the delights of German wool – and by the 1830s and '40s, knitting manuals began to appear. In the 1830s, the smart money was on wool. Berlin wool. Seeing the strong, bright colours, made from mill-spun merino wool, suddenly middle- and upper-class women everywhere wanted to knit. In York, Mrs Elizabeth Jackson set up the first of what was to become a chain of yarn shops, called "The Berlin Rooms." Jane Gaugain was doing the same thing in Edinburgh. Simultaneously, as hand knitting survived as industry, it began to flourish as a pastime. It was used as a tool for therapeutic reasons in some settings, and a punishment, in others. Knitting flourished in homes, schools and various institutions.

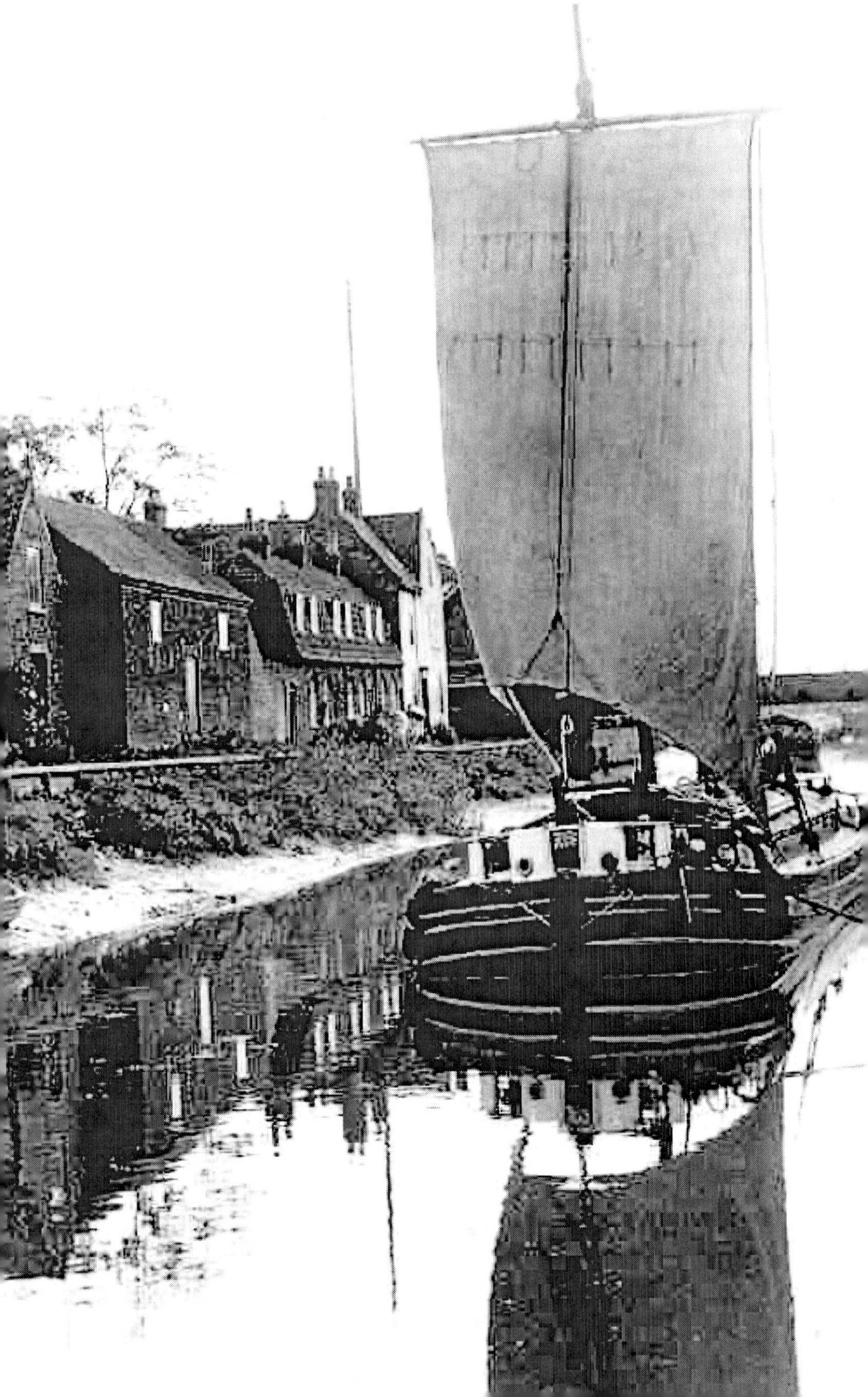

Inland Waterways Ganseys

From the West Riding to the Wild West; Humber Star to marshall's star. Furnishing the reader with tales of horse marines, gunslingers, gamblers, and Blue Coat boys. Of keely dogs and whistling up the wind. And in which we find a simple journey down the River Ouse, may put us in company with more dangerous and colourful people than we'd imagine possible in a book about the genteel art of knitting....

> The distinctive feature of their patterns is the central star pattern, exclusive to this tradition. I have never seen it anywhere else in all my travels.
>
> —*Traditional Knitting*

BOOKS ON KNITTING HISTORY HAVE LINGERED WITH THE COASTAL mariners. Here, I want to spend time with their inland counterparts to take us into uncharted territory. Michael Pearson's seminal *Traditional Knitting*, is the only book on the history of knitting so far that has tackled the patterns of the keel and sloop men of the Humber Estuary. And even Pearson had never heard of the inland watermen until, just about to submit the manuscript of his book, he got a request to send some of the ganseys in his collection to a knitting exhibition run by the Humber Keel and Sloop Preservation Society.

Years ago, the second I saw that hand-drawn map of the Humber Estuary in Pearson's book, I knew I had to find out more about the ganseys of the inland waterways. Why? Because the map showed the villages along the Ouse and Humber where all my mother's ancestors hailed from! At that time I had no idea I had any fisherman or mariner ancestors at all. But when I saw that hand-drawn map, I saw the places where I knew my family had lived for centuries.

ON FACING PAGE: A HUMBER SLOOP.
IMAGE COURTESY YORKSHIRE WATERWAYS MUSEUM, GOOLE.

74—*River Ganseys*

THE STAINFORTH AQUATIC SPORTS COMMITTEE.
IMAGE COURTESY OF THE HUMBER KEEL & SLOOP SOCIETY.

Inland Motifs and Knitting Methods

When we think of inland ganseys, we think of the Humber star motif. This gave me the clue that something slightly different was going on with the inland mariners. Mariners' ganseys were products of a distinct culture. Every design decision had ramifications and every symbol knitted on a gansey its own significance. This is where the true romance of ganseys can be found. To understand it, we will need to know a little of the inland mariners' lives. I'll start with a survey of the known pattern motifs and techniques.

Patterns varied from the simple, like the gansey worn by Admiral Foot from Hull, to the complex, as shown by the ganseys in the photo of the Stainforth Aquatic Sports Committee, circa 1914 (above). Some old inland mariners remarked that the patterns were plainer in their fathers' and grandfathers' day. Others seem to take rich and complex patterning for granted.

As for how these designs were constructed, keelman Harry Fletcher wrote just one paragraph in *A Life on the Humber: Keeling to Shipbuilding* about the ganseys he recalled his mother knitting. But that paragraph is so full of detail, it's worth quoting in full.

A Yorkshire 'tippie' or knitting belt. Image courtesy York Castle Museum.

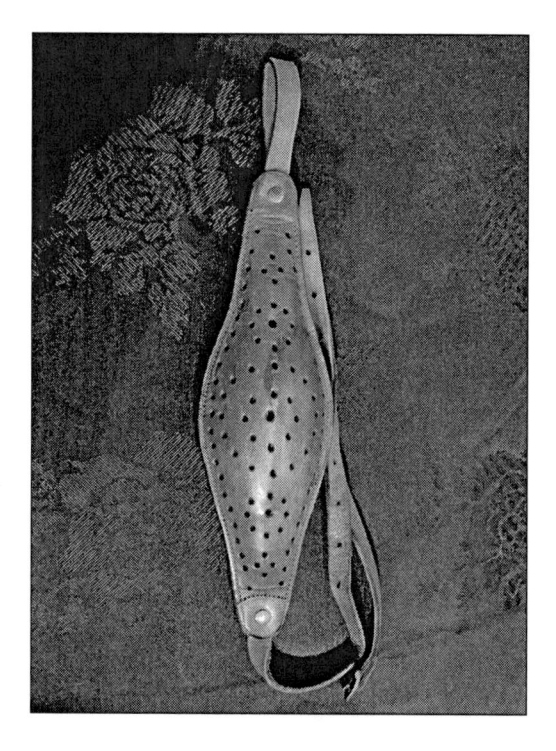

Their navy blue jerseys were home-knitted with a diamond pattern on the front and had high necks which fastened with two buttons on the left shoulder. Fastening had to be on the left as we carried things on the right shoulder. These guernseys had to be close-fitting and tight because loose clothing could so easily have caught on projecting parts of keel or lock.

My mother always knitted ours in one piece on four needles so that there were no seams, and even the sleeves, worked on three needles, were knitted into the garment. She used 14 or 15 ounces of fine worsted wool from Hammonds in Hull for each guernsey, and she was such an expert knitter that it was hard to tell the inside from the outside of the garment. To help her take the weight of the wool she always wore a knitting pad made of leather, stuffed with horsehair, one with brass eyelet holes let into it. She tied this pad onto her waist with two tapes and slotted the needles not actually in use into the holes, so that the pad held the knitting for her. She never used a pattern. No one did. They all made it up as they went along: ropes and cables and knots and diamonds, all kinds of patterns. Some keelmen wore a silk hanky tied in a knot on top of their guernseys rather like a tie or cravat.

Whether using the tippie was a personal preference of Mrs. Fletcher or was more common than a knitting stick along the inland waterways, we have no way of knowing. It is interesting that Harry saw no regional or family pattern or motif. His mother extemporized, which is in keeping with other accounts of Yorkshire knitters. Certainly, the diamond or mask crops up in a lot of photos of keelmen. So does the chevron. These are comparatively easy to knit from memory, as the patterns build logically. The round where you establish them is the hard part. The

76—*River Ganseys*

AN UNKNOWN SALTY SEA TAR FROM A SARDINE ADVERTISEMENT, WEARING THE EYE OF GOD MOTIF. COURTESY WHITBY RNLI.

detail about only buttoning on the left is very interesting, and so far as I know, this is the only place I have seen this point made.

You'd be forgiven for believing that Humber Estuary patterns were plain or just distinguished by the famous Humber Star, since the scant knitting histories to cover this point tend to give the impression that inland ganseys were just upper body patterned with moss stitch or some fairly straightforward Humber Star-based pattern. In fact, many of the old images of inland ganseys (although frustratingly low resolution) show what look to be elaborate all-over patterns separated by ropes. Even when the actual patterns can't be made out, you can see that they were often heavily patterned all over. One common pattern motif, called the English pattern in Holland, is The Eye of God. Also common to both Holland and Yorkshire, are the chequered pattern with purl stitch band motif that van der Klift-Tellegen attributed to the Ouddorp area. I found a version of this in Goole in the museum only yards from the Dutch canal. In Whitby's RNLI museum, there is a fascinating portrait of an unknown man wearing The Eye of God (shown above). This gentleman is actually a poster boy from an advertising campaign for sardines! At first glance, you'd assume the gansey might be machine-knitted. But it wasn't unknown for ganseys to have very fine gauge with stitch counts of 13 stitches and 19 rows per inch. The modern gansey runs closer to 7 stitches per inch. The result was a fabric that is difficult to believe is hand-knitted, with extremely crisp and well-defined patterns.

COURTESY YORKSHIRE
WATERWAYS MUSEUM, GOOLE.

The Yorkshire Inland Waterways Museum in Goole has one photo of an elderly woman knitting aboard a keel (shown above). On board a ship, as on dry land, the knitting was unremitting for many women, and stockings as well as ganseys would have been the order of the day. The woman in the photograph is pit knitting, as she has long needles and the working one is tucked into her armpit. She may well have had a knitting stick tucked under that arm. This is rare documentary evidence of technique.

There was a long-established trade of knitted goods between England and the Netherlands. Victorian historian Christopher Clarkson said of the landlocked Yorkshire town, Richmond, "This town had formerly a large trade in the exportation of knit yarn stockings and seamen's woollen caps to Holland and the Netherlands." From England to the Netherlands was a long established trade route, prior to the development of ganseys. A quick look at the ganseys worn in Holland confirms there are some similarities between the Dutch mariners and the east coast and Humber estuary British seamen. The patterns photographed and charted in Henriette van der Klift-Tellegen's *Knitting from the Netherlands* show many similarities in gansey design, not only structurally but also in the pattern motifs. The garments show many vertical patterns, six-stitch cables, masks, and quite commonly, the ganseys are patterned only over the upper half of the body and sleeves just as most of the inland waterway ganseys were.

Men who sailed the keels and sloops of the inland waterways would have worn ganseys identical to those worn by the seamen. In fact, many of the inland mariners also made short journeys across to Ghent, Le Havre, or other European ports, so it is hard to make a huge distinction between the coastal and the inland mariners of England's east coast. Yorkshire sloops were not made for the coastal trade, but occasionally, if the tides were right, they would make runs out to Whitby to trade sea coal. And as we have seen, the assignment of given motifs to certain geographical areas is sometimes spurious.

Looking at ganseys in photos, there seems to be no difference between coastal and inland styles. This runs counter to expectations. In fact, one of the best photos of Sheringham ganseys is a group shot of the Norfolk fishermen taken in Goole, on the Humber, in the inland waterways, which hints at a symbiosis between the coastal and inland patterns. There were relationships with more distant places, too. The Vale of York is flat as a pancake and much of it at sea level. My mother's farm was surrounded by man-made dykes, which drained the land enough to farm. In the seventeenth century, the great Dutch engineer Vermuyden came to Yorkshire to help drain our flatlands. The Dutch Canal in Goole was his work. There are Yorkshire folk with Dutch names and even Dutch vernacular architecture can be found dotted around the manor and farm houses of the Vale, including Cawood, one village my ancestors came from.

It is thought the Dutch ganseys came about at a later date (post 1860s) and were heavily influenced by the English. However, Dutch ganseys have barely been researched. Van der Klift-Tellegen remarked that when she brought up the topic, most people responded, "What Dutch ganseys?" As she uncovered photos documenting them, even museum curators were surprised to see there had once been a Dutch gansey tradition. Since she published her book in 1985, there has been no further research into Netherlands ganseys. For this reason, it is hard to draw any conclusions on how old the Dutch tradition really is and whether or not it influenced the Yorkshire tradition. Given the two countries' ancient trade in knitted goods, and close ties between the two, it could well be that the Yorkshire inland ganseys developed some of their pattern motifs from the Netherlands or that Yorkshire knitters created some of those ganseys photographed in Holland.

Compared to coastal ganseys, we have a paucity of evidence for the inland ones. There are fewer photos and images, presumably due to the fact that the coastal areas attracted tourists and so also had their fair share of professional photographers. These photographers had the equipment and know-how to capture crisp, sharp images in studio portraits so that we have a more complete and detailed record of the coastal ganseys. The inland photos, where they exist, tend to depict landscapes and boats more than people, and are more blurry and less detailed. It was a workaday, unglamourous, non-touristy environment.

A gansey at the Inland Waterways Museum shows a fairly simple pattern with horizontal bands of basket stitch, alternated with bands of plain knitting. It is knit from the usual millspun navy blue wassit. Keelman Harry Fletcher's mother

Inland Waterways Ganseys—79

ADMIRAL FOOT AT THE WHEEL. IMAGE COURTESY HULL MARITIME MUSEUM.

bought hers at a Hull department store. We know there was at least one yarn shop on Hull's Hessle Road, where most of the mariners lived. In the photo of Hull's *Admiral Foot at the* Wheel (shown above), we see the admiral wearing a simple, utterly plain gansey, which may or may not be commercially knit, with a pinstriped waistcoat over it.

Hull Museum also has some images of the defendants in a case where a young apprentice fisherboy was murdered on board a Hull ship. Two of the defendants were wearing ganseys in the shot the press used (shown on next page). Both appeared to be an all-over 1×1 moss stitch, possibly of the sort commercially available at the date: hand-knit, but not a sophisticated or customized-for-the wearer pattern. These are inland ganseys at their plainest.

80—*River Ganseys*

SUSPECTS AND VICTIM IN CRIME ONBOARD HULL SHIP – A RARE PROFESSIONAL PHOTO OF RIVER GANSEYS! IMAGE COURTESY HULL MARITIME MUSEUM.

Added to the lack of clear images, we hit other difficulties when researching inland knitting. By the early 1980s, the tradition had already died out, and Pearson remarked, "Keelboat jersey knitting is a memory." Patterns were hard to find. He noted that the Keel and Sloop Preservation Society had, in the past two years, started to revive the knitting. However, when I emailed their archivist, Brian Peeps, for this book, he said, "The only people that I know of that still do knitting are the people that sell them at Whitby." Bobbins, at Whitby, is a lovely shop in the old Methodist chapel. But they have no connection with the inland waterways!

Pearson documented ganseys that people showed him dating from the 1930s to 1950s. I have no real, live keelboat gansey knitters to turn to. So for the patterns and charts here, I will continue to analyze some previously unpublished photos. The Keel and Sloop Preservation Society also kindly gave me the pattern for a keelman's gansey based on a surviving one by Mrs. Phoebe Carr of Thorne, and the Leeds and Liverpool Canal Preservation Society generously shared some photos of canal ganseys with us.

The paucity of images of inland ganseys has proved a real difficulty in research. But we can piece some of the story together, from the scant photographs and written references we have, and the heroic efforts of the Preservation Societies to salvage what information they could. Also, Hull was a port that had strong links with other ports and fishing communities, and sometimes their gansey motifs are well recorded. We know that Norfolk, London, Scottish, and other Yorkshire coastal mariners were regularly on the docks and in the streets of Hull and some of their motifs would have found their way up the Humber.

If patterns like The Eye of God and Betty Martin have their roots in the keelmen's Christianity, there are other influences at work, too. Keelfolk developed their own lore and culture. Like the Vale of York farmers, they were famously superstitious. This could have had some bearing on the inland patterns. As Michael E. Ulyatt has written, "Keel and sloop men were usually honest. Some were extremely religious and superstitious" (Ulyatt, *Flying Sail*). This recalls the protective magic of patterns with names like The Eye of God and Betty Martin, which were thought to be a corruption of a mariner's prayer in Latin. This gives us a clue about motifs that embodied the inland mariners' strange fusion of Christianity and superstition. The Eye of God was more than just protective, though. For *Knitting from the Netherlands*, Van der Klift-Tellegen spoke to a woman from Ijmuiden who said the eye was seen as a warning symbol. "That eye looks after men in strange ports so they will conduct themselves properly. It used to be common, in a bar, to find a wall plaque with an eye painted on it. Under it were the words 'God sees you,' meant as a warning" (p. 19).

Horse Marines, Fishermen, Haulers

Looking for something else, entirely, I stumbled on these entries about the sons of an Ouse waterman in the original admissions books for the York Blue Coat Boys Charity School:

Admissions, 1846

1847. George Shillitoe. Acaster Selby. Born March 26 1837, admitted 1.4.

An industrious boy of fair capacity. On a vessel with his father. Waterman.

1848. Robert Shillitoe. Spurriergate. Born 19 March 1839, admitted 8.8.1848.

Sureties: William White, chemist, 5 Fishergate; George Shillitoe, waterman, 51st Water Lane. Of medium capacity and tolerably obedient. On a vessel with his father.

1855. William Shillitoe, Cawood. bap 21.9.1845, admitted 5.4. 1855.

Sureties: Wm Snow, Temperance Hotel, Low Ousegate, Wm Howe, draper, Low Ousegate. Died of consumption, 19.4.1858.

AINSCOUGH BOAT. IMAGE COURTESY OF THE LEEDS & LIVERPOOL CANAL SOCIETY.

These Shillitoe boys are all my relatives. By the 1851 census, both George and Robert were back home with their father who is listed as "farmer of 24 acres" in Acaster Selby, a village not far from York. The village fronts onto the west bank of the river Ouse. According to the charity school records, the boys' father is a "waterman." From this we can see the way people along the river alternated farming in a small way with working the river. Small farmers augmented their income by providing horses to tow the boats and the men to lead them. I'd imagine the Shillitoes were this kind of horse marine. Most charity school boys were apprenticed to a trade but the Shillitoes seem to have had one to return to. In charity schools, younger boys were often taught to knit and so even the inland mariners themselves were often the product of knitting schools. These boys would have been knitters!

The river defined people's lives. When the land was enclosed in the 1770s, and smaller farmers lost out, many turned to the river to make a living. The Shillitoes' grandfather had been a substantial farmer and churchwarden in the late eighteenth century. By the nineteenth century, many farmers had lost their land. In the 1930s, my family finally lost the farm that had been in the family for 100 years, when there was a catastrophic flood, wiping out our entire dairy herd. We were finished and off the land forever. This loss of the farm of her childhood was the single most defining event in my mum's life; I grew up, like generations of folk around the Ouse, knowing that the river gives, but she also takes away.

Along with inland waterway haulers and vessel owners, I found a couple of fishermen in my family tree. One was my great-great-great grandfather, William Richardson. He was born at Keyingham on the Humber in 1797. William moved to

The Lizzie Lee (1856).
Courtesy of the Reuben Chappell Collection, Goole Museum.

Ottringham and then later to Wistow on the Ouse, some thirty or so miles upriver. He was described in censuses and on other documents interchangeably as "fisherman" or "agricultural laborer." His wife, Ann Ablett, was the daughter and granddaughter of Humber fishermen, too. I descend from their daughter, Rose Ann, along a wholly female line. This probably explains my bizarre knitting style. I suspect it came along this mitochondrial line, along with the DNA, from the eighteenth century right down to the present. My mother learned to knit before she was school age (as I did, as presumably, her mother did, etc!) without the external polite parlour-style Victorian knitting having a chance to interrupt our technique.

Life on the Inland Waterways

The red sails of the keels are now no longer even in folk memory. Gone, like the folk who peopled the river. Keels and sloops plied the river trade between the Humber and York and at all inland waterways beyond. We forget now how busy the rivers must have been. In the age of steam, cities and towns had a massive appetite for coal, and everything you can imagine was hauled up and down the inland waterways. Freight included bricks and pit props to the coal mines at Castleford, cattle cake, timber, tiles, fertilizer, coal, slag, corn, and beet. Also woven woollen and worsted cloth from Bradford, Leeds, and Halifax. It was up to the vessels' captains to find a cargo. In his monograph on the Humber keel, John Frank wrote,

IMAGE COURTESY OF THE YORKSHIRE INLAND WATERWAYS MUSEUM, GOOLE.

"The Humber keel is supposed to be descended from the oldest line of sailing ships in the country" (p. 6). It was almost the last square rigged sailing boat left, descendant of the Viking boats that went down the Ouse in 1066.

The Yorkshire Inland Waterways Museum at Goole has the wooden interior of the vessel Sobriety. Sitting in the keelboat cabin at the museum, you get a sense of the small space, very much like a caravan, in which the keelboat men and their families lived. Keelmen and their families were often seen by landlubbers as gypsies. Harry Fletcher said the children from schools along the canals and rivers would chase him to fight him and shout "keely dog" after him. He described the keel's interior as "cozy" with a gleaming brass fireplace and Staffordshire dog ornaments on the mantelpiece. Harry attended the charity school at Thorne for a brief span of seven weeks each year, when the boat was frozen in. His parents wanted him to have an education, but he was needed as an extra pair of hands. Harry only learned to read and write when he had appendicitis and the nurses taught him, during a long stay in hospital.

Watermen had a hard life leading the horses as well as sailing on the vessels. When the wind failed, or was going in the wrong direction, the boats were hauled by horses. These haulers were called horse marines. Tow paths would frequently abruptly change sides of the river so they'd have to ferry across, horse and all, to the other side. There are several accounts of narrow escapes and fatal incidents on the river ferry crossings. Two of my father's Hemingway ancestors were drowned in the river Aire. One of my mother's ancestors was one of only three survivors of an accident on the Ouse when a coal barge's tow line bowled into a small rowing boat

CAWOOD DOCKS, FROM 'LOWER WHARFEDALE', EDMUND BOGG, 1923 (REPRINT).

full of church singers out carolling on Boxing Day in 1833. The hauling man that night was Stephen Green. The river never stopped. Not even on Boxing Day. The keelmen lived by the tides and, that day, the river had a sharp ebb tide, ideal to get a coal-laden barge up to York and back. The first victim of the apocalyptic cholera outbreak in York, in 1832, was Thomas Hughes, a waterman. He caught it from a boatload of Selby and Hull tramps he was ferrying across the river for the York Races. Cholera, of course, was spread by water, although no one knew it yet.

In villages all along the river, and York itself, the river was effectively an open sewer. All waste pipes led directly into it. As a child in the 1960s, I was always fascinated when I went to the bathroom at my great aunt's house in Cawood, as the toilet consisted of a wooden seat placed over a hole cut through sheer rock, falling about 10 metres into a stream that ran beneath. Straight into the Ouse, yards away. My other great aunt lost her baby when a babysitter accidentally dropped him into the river – down this hole? I've never been sure – in 1918. The poignant record of thirteen-year-old William Shillitoe's death is no surprise given the harshness of life. Even if your dad did rent twenty-four acres, life along the river was hard.

The relationship between farmers and keelmen was a co-dependency. Traveling up and down the waterways, the sloop men and women relied on the farmers along the way to sell them their provisions. They also foraged. One of the sloop men of South Ferriby recalled how families all lived aboard and foraged to supplement their income. "In some keels, women lived aboard. The families ate blackberries, mushrooms, eggs. They'd take a moorhen's egg then she'd lay one a day for weeks. Commonest food they had was eel. Boats had a kettle, frying-pan, stew pot, and beef kettle" (Day, *Humber Keels*, p. 10).

But even that had its dangers. In *The Mariner's Mirror*, John Franks recounted, "A keel called the 'Masterman' grounded on the plumb edge of sand at Whiton. The skipper went ashore poaching and left his wife and children on board, the ship

86—*River Ganseys*

ETHEL, BY REUBEN CHAPPELL, NO DATE. IMAGE COURTESY OF GOOLE MUSEUM.

rolled over and sank, and the woman and children were drowned" (Day, *Humber Keels*, p. 12).

Franks also interviewed Tom Burkill, aged 70 in 1996. Tom remembered his grandfather's sloop, John and Annie. "We were not very religious but were brought up with the traditional values of Methodism" (Day, *Humber Keels*, p. 14). Tom's uncle was a lay preacher, and many keelmen were ardent Bethel Methodists. These virtuous watermen were not the whole story, though.

From Humber Star to Marshall's Star

There were less law-abiding watermen. When you think of inland waterway Yorkshire ganseys, maybe the last association you make is with a gun-slinging gambler of the Wild West, and yet there were two such men who would have recognized the Humber Star as easily as they'd have known the town marshall's star.

One of the greatest gunslingers, gamblers, card-sharks, hired gun, and lawmen of the Old West was Ben Thompson. Bat Masterson rated him highly: "It is doubtful if in his time there was another man living who equalled him with a pistol in a life-and-death struggle" (Masterson, "Ben Thompson"). Ben was born in 1843 and in his childhood emigrated from Knottingley, in the West Riding of Yorkshire, with his parents and his brother, Billy, and sister, Mary Jane. Knottingley is on the highest navigable point of the river Aire and was an important port on the inland waterways. Ben's grandparents, William and Mary, owned or part-owned eight sloops which, like my own family's boats, worked the inland waterways and occasionally were seagoing across to Holland, France, or beyond. Ben's father, William, was a mariner.

In 1849, flush with an inheritance, William Thompson bought the Whitby vessel *Providence*. The Thompsons can last be found in Yorkshire on the 1851 census, shortly before they emigrated to Austin, Texas. They were at Little Marsh, Knottingley, close by the canal. Most of their neighbors were listed as "seaman," "mariner," or "master marine." William gave his age as thirty-three and his birthplace as Hull. In Texas, the once prosperous William Thompson made a scant living fishing the Colorado River, while his wife, Mary Ann, took in sewing. It's likely as a mariner's wife she was already acquainted with knitting.

Life in Austin, Texas, a frontier town, must have been very different to life in Knottingley, England. At some point around 1859, William returned to England to settle his affairs, but by 1860, he was back in Austin and recorded on the U.S. census as "mariner," despite the fact the river there wasn't navigable. Maybe he kept ownership of some of the family's vessels back in Yorkshire.

Family legend had it that William died at sea of yellow fever during one of these trips back to England. From that point on, Mary Ann and the children were alone and had to make their way as best they could. Ben became a card shark. Photos of Ben show a fashionably dressed, elegant man with top hat, cane, and well-cut clothing. In Costumes of Yorkshire, George Walker remarked that Yorkshiremen were renowned throughout England for their fancy and expensive taste in clothing. Inland mariners and Humber mariners alike could be dandies when off-duty. Card sharks, of course, plied their trade on the packet steamers on British inland waterways as well as American ones. Involved in numerous duels, Ben never fired the first shot, but relied on his opponents to miss. He'd take aim and then fire accurately and calmly, always keeping his cool. This gave him the excuse of self-defence. He seems to have retained a sense of himself as an Englishman abroad with stylish clothing and behaving in a gentlemanly way to women. Aged eight when his family emigrated, he may have retained some of his distinctive Yorkshire accent.

He was elected City Marshall in Austin in 1881. During his ten months in office the crime rate in the city dropped to zero. Ben was killed instantly when shot in the back by someone bearing a grudge, at the Vaudeville Theatre in Alamo City. He remained a Yorkshireman to the end. His gravestone reads proudly, "BEN THOMPSON, born in Knottingley, Eng." No doubt his fancy threads were in part paid for by the sale of his father's shares in the sloops.

Either way, ganseys are a part of the United Kingdom's and United States's shared heritage. Mariners, even inland ones, tended to be the nineteenth century's more adventurous souls. And many more, like the Thompsons, headed west.

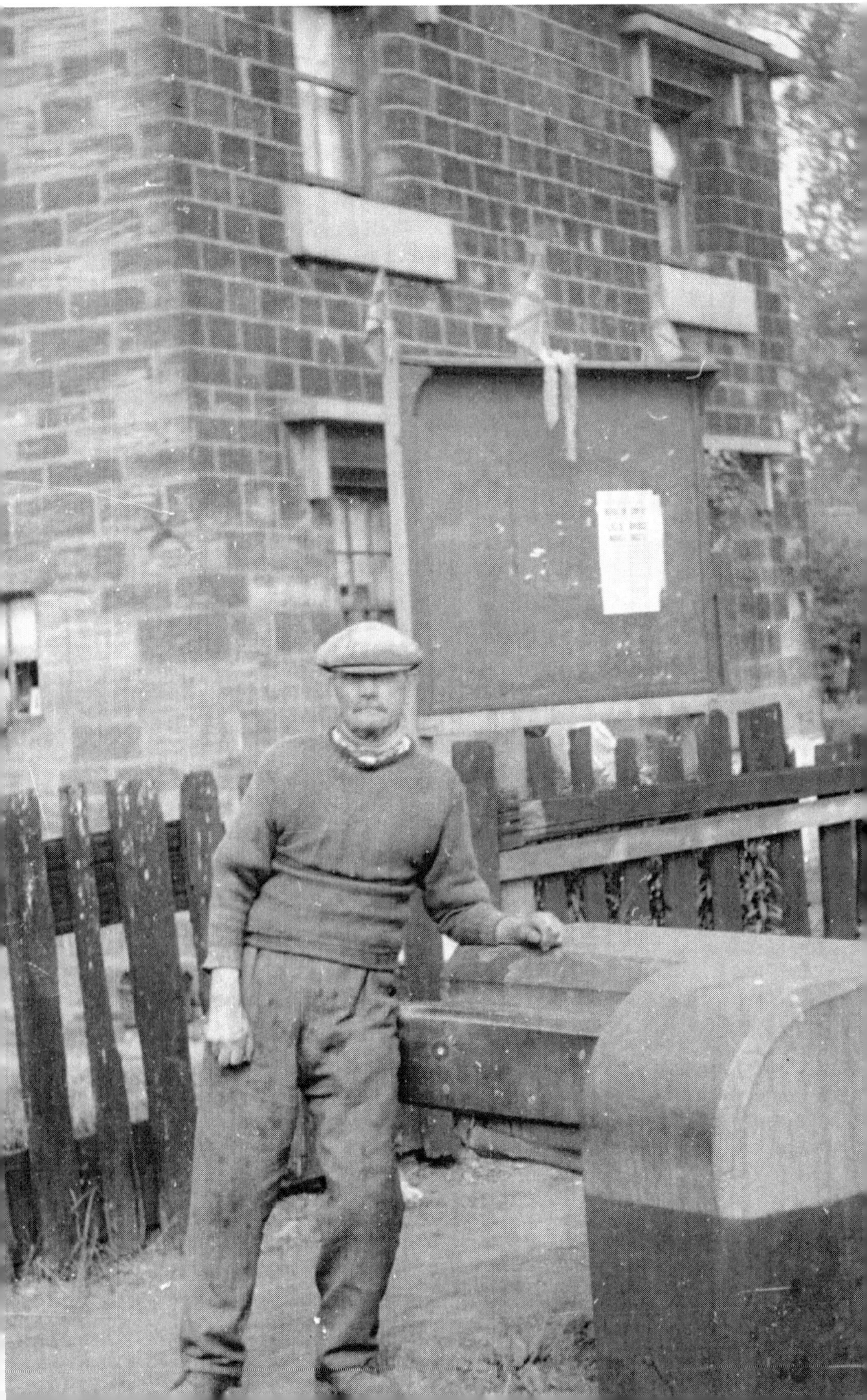

Motifs: Superstition, Folklore, and Inland Ganseys

In which we whistle up the wind, visit the Stalberg Ghost and Suicide Sid, and learn why one must never wear the Forbidden Colour.

> Keel and sloop men were usually honest. Some were extremely religious and superstitious.
>
> —*Flying Sail*

KEEL-FOLK DEVELOPED THEIR OWN LORE AND CULTURE. LIKE THE Vale of York farmers, they were famously superstitious. The inland mariners were a strange mix of Wesleyan Methodist and something older. Harry Fletcher said, "When I stayed with my father's father, I attended the Wesleyan Chapel, as did most keelmen. My grandfather was so keen that he once had a service aboard his keel, while it was moored at Thorne, and old keelmen still remember the occasion" (Fletcher, *Life on the Humber*, p. 69).

Alec Gill, MBE, studied the Humber fishermen's superstitions and folk magic and found hundreds of ritualistic behaviours and beliefs prevalent among the Hessle Road trawlermen and families in Hull. Those superstitions and beliefs are worth examining, as they go a long way to explaining the mindset that informed inland and coastal ganseys.

Keelmen, like the coastal mariners, went by nicknames. Anyone who has seen the captions on photos in books about gansey history, will have spotted Billy "Clubfoot" Mayes, "Tanker," or John "Snouts" Cox. For inland mariners, Gill recorded names like "Snowy Worthington," "The Stalberg Ghost," "Suicide Sid," and "Cod-Eye White." Giving objects or people their true names has sometimes been seen as bad luck in British folklore, and words have power. You can disempower bad luck or avert it by changing a name. What has this got to do with

FACING PAGE: A CANAL BOATMAN. IMAGE COURTESY LEEDS & LIVERPOOL CANAL SOCIETY.

90—*River Ganseys*

TYPICAL RIVER GANSEY CABLES.
IMAGE COURTESY HUMBER KEEL &
SLOOP SOCIETY.

ganseys? I suspect it may affect the naming of the gansey motifs as well as the knitters' choices and combinations of motif. Motifs were often given short, pithy names that were easy to memorize. And by naming something, you made it lucky; its magic was knitted in with every purl stitch.

One question contemporary knitters often ask is why the ropes (cables) are never mirrored in old ganseys. Again, I suspect the answer lies in folklore. One of the objects mariners were most averse to was mirrors. Going back to pagan times, places where a person could be reflected were liminal places, gateways to the otherworld. To reflect was to bring on bad luck. If all the symbols or motifs on a gansey could be said to evoke good luck, then to mirror a cable might create bad.

Diamonds, sometimes called nets or masks, were a very common motif on the inland ganseys. And yet, along the Hessle Road, seeing diamonds appear in the folds of your laundry was taken as one of the most dire omens. In February 1946, Joseph Gerrard took his first post-war job on a Hull trawler, *The Kingston Pearl*. On her return journey from the Norwegian fishing grounds, he was swept off deck by a sheer wall of sea. Joseph's son, Bernard, remembered, "For several weeks after losing dad, we kept finding diamond shapes in bed-linen, table clothes, tea towels." The diamond-as-death omen probably had its origins in the fact that it echoes the shape of a coffin. The diamond might also have been seen as a lucky omen, ironically, as that sort of inverse magic where you invoke the thing you most fear.

Motifs: Superstition, Folklore, and Inland Ganseys—91

GANSEY AT NATIONAL WATERWAYS MUSEUM.
IMAGE COURTESY OF LEEDS & LIVERPOOL CANAL SOCIETY.

For some reason, Humber fishermen held onto the superstition that they must not even say the words "pig," "rabbit," or "hare," which had once also been common superstitions among landlubbers, but had died out on shore long since. Even saying the words aboard ship would be as doom-laden as mentioning the Scottish play is to actors. Sometimes, perversely, the unmentionable was evoked to take the sting out of it as an omen, to dis-empower. So the wartime crew of Her Majesty's Trawler *Rosy Morn* were photographed, one of them holding a knitted white rabbit for luck (reproduced in Gill's *Superstitions and Folk Magic*). Maybe the diamond patterns were used in the same spirit, to take the sting out of the most feared event: death at sea. Also, it recalled the mesh of nets and maybe was lucky for that reason, as well.

Another common superstition was the idea that clothes put on inside-out must not be changed or you'll change your luck, too. Keelman Harry Fletcher touchingly remarked of his mother, "She was such an expert knitter that it was hard to tell the inside from the outside of the garment," maybe implying he put his on inside-out many times! To be honest, most ganseys look phenomenally neat inside-out as there are no woven in ends and no seams. But Harry's words showed his pride in his mother and his love.

Maybe one of the most interesting taboos for Yorkshire fishermen and mariners was the colour green. This was called the forbidden colour and not without reason. Even Winston Churchill had an aversion to green. A local yarn goes that when Churchill visited a bomb-torn boulevard off Hessle Road, he gave a man £10 to get rid of a jumper. It was green. Gill went on to say that in 1990 he had a phone call from someone at Hull City Council who had heard about his research into Hull superstitions. Apparently, whenever the council painted something, whether it was a tenant's door, a park bench, or a lamp post, they were flooded with complaints if they painted it green. Most complaints came from Hull's elderly residents, and after a while it slowly dawned on the council that it was something to do with trawling. Meanwhile, down on Hessle Road, the wool shopkeepers realized it wasn't worth stocking green yarn. "Green woollen jumpers and mufflers (neck scarves) caused problems at sea. Jenny Pattison from Easington, however, interviewed the *Spurn* lifeboat men, and they confirmed that there is still a strong superstition against green among east coast fishermen and themselves."

When the new vicar, Reverend Tardew, painted the pews green in his church, off Hessle Road in Hull in 1924, he was hated so much for his insensitivity to local superstition that when he had a fancy garden party with the Archbishop of York, the local kids pelted the vicar and his august guest with stones, eggs, dead cats, and huge lumps of rotting cod.

Avoiding green was a form of mimic magic. Green was seen as the colour of creation/god, so to avoid death, one had to avoid wearing it. Yorkshire churches are full of that figure of deep folklore, the Green Man. The Chapter House at York Minster is covered with medieval green men carvings. No one really knows why. But it points to the fusion of Christian and pagan in the Yorkshire mindset, where religion and pagan superstition often went hand-in-hand. Hull trawlermen wouldn't have green curtains or furniture in their houses. We can see that even the colours used for ganseys were dictated by folk belief. Likewise, the local hardware stores refused to stock anything with birds printed on it as all birds, not just the infamous albatross, were seen as bad mojo. It is striking that there are many motifs inspired from nature but very few refer to birds, in any way.

Another superstition relevant to knitters was the embargo on working on the Sabbath. "Sunday is another special time when certain domestic jobs are taboo. No one was allowed to knit. In Robert Ramsbottom's family no one was allowed to wind wool after darkness fell. You could wind a man overboard" (Gill, *Superstitions and Folk Magic*, p. 106). Yorkshire inland mariners referred to their Methodist chapel buildings as fishermen's bethel, and seamen's missions were often called bethel. This might be the long lost key to the symbol of the Humber star, as a star was a symbol associated with bethel, and, along with a dove, was on the flag of the British and Foreign Seamen's Society and Bethel Union. Doves would be tricky to depict at sea, given the deep aversion to anything with an image of a bird, but the star could also have been seen as protective. Mariners could navigate by the stars, of course, but also the bethel star was associated with their Wesleyan faith. The bethel flag was often displayed at prayer meetings in the 1820s. One of our family's second wave of Illinois immigrants was even named Bethel Cleveland! Sunday was the Lord's day. Keelman John Frank mentioned whistling up the wind. "Some old keelmen believed it was unlucky to sail on a Sunday; they said money earned on a Sunday went to the devil on Monday. If you were short of wind you could get a

Motifs: Superstition, Folklore, and Inland Ganseys—93

Mug shot of a prisoner, mariner Thomas Haigh, wearing a Betty Martin variant. Though convicted in Tyneside, Haigh was born in Askern, Yorkshire – as his gansey shows! Image courtesy Tyne & Wear Museums.

breeze by whistling for it or by throwing a half penny overboard, but it was unlucky to throw more than one" (Day, *Humber Keels*, p. 7).

Coins and shells are gansey motifs that reflect the luck of money as shells in European culture long were symbols for cash. Italian Tarot decks had four suits; one of them was coins. Sometimes the coins were rendered as shells in art, as if the two were interchangeable, the shell a symbol of bountifulness and wealth. Salmon fishing in the Vale of York Rivers was seasonal. Men in Cawood could make enough money from the salmon to subsist the rest of the year as day labourers. There was a lot of money in fishing but only at certain times of year. Coins or shells knitted into the ganseys would invoke luck and weave in the magic.

It's impossible to trace the origins of any motif. But I did have some fun chasing up one motif's name – the elusive Betty Martin. I had always assumed it was the name of a vessel, and sure enough, eighteenth-century shipping reports list a vessel of that name. In the eighteenth century, there was a commonly known phrase: "All my eye and Betty Martin!" These days that's been reduced down to "My eye!" Now, I suspect the Betty Martin pattern started out as one with the word eye in the name, like The Eye of God or bird's eye, etc., and that became "My eye and Betty Martin" – which figures.

The earliest known reference to Betty Martin had previously been from 1781. I managed to find one from *The Morning Post*, December 15, 1770. "My eye, Betty Martin! What have we here? What say you to this White Bantum? He is the only cock that ever laid an egg." And no, I have no clue what it's all about, but it looks satirical. Clearly the phrase was well known already by 1770. Various adverts and letters to the newspapers were signed Betty Martin, usually in the context of political satire. So it's hard to believe it wasn't used with at least a nod to the saying. I suspect this tells us that "Betty Martin" was sometimes used to mean "filler," or a bit of nonsense.

However, there was also this from *The Morning Post* on December 15, 1814:

> Oh! My eye, Betty Martin! Many of our most popular vulgarisms have their origin in some whimsical perversion of language or of fact. St. Martin is one of the worthies of the Romish calendar, and a form of prayer to him begins with the words – "Oh! Mihi Beate Martine," by which some desperate fellow, who was more prone to punning than praying, has furnished the plebeian phrase, so well known in these modern circles of horse laughter.

And the aforementioned 1781 reference suggests it's a nautical term, although no one knows what for. (Could it be a knot?) If the prayer reference is right it's a sort of good luck charm, bringing good luck at sea – again reflecting that peculiar fusion of religion and superstition that seems to have characterized mariners. The term also seems to be referenced in countless songs or parodies of well-known songs. Much of British folk culture was better preserved in the United States than in England. Note this passage from *American Notes and Queries*:

> The bit of "an old song" would seem to be a corruption. There was a famous Maryland belle and beauty, Elizabeth Martin, familiarly known as "Pretty Betty Martin," in whose honor a song was written, beginning with or having for a refrain, I am not sure which, the lines:
>
> *Pretty Betty Martin, Tip-toe! Tip-toe! Pretty Betty Martin, Tip-toe fine!*
> *Pretty Betty Martin, Tip-toe! Tip-toe! Couldn't find a husband To suit her mind!*
>
> The story is that "Pretty Betty Martin" was born in England and when she came to this country, a young woman, had so many suitors on the ship in which she made the voyage that she could not choose among them, so, consequently, rejected all. It has been said that she was a niece of the Duke of Marlborough, but even this reflected effulgence of glory can add little to her fame as the heroine of the jingle just quoted.

From this it seems that some motif names might echo long-forgotten songs or satire in the broadsheet newspapers. By the later nineteenth century, music halls provided popular, vaudeville-style entertainment in the UK, and one of its stars, Lillie Langtry, was famous for wearing a gansey.

Ganseys were inextricably bound up with popular culture, and the names of some motifs might reflect these long-forgotten songs and jokes. Gansey motifs might have had a sort of totemic function in a highly superstitious, sometimes religious, culture. Although I believe many motifs developed flowery names for good reason (an *aide mémoire* to knitters), some motifs' names also had a deeper significance. Still other motifs depicted the more prosaic aspects of a mariner's everyday life, with its ropes, ladders, starfish, anchors, and flags. (The inland vessels often flew pretty pennants with the ship's name emblazoned.) Some motifs are pure geometry:

Motifs: Superstition, Folklore, and Inland Ganseys—95

"IMMITATING [SIC] A BAND ADMIRAL FOOT AS BAND MASTER."
IMAGE COURTESY HULL MARITIME MUSEUM.

zigzags, triangles, chevrons, and diamonds. Space-fillers like Betty Martin – a bit of "summat and nowt." These geometric shapes might have had less significance, culturally. The vertical pattern of double zigzags, often called marriage lines, were a commonly recurring motif on the rivers, as are horizontal waves maybe reflecting the tidal rivers.

And then there are the symbols with a religious significance. The Eye of God was a very popular, imposing single motif, which seemed to have been exported to Holland from England in large quantities. The Dutch called it "the English pattern." Again, this is a powerful symbol in eighteenth-century English culture, where it is often called "The Eye of Providence." The motif depicted an eye surrounded by rays of light, often enclosed in a triangle. The Eye of Providence appeared on all kinds of eighteenth-century items from long-case clocks to the inside base of chamber pots. (My aunt had one of these which was from the eighteenth century. Chances are it came from the Clevelands or the Moses ancestors.) The Eye of God could even stare up at you on the potty, offering a bit of an insight into eighteenth-century English humour. I'm not sure it's a flattering one. In the United States, the Eye of Providence has even more potent connotations, also with its roots in eighteenth-century culture, as it appears on the dollar bill and the reverse of the Great Seal of the United States. It must have been seen as a potent protective symbol. With providence on your chest you were less likely to drown, which no doubt explains why Providence was a common ship name.

Ingenuity, observation, and shibboleth seemed to combine in various gansey motifs. And all varieties of motif could be combined in any single gansey, making each garment reflect the local culture.

If my theory is right – that ganseys were a by-product of the Industrial Age, springing from the late-eighteenth century and Regency period – then they were also a knee-jerk reaction to that same industrialization that produced the millspun to make them. The dawn of the Industrial Age coincided with the Romantic movement, in which poets travelled to picturesque but wild northern places (like Westmorland) and immersed themselves in nature. So the botanical and other natural motifs on ganseys were in the spirit of the Romanticism that was everywhere, as the gansey developed during the first decades of the nineteenth century. Many motifs were drawn from nature: hoof print, ridge and furrough, snakes, trees, ferns, leaves, stars and flowers, hailstones, and cobblestones, which in Yorkshire were sometimes made from the large, rounded cats' head stones found on beaches.

When I look at ganseys in faded photographs, I always wonder about the identity of the knitters, and I find myself thinking of those forgotten knitters like Lucy, the girl who "dwelt among th'untrodden ways," in Wordsworth's poem *A Slumber Did My Spirit Steal*.

- No motion has she now, no force;
- She neither hears nor sees;
- Rolled round in earth's diurnal course,
- With rocks, and stone, and trees.

Motifs: Superstition, Folklore, and Inland Ganseys—97

Unknown crew. Image courtesy Yorkshire Waterways Museum.

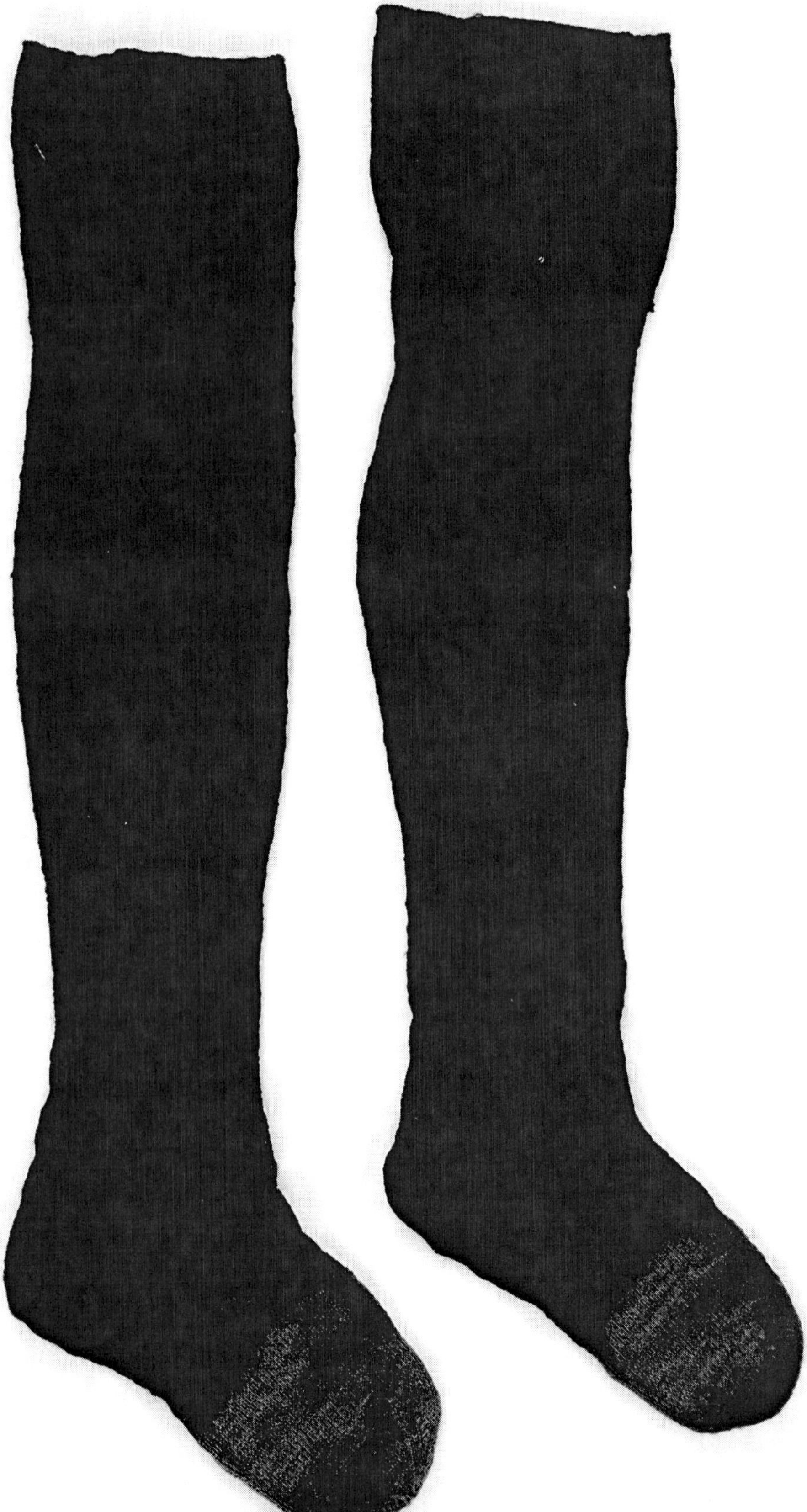

Pioneer Yorkshire Knitters in the New World

In which we learn it may not be prudent to leave one's belongings in sea-chests by Lake Erie..

> We did set an red dye and I did card a bit of wool whilst Mary did wrap the silver and did store it away in the chest. I did set up an stocking and did finish it by early candlelight. May, 1834.
>
> —*Prairie Smoke*. Based on the lost journals of Jane Moses Wood Roodhouse, pioneer.

WHY AM I WRITING ABOUT ILLINOIS PIONEERS WHEN YOU settled down to read about Yorkshire mariners? Because inland mariners in Yorkshire led lives they felt were so unremarkable, generations passed by unrecorded. But some of my inland mariners emigrated to Illinois in 1830. As founding fathers of a city in the New World, this family's lives are better documented than they ever would have been back home. Leisurely crafts at home, like knitting, became a matter of life and death on the prairie. As we have seen with the story of Ben Thompson, Yorkshire inland mariners could and did take their families in search of a fortune in the Americas. Sometimes they turned away from the waterways as a source of income. But the women brought with them the skills they'd learned by the river – to knit and even to spin – and turned to these skills when it became a matter of survival. So the skills were preserved, for at least a generation or two, and have been better recorded than they would have been back home in Yorkshire. As we spin the yarn of the life of pioneer, Jane Moses Wood Roodhouse, my sixth great aunt, I will share with you some of the gansey motif patterns that Jane would have known.

Jane was born in Cawood, by the river Ouse, in 1791, the daughter of gentleman farmer and hauler, Isaac Moses, and his second wife, Jane Brown. Isaac seemed to have had bases on the rivers Derwent, Ouse, and Humber, with family working for

FACING PAGE: COURTESY POLISH MARITIME MUSEUM, GDANSK.

him in various places along the inland waterway network. Port records for York are scattered and few and far between. No records of Isaac's vessels survive, but when he died in 1820, he left his share of the vessel *Ebiezer* to his son. His grandson went on to become master mariner on the inland waterways of Nottinghamshire. Mariners preferred to own shares in vessels rather than own the entire boat as owning the whole vessel meant you shouldered 100% of the risk if a cargo or ship were lost. Though Ben Thompson's father, William, did buy all sixty-four shares in the two-masted schooner *Providence* built by William Hobkirk at Whitby in 1843 – shouldering all of the risk in a shipping venture was relatively unusual.

Shipping records show that Yorkshire inland mariners travelled every few weeks to Ghent, Le Havre, Abbeville, and various English, French, and Dutch ports. This gives a sense of the links not only between inland mariners and other European ports, but also between Norfolk and Yorkshire (seagoing schooners were present on the Humber). I have been unable to find any records of *Ebiezer*, or any other vessel owned by Isaac, and he had a long career, so it's likely there were many. Still, some of Thompson's records are extant and are fairly typical of the river/ocean-going runs between Yorkshire and Europe.

Hard to believe that Cawood, now a sleepy, almost empty stretch of river, with a scant bit of leisure cruising, had its own busy little wharf that supported basket makers working in the days before cardboard boxes and crates. For such a tiny village, it had a surprising number of pubs. Now all that remains of the village's days as a dock is a jagged line of the stumps of the piles once driven deep in the mud flats, only visible at low tide, like a row of rotten teeth. Many other busy wharves are now long gone. Kirkby Wharfe, even Tadcaster, don't have landing stages any more. Once, freight was being hauled up and down, day and night, maybe only letting up once a year on Christmas Day.

Isaac Moses was born a yeoman farmer's son. The river Derwent threaded through his village, and he must have watched the vessels come and go as a child, and decided the waterways, not the land, was where he would one day make his living. Isaac's daughter, Jane Roodhouse, was middle-aged and had nine children from two marriages, when she emigrated to America in 1830.

Jane's first marriage had been to Captain Abraham Wood. Their children came with Jane to the United States: William Moses Wood (b. 1810), Mary Ann (b. 1812), Isaac (b. 1816), and Abraham, born 1818 at North Street, York, and named after his father, who had just died. I was able to trace Jane and Abraham's lives in Regency York, via parish records, their marriage bond, and other documents. Jane seems to have moved between the village of Cawood and York, where she lived on Bishophill and North Streets. Bishophill is a hilly street lined with imposing Regency buildings; North Street has a stunningly beautiful church, lined on either side with huge warehouses with the river literally lapping at one side of it. All Saints North Street seemed to have been one of the watermen's churches. York has a church on every street corner. North Street church was famous at that time for its

CAWOOD CHURCH (WITH RIVER BEHIND IT, IN FULL FLOOD).
ABRAHAM WOOD DROWNED NEARBY AND IS BURIED HERE. CREDIT: NATHANIEL HUNT.

very low-church, evangelistic services. This too, would have been a pull for the mariners.

On his children's birth records, Abraham Wood is listed alternately as "mariner" or "waterman." He is described as "captain" only in Isaac's will. Captain was the final stage before becoming a "master"; sometimes captains too had shares in the vessels. It's likely Abraham worked for Jane's father, Isaac Moses, and maybe Jane and Abraham ran the family haulage business for him at the York end. Isaac himself had bases at Barmby on the Marsh at the confluence of the Rivers Derwent and Ouse and also at Cawood on the Ouse. Isaac's older son, Jonathan (my direct ancestor), had been based in Howden, also on the Derwent. All these waterways link to Hull and the Humber.

I have been unable to find a birth record for Abraham Wood, but various documents put his birth around 1786 to 1787. He died aged thirty. Abraham and Jane married by licence. Most people married after the banns were called. The advantage of ancestors being married by licence is that you get extra documentation. On the marriage bond and his marriage record, Abraham signed with his mark, indicating that he was not literate (as a river mariner, he did not need to be), while Jane signed her name neatly. When Abraham drowned in 1817, he was buried at the village of Cawood, but the parish record says his "abode" was York.

At some point after the birth of baby Abraham, Jane probably returned to Cawood. Jane's father, Isaac Moses, died in 1820, taking the unusual step of leaving the bulk of his estate to Jane, although she was in fact his youngest daughter and he had a son still alive. Much is made of the fact that nineteenth-century women were technically "possessions" of their husbands and could own no property in their own right. But parents could will property directly to a daughter, and ring-fence it with various legal provisos to protect it, if necessary. Jane was landed and well set up in her own right, with or without her first and second husbands. Her father saw to that. It seems Jane was his favorite.

In 1822, Jane married her second husband, Ben Roodhouse, described in parish records as a "butcher" in 1801 and a "mariner" in 1802, but by 1807 he was listed in the Yorkshire poll book as one of only a handful of men with the vote in Cawood. In that list of the enfranchised, we also find his brother Peter Roodhouse, brother-in-law John Cleveland, and father-in-law Isaac Moses. It's likely Ben amassed the portfolio of farms and houses he sold in 1830 by making a fortune on the vessels. In other words, Ben's time as a Yorkshire mariner probably paid for his large farm in Illinois, years later. By 1823, Ben was described as a "farmer."

While reading the parish records for St. Mary's Bishophill Senior in York, I stumbled on the burial of one Thomas Cleveland, mariner, of Skeldergate, aged thirty-six. Thomas was Ben Roodhouse's cousin, born in Cawood in 1774, and a mariner around the same time. All this tells us is that the extended family spent some time in the bustling city of York, England's "second city" in Regency times. St. Mary's Bishophill was around the corner from North Street, where the family lived.

I descend from Jonathan, Jane's half brother but also, by coincidence, Ben Roodhouse's sister, Hannah, was my fourth great grandmother. The witnesses at Jane and Ben's wedding were Benjamin Thompson (not that one!) and Elizabeth Cleveland. As late as the 1870s, farming Clevelands were to join the Roodhouse and Woods in Illinois. It seems our family stayed in contact across the Atlantic for at least two generations after emigration, although no letters are extant. Five children were to join the four from Jane's first marriage, this time all of them born in Cawood: Jane (b. 1823), twins John and Ben (b. 1825), Peter (b. 1827), and James (b. 1830). These little Yorkshire boys in particular were to become prominent in Illinois life. Old Isaac left his shares in *Ebiezer* to his son, William, but only on the condition that William paid all debts and ran the business well.

If the family had stayed in England they'd have been haulers and farmers. Instead, Jane's twin sons went on to have the town of Roodhouse named after them. U.S. dollar bank notes bear their image. Quite something for two little Cawood boys! Abraham Lincoln is thought to have stayed with the Roodhouses, in White Hall, Illinois, and the boys' connections were later to help them re-route the railroad to Roodhouse, which made the town economically viable. Springfield was forty miles away from Roodhouse, and Abraham Lincoln also turned up in Illinois in 1830 and was in his early days, an attorney, like some of Jane's friends.

So Jane and her sons were to mix in influential circles in the United States. Had they stayed in rural Yorkshire, they'd have been unlikely to meet, say, an ordinary member of Parliament once in their lifetimes. This part of the family is thus much better documented than their cousins who stayed home in the Vale of York, quietly farming, maybe meeting no one more influential than a local magistrate or two.

Jane was a middle-aged woman when she emigrated, at a time when life expectancy for some in the industrial West Riding of Yorkshire was as low as eighteen years of age. (That particular low was achieved in Bradford, centre of the Yorkshire woollen trade.) Positively elderly by some standards, Jane's crafting skills and habits would have been well established.

Leaving England, it's likely the Roodhouses proceeded to London to meet their ship by river boat. Vessels went daily from York and Selby, down the inland waterways, to London. It was slower than stagecoach but kinder on the furniture if you were moving your possessions. In London, there was a mishap when the ship was still docked. Family legend has it that one of the twins fell into the water. Their 14-year-old half-brother, Isaac, dived in to rescue him.

Jane's journal of her struggles as a pioneer woman did not survive. The journal was thought to have been lost in a fire in Roodhouse, Illinois, in the 1930s. However, a novel based on Jane's experiences, written by a descendant in the 1930s who we believe might have seen the lost journal, does survive. This manuscript was called *Prairie Smoke* and remained unpublished in its author's lifetime. When maiden aunt Nelle Strang died, the manuscript of her novel based on Jane's life was found in her attic and privately published. We have to be cautious using a secondary source like this based on a long-lost primary account. Still, mixed in with the romantic notions of the 1930s Aunt Nelle are some startling details of pioneer life that ring true. There is every reason to believe that the sequence of activities detailed in *Prairie Smoke* has some basis in the facts documented in Jane's long-lost journal. Indeed, *Prairie Smoke* is full of convincing detail – until it touches on anything to do with Regency England.

Little Cabin on the Big Prairie

When they arrived in New York late in 1830, Jane described it quaintly as a "sea port town!" The family then travelled, via the Erie Canal, to Greene County, Illinois, shortly before the deep snow set in. The family bought a farm for $3,000. The house was little more than a long, low log cabin but that had more acres of land than they'd have got for the money in Yorkshire. Their home was a far cry from the imposing, brick-built eighteenth-century home they had in England. The previous owner, Thomas Rattan, "len'" the English folk his servants to help them settle in over those first months. Jane grew very fond of them and learned a lot from them over that first winter in Illinois. Just as well as the winters had been mild for several years but, according to IllinoisHistory.com, the winter of 1830 was later remembered as "The Great Snow."

104—*River Ganseys*

> The Winter of the Deep Snow became a dating point in pioneer legendry. [sic] Residence in the Illinois country before that date was qualification for members in Old Settlers' associations and special designation as a "Snow Bird." One pioneer wrote, "I have my Snow Bird badge which was given me at the Old Settlers' meeting at Sugar Grove. I prize it very highly and would not trade it for 100 wild turkeys running at large in Oregon." Among those who qualify was Abraham Lincoln. He came from Indiana with his family in 1830 and tells of spending the "celebrated 'deep snow' of Illinois" at a spot 10 miles southeast of Decatur.

In *Prairie Smoke*, and very likely in real life, Jane's knitting wires were busy from the get-go. In November 1830, for her eldest son William, she said, "I did knit him neck-scarf." Then she added, "The lads do assist in the felling of the trees and with the care of the stock while Mary and I do spin and knit. Jane does mind the small lads for they are ever in mischief as small lads do ever seem to be. Many stitches must be taken for we do number nine and no seamstress is at hand as in the Old World."

After that first hard winter, Ben made his way back up to Lake Erie to retrieve some of the family's possessions they'd left in a secure building, locked in sea chests. Ben arrived at Lake Erie only to find that many of the family's treasured possessions from home had been looted and the building had burned to the ground. At Christmas 1830, the family celebrated Yule "in the English manner" – fetching in Yule log from the forest (pretty much as my family continued to do in the woods near our farm here in Yorkshire, more than 100 years later). Poor Jane bemoaned the loss of her sea chests. "This fine silver tea set and the salt dish were marriage gifts from mine husband the Captain and it is indeed rare I bring these gifts forth for mine husband Benjamin does not wish to see them but I hold them for Mary that she may have them in memory of her father long ago lost at sea." The "long ago lost at sea" could be a fiction. As we have seen, Captain Wood was buried inland, at Cawood, in 1817. There were no death certificates in 1817, and, especially for a mariner, place of burial does not always equate to place of death.

Months after his return from Lake Erie, Ben sickened with a fever and died, leaving Jane to raise nine children alone, thousands of miles from home. Fortunately, her sons from her marriage to Captain Wood were old enough to run the farm, leaving Jane immersed in domestic chores, a common situation for pioneer women. These routines give us a brilliant insight into the capabilities of an inland mariner's daughter/wife, in extremis. Spinning and knitting were a relentless part of her daily routine and are mentioned frequently in *Prairie Smoke*. We get another insight into the lifestyles of the Humber ship captains of the Regency period when Jane says, "I do greatly regret the loss of the great brass ship lanthorns I did possess for much light would these have given in our dim cabin." Along with spinning, sewing, knitting, and even learning how to make straw hats, Jane had to learn how to make her own candles and rush lights. The big brass lanthorns (lanterns) would have been missed, especially when you recall that the women had to knit at night in poor rush light.

The Roodhouses had brought some of their belongings with them in what Jane called a "canvas covered wain" (again, this strikes me as authentic language for an Englishwoman as opposed to the more expected "covered wagon"). These belongings included a large mirror, a clock, and a spinning wheel. As we have seen, working-class women could only rarely spin, and the raw wool was already hard to acquire, by the time Jane was growing up. However, Jane was also privately educated in York. Her background was more Jane Austen than Calamity Jane. Maybe her practical, Methodist upbringing meant she could, indeed, hand-spin from childhood. We can't know.

A new skill that Jane learned from the servants – the servants they had inherited from the land's previous owner, Rattan, were former slaves – and from locals, was that of dyeing. "Jennie's mother did make promise to set the dyes for us for it is soon we will need the garments stitched for mine household. She does handle the dyes with much skill. Each year she does go questing about in search of madder and logwood and sassafras also. She has even used the dark juice of the pokeberry and she knows even goldenrod and iris will yield up a bit of juice for her use." I suspect Jane enjoyed the chance to do things she never could have done in Yorkshire. The New World yielded some new and excellent dyes like pokeberry and sassafras, which would have been unheard of back home. The endless socks and stockings Jane knitted were probably much more fun and colourful than those she'd have bought in England.

In Yorkshire, spinning was for charity school children, not a "genteel" or acceptable skill for a middle class girl like Jane who had inherited land as well as property from her late father. In England, handspinning still happened, but it was largely superceded by spinning jennies, where one unskilled operative could work 28 or more spindle heads at once. That said, York, where Jane had spent her school days and her married life with Abraham, was home to the manufacturers of England's finest quality parlour wheels for middle-class ladies like Jane. Dyeing had long been an industrial trade in England, and hand-spinning a dying art.

John Jameson made the finest parlour wheels in the United Kingdom and happened to be based in York around the same time Jane went to school there. Jameson set up his factory to employ "the industrious poor." One of Jameson's trade labels read, "JOHN JAMESON his TOY & TUNERY MANUFACTORY in Carlisle Buildings, Little Alice-Lane, in the City of YORK." Jameson wheels survive in York Castle Museum, and there is a surviving Jameson boudoir wheel in the Pitt Rivers Museum at the University of Oxford. As Jameson wasn't a Freeman of the City he couldn't trade within the city walls, so he set up at Carlisle Buildings (now St. William's College) in the shadow of the minster. Jameson traded until 1806, selling the entire contents of his workshop and shop. York would have been flooded with Jameson wheels for a while, maybe even still in 1809 when Jane moved there and certainly during the time she was at school in the city. Jameson's place was taken by Joseph Doughty, of 6 Coney Street, York, who made a fancy parlour wheel with a modification to add speed. Doughty's wheel seemed to have been based on a wheel mentioned in the *Transactions of the Royal Society of Art* in 1793.

> Twenty guineas were this year voted to Mr. John Antis of Fulneck (the Moravian settlement) near Leeds, for his ingenious method of causing the bobbin of the common spinning wheel to move backward and forward by which means, the time lost by stopping the wheel to shift the thread from one staple, on the flyer, to another, as hitherto constantly has been practiced, is avoided.

Moravians were a progressive, evangelical protestant sect who set up their own community near Leeds. Jane would no doubt have been all for the Moravian connection.

When Mr. Doughty died, his wife, Martha Marshall, took over making the spinning wheels until she sold to John Hardy in 1824. Hardy's wheels ceased trading in 1832 – two years after Jane had left for the New World. His trademark was an ivory circle inscribed "DOUGHTY YORK." You'd think Jane must have prepared for pioneer life either before she left England, or shortly after she landed in the New World. But I suspect, as a mariner's daughter and wife of Captain Wood, she would already have been well acquainted with knitting. In England, Jane would have been able to afford to buy hosiery. But thrown on her own resources in Greene County, she, along with her eldest daughter, Mary, would have been on an endless treadmill of stocking knitting.

She did some fancier stuff, too. In May 1834, there's a reference to her learning to do beaded knitting, using recycled beads, taught by a fellow pioneer woman. "Mistress G. did also teach us to knit silk purses and did tell daughter Mary she might knit one for her lover. I did knit some purses and did knit also watch ribbands of black and I did garnish my knitting with gilded beads. Beads are indeed rare but Mary did remove our beads from an old tablemat festooned with them and these beads were of divers colors" (quoted in Brears, "York Spinning Wheel Makers").

For most pioneers, for whatever reason, knitting ganseys did not figure. In her 1930s memoirs of pioneer life, Etta May Lacey Crowder wrote that "knitting, which was done by most of the women, was usually confined to the necessities – socks, stockings, mittens, mufflers, and wristlets. A few did fancy knitting, such as lace edgings, chair tidies, and even bedspreads" (Crowder, "Pioneer Memoirs").

I like to consider this thought in light of the observation made in *The Dalesman* that not a single gansey or jumper of any description can be found in a nineteenth-century photo of Dales farmers. Even though ganseys seem curiously absent, pioneer knitters must have made warm woollen undergarments. How can snow birds not have? Back home in England, in the *Wrexham Advertiser* of 1884, an ornery feature writer gave out an *ad hoc* pattern for making some sort of body comforter. This item was widely syndicated, including in Yorkshire local newspapers.

> KNITTED VESTS. Again, I must beg my readers not to overwhelm me with any more applications for the loan of a pattern vest I promised. I cannot supply one-half of them if I despatched two patterns a week for more than six months, so numerous are they! I cannot make any written description plainer than my first one. Knit a strip of coarse loose elastic warm knitting, about 11 inches wide, and 38 or 40 inches long; sew the two ends together, then sew the middle of the two sides together for about 12 inches, leaving the rest unfastened at each end. These two holes form arm holes; put your arms into them backwards. Your head has nothing to do with it; the vest doesn't go over your head at all. When the arms get into the holes, pull the knitting across your chest and down to the waist at the back, and up around the neck. It should fasten across the chest with three buttons and loops, but is open at the neck.

Apparently, the "Our Ladies" columnist was overwhelmed by the response to her ambiguously worded "recipe," as two years later, she wrote testily:

> When I wrote about the knitted vest some years ago, I gave all the directions in my power, but ever since then I have been pursued by a certain number of knitters who say they cannot find out exactly what I mean, while others do so with the greatest ease and satisfaction. I can add nothing to the directions I have already given, and I have made many of these vests myself without any difficulty. Knit your 38 inches of 11 wide, follow the recipe exactly, and you will find a comfortable sleeveless jacket is the result. I never answer letters by post, and I cannot lend you a pattern; you must work it out for yourself, as I have done with perfect success.

In Illinois, in November 1834, Jane noted, "Already I have an vast number of socks and stockings knit. Mary has knit mittens and she did double-hook and peg an pair for each lad and she is now knitting braces for the lads to present them at Yuletide." With characteristic Yorkshire bluntness, as she watched her younger daughter, Jane, knit and compared her to the older, Mary Ann, "Jane does knit both rapidly and well. She oft sits on an hassock close by mine knee and recites her lessons while she does knit. The lass has already husked the nuts and sugared persimmons. Now she is not quite so handsome as Mary but she is neat and industrious and in a few years will make a fine woman."

Jane's upbringing had suited her to life on the prairies. Although sometimes even fetching her knitting could be fraught with danger.

> While the frolic did go on I did slip out to fetch mine knitting and when I did open up the chest an voice from within did say "Woman, what seekest thou?" I did draw back afrighted and did bang down the lid. I did return to mine chair and did sit a bit and did ponder on it and I did think mine ears had deceived me and I did again go to the chest and the voice within did say – "Woman, why fleest thou from thy fate?" Quickly I did turn about and when I did return I was greeted with a shout of laughter. The lad did then come to me and did plead for mine forgiveness for his trickery and when I did grant him this he did make the fire – dogs hark and an robin did chirp upon the window sill and there was an mewing beneath the table and no pussy cat was there. He did have the power to cast his voice where he did choose and did much enjoy playing tricks on those about him.

When old Isaac died in 1820, Jane's beloved Mary and the other Wood children inherited clocks, silver, and furniture from their grandfather. I wonder if Isaac's bequests were among the silver and furniture lost by the disaster at Lake Erie back in 1830? As it was, most of Isaac Moses's fortune made on the Yorkshire rivers and canals ended up stolen by Lake Erie or treasured in Greene Valley, Illinois, with the Wood and Roodhouse children.

Jane's children were also to inherit some money and a clock from their Uncle Peter, Ben's brother, who was close to death when the Roodhouses sailed for the New World. Peter left his farm to his nephew, the son of his long-dead sister, Hannah Cleveland nee Roodhouse; his only other bequests when he died in the winter of 1830 were to the children of "my brother now in America." Ties between the Yorkshire folk and their Illinois cousins remained strong for at least a generation. There must have been many letters home and also out to Greene County from home. As late as the 1870s, my great, great uncle, Aetheling Cleveland, and his large brood, joined the family in Illinois.

The Illinois Yorkshire folk also maintained some mariner connections. Jane writes about the two young sons of Dr. S., formerly the apothecary (doctor) on her father's vessel going out to Illinois for a year and living with them at the log cabin. The English boys were enormously popular immediately and taken out on a hunt. Being Englishmen, they expected something like a fox hunt but got a wild chase across thirty miles of prairie – after wolves! One of the lads took ill with a fever and was buried on the farm. The other returned to England alone. I have been unable to trace Dr. S. and his sons.

For years, Jane lived in a wooden shack on the site until she could afford to send to Boston for an architect. Brick by brick, she had built from memory a copy of her old house in Cawood. (The house, also called Cawood, still stands and was only sold out of the family in the 1990s.) This well-educated Methodist woman, widowed and alone with her children thousands of miles from home, had to call on skills no woman of her background would have needed in 1830s Yorkshire. In one of the more fanciful later passages of *Prairie Smoke*, purporting to be from 1854, Jane (or Nelle) wrote of her memories of home. If nothing else, it gives a sense of this Illinois farmer's youth, among the community of mariners.

> Old seamen did oft sit by our fires and smoke their pipes and tell great tales of the sea. Oft mine father fetched home with him officers from the trading vessels anchored for a bit in the harbour. These were strongmen and fearless and mine father would chaffer with them for hours for the choice wear of their cargo. Then he would come and go making preparation for his journey. The great bales he did mount upon pack horses and he did rope them to hold these precious wares secure and tight and he then mounted his fine saddle mare and away she did go at the head of the pack train to lead them into the distant inland cities. Each morn I did pray for his safety and at eventide also.

Even if these aren't Jane's words, there is an element of truth in this. Either way, there is no doubt that a bit of Yorkshire knitting expertise made it to Illinois in 1830. We can't know whether Jane just knitted stockings, scarves, and purses. I'd assume she possibly could knit a gansey, as daughter and wife of mariners.

I think of the Stainforth hearts gansey, which bucks everything we thought we knew about inland ganseys. And also of the hearts design I knitted during my own father's last illness. In the words of his will, you can see Isaac Moses was a thoughtful, intelligent, liberal, and kind man, much concerned that his daughter should inherit more than his son and that his granddaughters be as well educated as his grandsons. Much like my own dad. And in the time when I knew he was dying, I knit this gansey where suddenly the full hearts wanted to alternate with empty ones. This pattern might have been in Jane's mind or available in the lexicon of motifs. She must have often thought of home, her long-gone much loved father, and his love of the river, and her heart, too, would have felt sometimes full, sometimes empty maybe when she missed home.

In May 1837, before she had had a new brick home built, Jane looked around the old log cabin and thought:

> Crude is our cabin and of simple construction but more commodious than most wilderness homes and we have had much happiness within these walls. As I gaze about me two beds do I see. There is an vast hearth and an deep chimney of field stone. There is mine spinning wheel close by the window of crystal glass fetched, all the way from Saint Louis by the river Illinois. Table boards and benches are shoved beneath the shelf holding the bucket of water and gourd dipper. The wash basin is on the shelf and clean towel spread on an roller above it. The English clock does tick on these strange walls as it did in the Old World in the days of mine youth.

For me, Jane's most poignant words are these, from the autumn of 1830, when she was only really a matter of weeks out of England. You can almost feel her aching for home: "Tonight there is a fine sunset in rose and gold and I do long to be once more in England. I can most see the street of our quiet village and the sound of the bells from the steeple I can most hear." In the end, many Woods, Moses, Roodhouses, and Clevelands ended up a world away from home in Greene County. For my part of the family, who stayed on the Vale of York, our world changed forever one night in the 1930s. One hundred years after Peter Roodhouse left the farm to John Cleveland, the river flooded. We lost our uninsured dairy herd, and left farming forever.

GANSEY TECHNIQUES

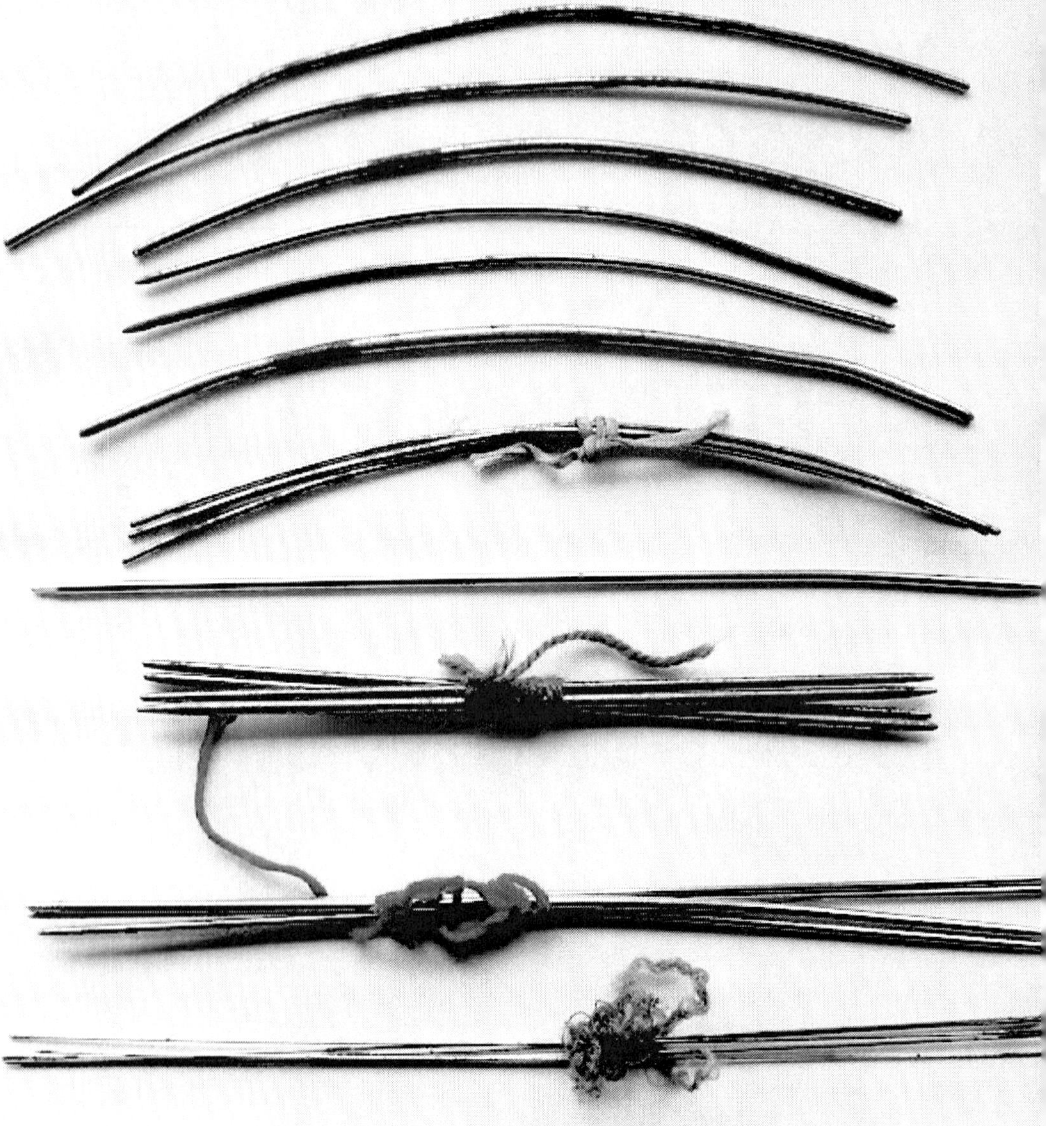

Gansey Knitting 101

Early and correct information and skills to complete a knitted gansey.

IN THIS CHAPTER I OFFER GUIDELINES FOR KNITTING ANY GANSEY YOU like, combining the motifs in this book, to make your own. Determine your gauge before you start. Standard needle sizes for gansey knitting are US #1½ and 2 (2.5mm and 2.75mm).

There are many ways to cast on, mark a fake seam, and work a shoulder or neck treatment. Once you have made one or two ganseys you can explore these with impunity. I will give you one or two alternatives here, rather than the whole smorgasbord. As you gain experience, you'll find your own tricks and workarounds, too. There are no wrongs or rights. Let's get up and running.

A gansey is a circular, seamless jumper. It is knit from the welt upwards, and the sleeves are knit down from the shoulders. This was so they were easier to frog and re-knit when the gansey wore out at the elbow or cuffs. Because we're used to twentieth-century style, tailored knitting – highly shaped pieces knitted as separate panels and sewn together in the finishing – some contemporary knitters find ganseys daunting to knit. A 300-plus stitch cast on, on what seem like infeasibly tiny needles, does look a bit scary before you try it. In practice, it is way less formidable than it looks. Ganseys are great news for the sewing phobic as they cut out that entire phase of finishing. Traditional methods of construction factor out the slightly amateur look that comes from poor finishing.

One word to the wise: Don't shy away from more apparently complex pattern motifs for your first attempt. A plain gansey can be boring to knit. Watching a motif emerge tends to spur most knitters on. People will be amazed by the end result, too, and think you're an Olympic class knitter. In fact, it takes very little extra effort to make a heavily patterned gansey than a plain one. If in doubt, make a really traditional river gansey – knit plain to the halfway point and then go crazy with patterns and motifs. I promise you that by the time you hit the patterning, you'll be desperate for some interest.

FACING PAGE: NEEDLES WERE SOMETIMES BENT SOMETIMES STRAIGHT, DEPENDING ON THE KNITTER'S PREFERENCE. IMAGE COURTESY DALES COUNTRYSIDE MUSEUM, HAWES. CREDIT: BELINDA MAY.

Welts

Before you cast on, think about what kind of welt you want. The most traditional is the 2×2 ribbing. But you could try 1×1 ribbing or two garter stitch panels each with half your overall stitch count, joined onto one circular needle (or four gansey needles) at the top of the welt. Your choice. Welt depth is usually 3–4 inches. The sign of being a fisherman was to turn the welt up, so the working gansey's welt was often deeper than modern taste dictated.

Casting on

It's sometimes hard to figure out a cast on from written instructions. If you're having trouble, all the gansey cast ons can be found in online tutorials. Many cast ons can be used for a gansey, including knotted, Channel Island, and just about any elastic cast on with the yarn held double for the first few rounds to give the gansey's edge strength.

One contemporary Yorkshire knitter does a provisional cast on (also called open cast on), then comes back at the end and knits down from it in a rib. The principle is that the ribbing can easily be frogged and re-knit if the edge wears out. This is not a traditional technique but is worth bearing in mind if knitting for a child who wears her clothes out or might get a bit more wear out of a gansey if the welt is frogged and knitted a bit deeper.

Traditionally, the yarn is held double both for casting on and for working the first two or three rounds of the body. Also, sleeves were bound off with yarn doubled, just to reinforce the most stressed point in your work.

However you cast on, be careful not to twist your stitches. I find it is easier to cast on with two straight needles and knit the first couple of rounds as flat rows, then join into the round, using the tail of yarn later to sew the gap invisibly.

If you want to make an almost invisible and jogless join on your first round, you can simply swap the first and last stitches of the round. Knitting in the round is essentially knitting a spiral. By transposing the first and last stitch on the first round, you close that spiral. Another way to do this is to cast on one stitch more than you require, then at the beginning of the first round knit together the first and last stitch that you cast on.

The welt is usually made on about 90 percent of your stitches for the main part of the body. For example, if I want a gansey that will need 260 stitches for the main part of the body, I would cast on around 90 percent of 260, for the welt. In this case: 234 stitches. I would knit the welt on these 234 stitches then, when it is complete, increase the required 26 extra stitches evenly across the first plain round of knitting. (Plus 2 seam stitches).

Your Usual Cast On

If you have a strong cast on that you like and normally use, there's no reason why it won't work for a gansey so long as you knit the first several rounds with the yarn held double. This will lend more strength to your welt edge. It might not be as pretty as the traditional knotted or Channel Island cast ons, however, so they're worth adding to your repertoire.

> **Tip**
>
> Knit one round plain (stockinette stitch on right side) after the cast-on round, before commencing ribbing. This makes the cast-on knots pop.

Some of the cast ons that are viable for ganseys are the long-tail and cable cast ons. Long-tail cast ons work especially well. For a variation, you could work a long-tail cast on with two colours, putting Colour 1 in front of Colour 2, then work a couple of rounds with both before knitting the rest in your main colour.

Whichever cast on you use, be careful to pause after every single stitch and take the time to pull the yarn so both threads look even. It is harder to manage any cast on with two yarns, but it is worth taking it slowly and persisting as this could add years of life to your gansey.

Here are two additional, brilliant gansey cast ons that are worth knowing as they work great for smaller projects like socks.

Knotted Cast On

Use the thumb (one-needle) method to cast on two stitches. With the left needle, lift the first stitch over the second, leaving one stitch. Work two new stitches, and again pass one over the other as if you're binding off. Continue until you have enough stitches. When you've knit the first couple of rounds of welt, eyeball this and decide which side of the cast on looks most decorative. Turn your welt inside out if necessary to show the cast on to the best advantage.

Channel Island Cast On

This is the prettiest cast on to use for ganseys, as it gives a firm, decorative, but strong edge. People think you're cleverer than you are when you use a Channel Island cast on.

This cast on has a bead of yarn between stitch pairs. If ribbing, the beads will only pop if you place knit stitches over them – not purls – so beware! Again, you can knit one round plain after casting on if you want to make the most of those beads.

Work with the working yarn held single, and set up as if for a long-tail cast on. Double over your yarn for the tail. This doubled over yarn will form the beads.

Go back to the beginning and fold over a third time. The single strand of yarn (working yarn) will be wrapped round your index finger; the doubled tail yarn round your thumb.

116—*River Ganseys*

THIS GANSEY'S SEAM STITCH WAS BASED ON ONE FROM A SEVENTEENTH-CENTURY STOCKING. CREDIT: NATHANIEL HUNT.

Make a slip knot with all three strands of yarn and place on right needle. You can take this slip knot out when you're finished. The tail (two strands of yarn) will be treated as one strand, and the working yarn (lone strand) goes to the ball. Put the tail over your thumb and wrap around twice. You'll be casting on in pairs. Place the right needle up into both thumb loops from underneath, catch up the loop of single (working) yarn from index finger, and pull the doubled loops over the stitch. Pull to an even tension. As the bead is made from the doubled (thumb) yarn, make sure both strands of it are equal tension.

Seam Stitches

Seam stitches were such a regular part of nineteenth-century knitting that Victorian knitting manuals often called a purl a seam stitch. And *to seam* was synonymous with *to purl* as a verb. Before ganseys came about, most knitters made stockings and most eighteenth- and early nineteenth-century stockings had one seamed (purled) stitch per round or alternate rounds. Increases and decreases could be made on either side of the seam stitch, either right next to it or one stitch away from it, on either side.

In ganseys, fake seam stitches serve a purpose. They mark the start of a round, but they are also the place where shaping can happen. They are usually mirrored on either side of the seam stitch. In stripy knitting, they were used to change colours and to mask a jog at the point of colour change.

For the ganseys in this book, a single purl stitch on each side will mark the seam the whole way up to the arm gussets. You can make your seam stitch as simple as one purl stitch or you could border the purled seam stitch with a column of 1×1 moss stitch on either side, which makes a decorative narrow border on either side of your underarm gusset.

Establishing the Main Body: Lots of Cables?

If you are aiming for a heavily cabled main pattern, it might be worth experimenting with swatches to see how much your cabled fabric pulls in. Some knitters need to factor in extra stitches at this point, after the welt and before the main body, to compensate for the way the cables pull in their work. Others are able to proceed without having to add in stitches to compensate. As a rule, most of my gansey knitting is cabled but not too heavily. I do not factor in extra stitches before starting the main pattern. If you end up needing to add extra stitches to compensate for your cables, you can most easily accommodate those stitches in filler sections. For example, columns of moss stitch at the start and end of the gansey's front and back.

Starting the Main Body

Complete ribbing then commence knitting in stockinette stitch for one round. This is where you need to bring your number of stitches up to 100 percent.

On this first plain round, you can get in your increases and also establish your seam stitches. In our example, we cast on 234 stitches, but we know we want to increase to 260 stitches for the main body. That means we need to make 26 new stitches somewhere across the first plain round of 234. But we also need to add two seam stitches, which means we actually need to increase 28 stitches evenly across the existing 234.

For the seam stitches, you can make one stitch purlwise (m1p) to mark both the first stitch of the round and the exact halfway point of the round. Between those 2 purls on this round you will need to make 13 new stitches on the front and 13 new stitches on the back. At the end of the establishing round, you will have this configuration of stitches: 1 purl, 130 knits, 1 purl, 130 knits – 262 stitches total.

> **Tip**
> Use two different stitch markers so you can remember which seam stitch is the start of the round.

Increase by evenly dividing the number of increased stitches (13) into the welt's number of

118—*River Ganseys*

front stitches: 117 stitches divided by 13; increase every 9 stitches across the front and then the same across the back.

Establish your seam stitches on this round by working an m1p in the space before your first stitch and then another m1p for stitch 131 (exact halfway point), taking into account the stitches you have just made. Double check that you have an even number of stitches, front and back, between the two purls.

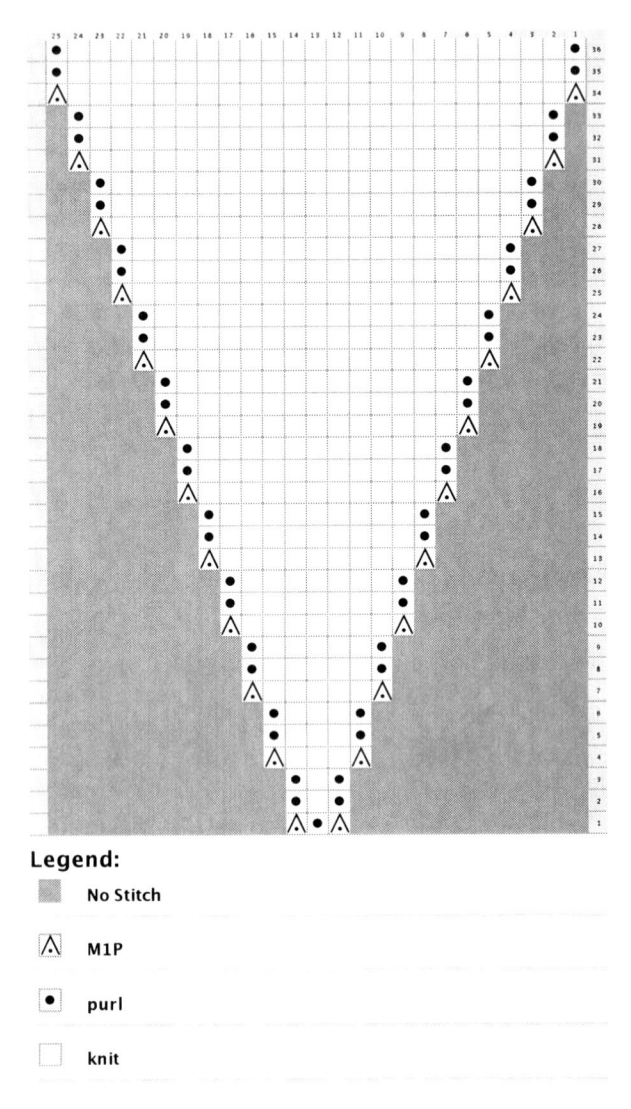

Legend:

- No Stitch
- M1P
- purl
- knit

Initials and Starting the Main Body

If you have decided not to knit initials, start the main body pattern here. Or work plain if not patterning until the yoke, remembering to maintain your purl faux seam stitches on every round.

If you want to knit initials, first knit 4 rounds of stockinette stitch. Then begin working initials, usually on the left front but you can put them wherever you like. Initials are worked in purl on a background of knit stitches. Some knitters prefer to work initials in moss stitch (seed stitch), as they believe the initials pop better from the background. Swatch both purled and moss stitch initials and see which method you prefer.

When you have completed the final round of initials, knit 4 rounds of stockinette stitch, still maintaining your side seam stitches.

Main Body

If making a fully-patterned gansey, start your pattern four rounds or so after the initials have been completed. There is no hard-and-fast rule for where to start; just do what looks good to you. Remember to maintain your purled seam stitches. Stitch markers on both sides help.

Work up to the yoke either in pattern or plain if doing a half-patterned gansey. Start the gussets 4 inches or so shy of where you want to divide for the underarms.

Underarm Gusset

Here's a chart to help you with underarm gussets, for those of you who feel safer holding my hand, first time out.

For those who just want a description, so you can get the gist of it, read on.

When you get to the start of a round, increase 1 purlwise in the space before the seam stitch. Knit 1 (this was your seam stitch), increase 1 purlwise (2 new stitches made). Now all you have to do is keep these 2 purl stitches that outline the diamond of your underarm gusset consistent. Repeat this again when you hit the second seam stitch on the other side. Knit 2 rounds, maintaining the purl stitches by purling when you get to them and knitting the stitch between the 2 purls.

On the third round, when you reach the gusset, purl the purl stitch, m1, k1, m1, purl the purl stitch. Do the same with the second gusset. Knit 2 rounds. Increase 1 stitch after the first purl and before second purl, at each underarm, and every third round. Keep increasing until you reach the underarm. As a guideline, I usually have around 17 stitches between the 2 purls, at the fattest point of my diamond.

When you reach the underarm, put both purl stitches and all the knit stitches between them on waste yarn.

Some people make their increases on every third round, some on every fourth. If you are not following a specific pattern, do what works best for you.

Bear in mind that the gusset stitches should be taken into account when measuring the sleeve. So when the time comes to pick up stitches for the sleeve, you will be picking up those gusset stitches currently waiting for you at the underarm. Don't forget to factor them in when figuring out how many stitches you need to make your sleeves.

You can put initials on the gussets or even a design that will work within the confines of the diamond you have made.

Back

Continue in pattern until you reach 2 inches short of desired depth. Don't be too precise about this. If you are mid-pattern and the pattern isn't too deep, try to end after a complete pattern repeat. If the pattern is many rounds deep and you must cut a vertical repeat of a motif, then try to cut it precisely in half. Transfer stitches to waste yarn.

I always err on the side of completing pattern repeats, both vertically and horizontally, if at all possible. For this reason, knowing your round gauge comes in handy. You can adjust patterns, taking into account the depth of your pattern repeats, if you are confident that x number of rounds = y inches of knitting, using your needles and yarn, working to your own gauge. You can calibrate this so that motif repeats end neatly, by knitting in plain stockinette stitch for slightly longer after the welt, if necessary. For this reason, deep motifs that need many rounds, such as the Humber Star, are much harder to work within a design than a shallow motif like a heart.

Front

Work to match back and again stop 2 inches short of desired depth for a simple shoulder and 3 inches short of desired depth for a fancy shoulder saddle. Again, try to make pattern repeats intact, if possible. Don't beat yourself up if you can't. It will only drive you mad and no one else will notice. Transfer stitches to waste yarn.

Shoulders

If there's more than one way to skin a cat, there are also several ways to work a shoulder treatment. You can get into all kinds of shenanigans with shoulder straps, but here I will give you the most simple and the most complex way. Choose whichever you prefer!

Simple Shoulder

Divide the front into thirds. Place the first third of the stitches on a piece of waste yarn, the central third (this will be the neck) on another piece of waste yarn, and leave the final third on your needles. Now take that final one-third and work it in pattern.

Shoulder Speak

I attended a talk with a speaker who is very knowledgeable on the history of ganseys but is not a knitter. Much of the lecture hinged on the ultimate expression of artistry and hard-core knitting which, to the speaker's mind, was exemplified by this kind of fancy shoulder saddle. A central cable becomes a feature of the shoulder, and the shoulder is closed by the whole thing being knitted sideways. I resisted going up to the speaker afterward and letting drop that this is actually one of the laziest and easiest ways to treat a shoulder. Whisper it quietly: it just looks impressive! The reality is, it is no harder to do than any other method. Non-knitters will think it miraculous. Let's not tell them it is the lazy knitter's way to do it.

For me, which shoulder treatment to use is a design decision. Nothing more. A simpler gansey might demand the simple bind off on the right side of the work shoulder. A more complex gansey looks better (and is fun to do) if you work the fancy shoulder saddle.

These are not the only shoulder treatments. These are just a sample of two methods to close a shoulder.

I usually run a six-stitch simple or braided cable down the centre of the shoulder. Calculate how many inches of knitting you will need to cover the gap between the front and back. If you stopped roughly 3 inches short on both front and back, that gives you 6 inches width to play with.

Here's a chart for a bog-standard Fancy Shoulder. (Try filling it in the chart with your own stitch pattern.)

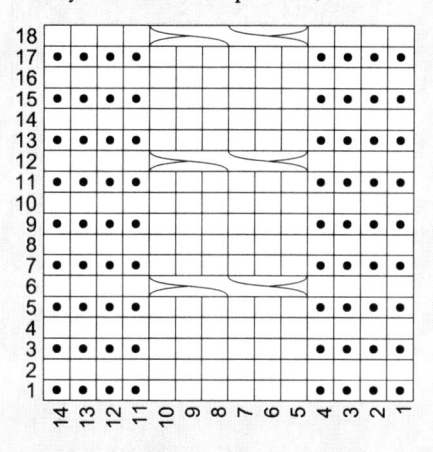

When working this shoulder, on the first and last stitch of each row, you work the first stitch together (K or P according to chart) with a live stitch from the jumper's Front and Back. This obviates the need to do any sewing, and neatly closes the jumper at the shoulders, as you incorporate Front and Back sts into the shoulder strap knitted sideways and down from the neck, towards the armscye, as you go.

Stitches
- RS: k; WS: p
- p
- WS: 3/3 LC (rev)

THIS FILEY SHOULDER TREATMENT SHOWS FRONT AND BACK WITH DIFFERENT MOTIFS, CAST OFF ON THE OUTSIDE. CREDIT: NATHANIEL HUNT.

Now you can continue in pattern or finish in ridge and furrough. (Ridge and furrough alternates purl rows/rounds with knit rows/rounds. The simplest version of ridge and furrough is garter stitch. Alternatively, for a different version of ridge and furrough, one purl row/round could be followed by two knit rounds to make the purl ridge stand out more. It is a matter of personal preference how you alternate bands of purl and knit to make your ridge and furrough.) The beauty of ridge and furrough is that you can bind off on the outside of the work, which gives a decorative finish and makes the ridge created by an outside cast on look intentional.

Work 2 inches in ridge and furrough or continue consistent with the gansey's pattern. When you have worked 2 inches, transfer stitches to waste yarn.

Do the same for the back at the corresponding side, the final one-third on a needle. Knit in pattern for 2 inches. Now for the fun. I find it easier to have the tips of the needles at the neck side, rather than the armhole side. That way if I fudge it and there's a slight discrepancy between front and back needles when I bind off, I can hide it in the armhole.

Bind off front and back together. Knit 1 stitch from the back needle. Knit 1 stitch from the front needle. Bind off by passing back stitch over front stitch. Do this until you have used all the front and back stitches on your needle. Cut yarn, leaving end long enough to weave in later when you knit arm.

Repeat this on the other side, working 2 inches front and back, then binding off loosely but with a consistent tension across the ridge of the shoulder.

Fancy Shoulder Saddle

Here, we're going to stop our front and back 3 inches shy of where the shoulder seam would be. Leave everything on waste yarn or stitch holders. We're going to knit down from the neckline to the armhole, placing a cable and a filler pattern on either side of it so the cable runs down the shoulder, uninterrupted from neckline to wrist and at a 90-degree angle to the body.

This is my all-time favourite shoulder treatment. I'd do it every time if I could. You end up with a spectacular looking shoulder that is really a lot less complex than it looks. These always fit well, too.

Left Shoulder

Use the same size needles that you used for body. I tend to work these shoulders using two needles, but some people like to use a third needle, a double-pointed needle, or a circular to hold the new stitches they cast on while they keep the front and back stitches on ordinary needles. I find the third needle unwieldy and unnecessary. I cast on my shoulder saddle onto a third needle, but once it is transferred to one of the main needles, I dispense with the third needle entirely. There is no right or wrong way, as ever.

Pick up the front stitches and place on a needle with the needle tip at neck side. Pick up back stitches and place on needle with the needle tip facing neck side.

Cast on required number of stitches to give you a 6 inches width of knitting. Establish cable and filler pattern, placing cable centrally. With right side facing, knit across these stitches. At final stitch, pick up first stitch of back (at neck end) and knit that stitch together with last stitch of cable. Knit back across your new shoulder stitches. At final stitch, knit last stitch together with first stitch of front (at neck end).

Continue like this, knitting final stitch of each row together with first stitch on back and then front needles.

When all back and front stitches are consumed, you should be at the armhole. Leave all stitches live on waste yarn. Make a note to yourself of which round you were on so that when you come to cable down the arm you remember where you were.

Right Shoulder

Complete right shoulder to match left, working down from the neck side to the armscye side.

Sleeves

Pick up required number of stitches evenly around front and back. If you used the fancier shoulder saddle, don't forget to pick up shoulder stitches from your waste yarn.

One trick to make this step easier is to measure the depth of the back armhole then divide that measurement into four. Take your overall number of stitches for the entire sleeve. Divide that number by four and then place stitch markers at each one-fourth section. So long as you're getting the right number of stitches into each quarter, the pick up will be uniform.

Another trick is to start on the back rather than the front so by the time you get to picking up stitches on the front, you have a fair sense of how far apart they're going to be. Don't forget at the underarm to pick up the purls that have been waiting for you for so long and the underarm gusset knits between them.

I mark the start of an armhole gusset, before the first purl, with a stitch marker. Remember, you're going to want to start decreasing that gusset down to complete the diamond shape as you knit down the sleeve. I usually knit a couple of rounds plain at this point before I start to establish the pattern, although I do continue with the shoulder saddle pattern as per chart.

If knitting the fancier shoulder saddle, continue on with your filler pattern and cable (hopefully integrating them into the pattern of the sleeve, if you have one). Keep the integrity of that cable.

Remember that you won't be able to keep repeats whole at the gusset/underarm seam stitch because you're going to be decreasing every third round for a long time yet. So start your pattern chart after the underarm gusset. As the first and last stitches of each round eat into your motif, you will remember where you start. Promise.

Gusset

All you're doing here is mirroring the first half of the gusset. So where you were increasing 2 stitches every third or fourth round, you're now decreasing 2 stitches every third or fourth round. You can mirror decreases by starting decrease rounds with a k2tog (right-leaning) decrease and ending with a sl1-k1-psso or ssk (slip 1 knitwise, slip 1 purlwise, k2 slipped stitches together), which is left-leaning. Some traditional gansey knitters mirrored decreases; some didn't bother, and did simple k2togs anytime they needed to work a decrease.

However you decrease, keep those decreases immediately inside the diamond formed by your 2 purls, or just one stitch away from the purls. Once you have only 3 stitches of gusset remaining including the purls, do the final decreases by purling 3 together. This gives you the purl stitch that will be the apex of your diamond.

Continue to decrease every fourth round or so (frequency of decreases will depend on length of arm and your gauge) until you have about 20 percent of your original main body number of stitches. In our example, that would be 52 stitches.

The only other design decision is whether to end your pattern at the elbow or continue the entire length of the arm. If you decide to end it, top off your pattern with a transitional one such as the waves motif. Then continue straight, either still in pattern or knitting plain stockinette stitch, until you hit the cuff or 3 inches or so short of the wrist.

Now change to smaller needles and work in rib to match your welt. Again, 2×2 ribbing was the most traditional. It's usual to mirror your welt stitches at the cuff so if you did a 1×1 ribbing at the welt, do the same again here. At the end of the cuff, work the last 2 rounds with yarn held double, and bind off sleeve loosely but consistently with yarn still held double.

Neck

Necks were often just one-third of the body stitches, centred, with no short rows or special shaping to raise the back of the neckline. For kids' ganseys, you may need to go up to 50 percent of the body stitches for the neck opening, and therefore shoulders will be narrower. For older kids and teenagers, use the 33 percent formula, same as for an adult gansey.

Crew necks are a contemporary thing. Most ganseys in the nineteenth century had necklines 4 inches or so deep in 2×2 rib sometimes topped off with a couple of rounds of garter stitch – which were simply left as is, no shaping, and no turning over and folding and sewing into a crew neck. The real traditional plain neckline has the advantage of being draught-proof and not as itchy as you'd imagine. On the river, ganseys were usually worn with neckerchiefs under them.

If you have done the fancier shoulder saddle, you can have all kinds of fun by continuing your cables up into the neckline ribbing. I love doing this. It is non-traditional, but it looks pretty.

Necks can be worked in the round but also could be knit flat, with a narrow garter stitch band at one side for buttons and buttonholes on a garter stitch background on the other side. Yorkshire keelmen's ganseys were fastened with small pearl buttons bought from a department store. Most of the keelmen's ganseys seem to have had flat knitted necklines. If you want to do this, it's a simple matter of finding a small, simple buttonhole, figuring out the spacing (number of inches to be covered divided by number of buttons used; two or three was a common choice).

Two-Row Horizontal Buttonhole

Decide how many stitches you will need to bind off to make the hole fit your buttons. It's likely to be 3 or 4. I'll write this as if your horizontal buttonhole is 4 stitches long, but adjust this if necessary.

- » On the first row where you want to place hole, work to where you want to place the buttonhole, and bind off 4 stitches.
- » On the next row, work to the bound-off stitches. Cast on 4 using backward-loop cast on.
- » On third row, knit as normal, but work the 4 cast-on stitches through the back loop.

Work several short rows at the back neck if you prefer your gansey to sit higher on the back than the front. If you like, you can knit a small triangular gusset at the base of a neckband on either side where the centre shoulder hits the neckline. These

Mysteries of the Neck and Head

Keelman Harry Fletcher answered a question that has puzzled many gansey historians for a long time: Why are the necks of ganseys in old photos always fastened on the left side?

> Their navy blue jerseys were home-knitted with a diamond pattern on the front and had high necks which fastened with two buttons on the left shoulder. Fastening had to be on the left as we carried things on the right shoulder.

On the Vale of York, we had a saying about our neighbouring Yorkshire Woldsmen: "Wolds born, Wolds bred. Strong in the arm, thick in the head." As a result of this stereotype, labourers from the Wolds were often employed on the railways to act as porters. I have a horrible suspicion that the Vale people thought the same of the average Hull trawlerman or river mariner. Men working at the docks in Hull, and the small wharves along the rivers, would also have had to be strong – not just mariners, but also effectively, porters, loading and unloading heavy cargo.

are supposed to give a snugger fit, but I find that if I knit a simple, deep tubular neckline, I tend to factor out draughts anyway. Another tip is to switch to slightly finer needles for the midsection of your neck – say, 1 inch. Then revert to the regular sized needles to complete.

I hope beginning gansey knitters can combine these instructions, with the sizing information, to knit their own river ganseys. Beginner and intermediate gansey knitters can refer back to sections of this chapter, for hand-holding and brow-soothing when needed.

As Elizabeth Zimmermann remarked, nothing in knitting is entirely new. When we think we are adding something new to knitting's repertoire, we actually "unvent" rather than "invent," she said. In gansey knitting today we are playing with some patterns that are more than 200 years old. But nothing is stale, as everyone can combine and recombine, refine and evolve what appeals to them from within the tradition. All I want to do here is empower you to feel confident enough to do just that. Learn the tradition, and then have fun with it! Make it yours. It is yours.

Blocking

> Blocking is the process of wetting, pressing, or steaming finished knit pieces to give them their permanent size and shape. You should give this process as much care and attention as we do to knitting.
> —*Vogue Knitting: The Ultimate Knitting Book* (2002), p.94

> The smart woman of today knows that "It's the line that tells the tale."
> —*The Penguin Knitting Book* (James Norbury, 1957), p.57

When you have finished your gansey, do not despair if it looks a bit wayward. Don't panic! You need to block, is all. Blocking tames the savage gansey – evens out stitches and shapes the entire garment, so you can make it conform to how you want it to look. It also sets the stitches and size. And sometimes you can use a bit of judicious blocking to fudge a problem.

As ganseys are knitted in the round, the only sort of blocking we need to concern ourselves with, is wet blocking. Wool is one of the most elastic types of yarn, so lends itself well to wet blocking.

You need:

» A flat, clean, absorbent surface that you can pin to. I improvise blocking surfaces with large cork pinboards and towels. Cork tiles on a firm backing would work, too. Lay a towel or two over the cork. It helps to find a space where the work can stay undisturbed until it's dry.
» Measuring tape.
» Long, glass-bead-ended pins or T-pins (rustproof).

Using your delicates detergent of choice; wash the finished gansey by hand, gently. I always like to pretend I am washing my firstborn.

Rinse thoroughly in water at the same temperature you used to wash. Roll up gently in a clean towel and carefully squeeze out the excess water.

Pin to your blocking board, using the tape measure to help the gansey block to your specification.

Leave to dry naturally – not too close to a source of heat and not in direct sunlight. This may take a couple of days.

In the same way that fine lace knitting transforms from dodgy-looking "cheesecloth" to stunning lace during blocking; a gansey will also bloom, when blocked.

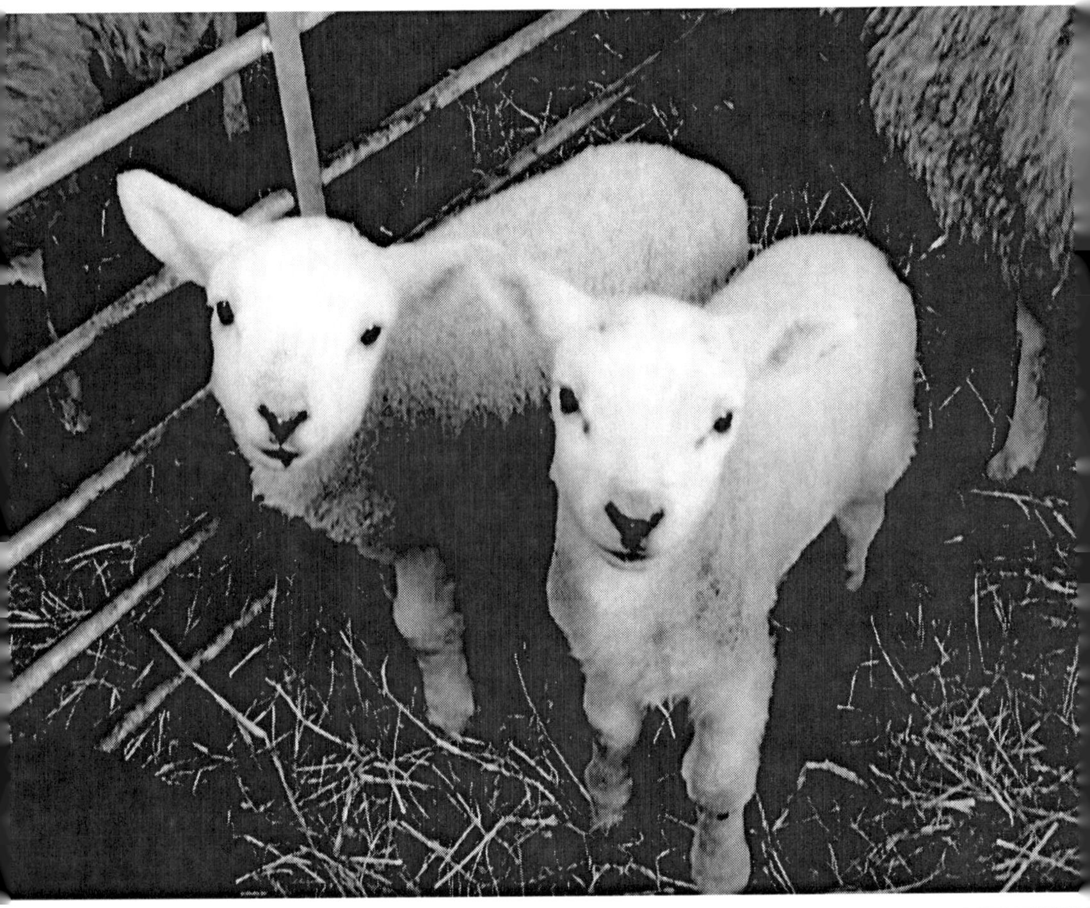

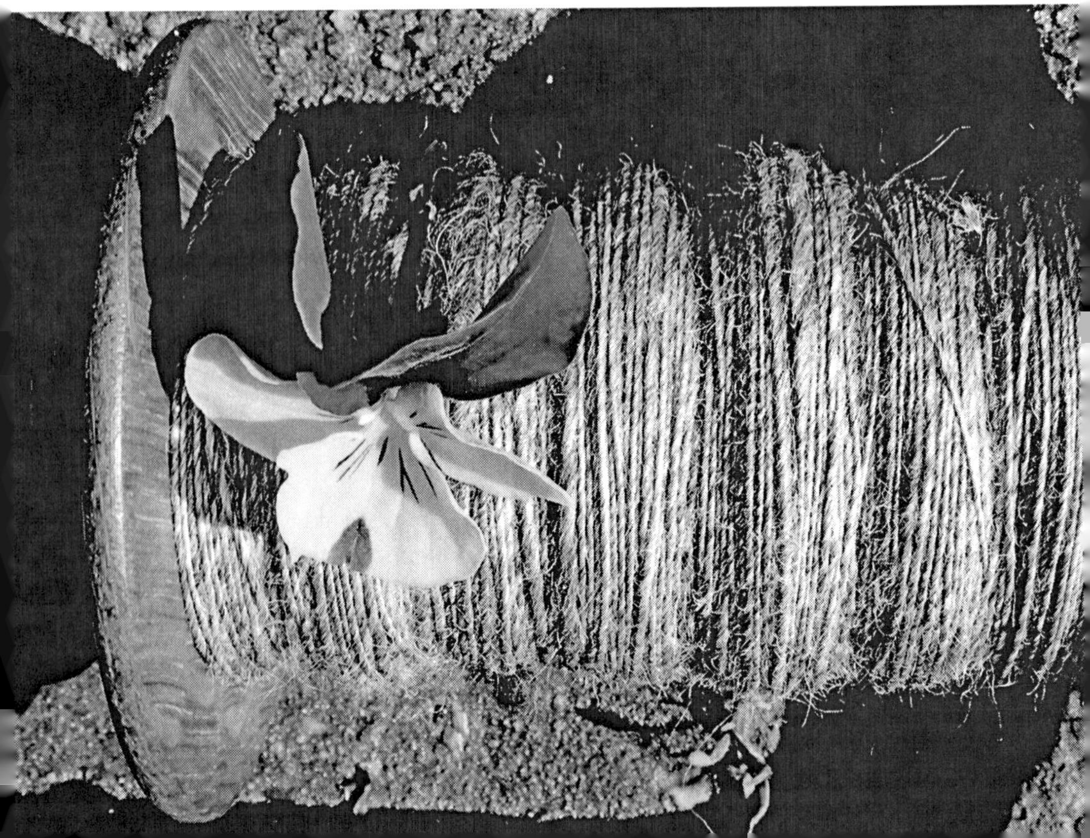

Hand Spinning for Traditional Knitting

In which the reader may learn to spin a satisfactory, lustrous and strong gansey yarn.

> For instance, if a child spun thick, be idle or wasteful of wool, it may be useful for the mistress to turn her bed gown or to pin some of the thick-spun wool to her shoulder, threatening if she be not more careful and more industrious, she shall be exhibited to her patroness, or other accidental visitors to the school.
>
> — *An Account of Two Charity Schools For the Education of Girls*

COMMERCIAL YARNS WORK JUST FINE FOR THE PROJECTS IN THIS book. But here are some guidelines for the adventurous – ambitious? mad? – hand spinner, who wants to turn her hand to making the yarn to knit traditional garments.

Ganseys were a product of the Industrial Revolution, the ultimate flowering of an age in which millspun worsted could be faultless, uniform, predictable, and have all the properties that lent it to producing a damask pattern – relying on texture, rather than colour, for effect.

The overwhelming majority of extant UK hand-spun yarns from the nineteenth century and earlier are singles or two-plies. Find me a single extant thread for the entire history of Europe that is a five-ply or that predates 1500. Can you do it?

Yorkshire was the epicentre of the world's textile industry, and so provides us with a prime example of how quickly the knitting craft changed in the nineteenth century. Already at the dawn of that century, an anonymous commentator from the York charity schools remarked, "By 1806 the spinning of wool by machinery having become general by manufacturers, it was difficult to obtain wool for spinning"

FACING PAGE, TOP: DALES LAMBS, FROM A FARM NEAR LEYBURN, YORKSHIRE DALES. BOTTOM: WORSTED-SPUN, OATMEAL BLUE-FACED LEICESTER (BFL) SINGLES. BFL IS PERFECT FOR GANSEY YARN AS IT IS LONG, VERY LUSTROUS, BUT SILKY AND BUTTERY. BOTH PHOTOS, CREDIT: NATHANIEL HUNT.

(Anon., "Souvenir of the Bi-Centenary"). That may seem incredible in such a sheep-infested county as Yorkshire, and yet it was the case. We can forget cottagers spinning in rose-bedecked doorways. Most of the county's clip went straight to feeding the vast juggernaut of heavy industry, which is precisely why ganseys only happened after industrialisation. Once machines could handle many plies, they did – for the hell of it. And it's only when you get above three plies that you get the stitch definition that makes a gansey worth doing in hand-spun. But if you are a hand spinner, plying more than three singles together means wasting your time. The hours spent spinning those two extra singles are three hours lost. (That said, with just three plies of hand-spun, you can reproduce five-ply millspun gansey yarn adequately.)

In short, England's Agricultural and Industrial Revolutions of the mid-eighteenth and nineteenth centuries combined to make a garment like the gansey possible. That said, I am talking here about English ganseys – more specifically than that, Yorkshire ganseys. In Scotland, ganseys were sometimes hand-spun and often from black worsted as opposed to navy, grey, or cream-coloured worsted that prevailed in England.

So let's be under no illusions that a hand-spun English gansey is authentic. It isn't. Worsted used for ganseys was five-plied because machines churned out worsted spun yarn at a given grist so as to make it the optimum thickness for ganseys. The number of plies in itself is almost immaterial. It just took five machine-spun plies to achieve the right yarn. Standard weight for most jumpers was four-ply. The term *double-knit* denoted four-ply doubled. Five-ply made a heavier-duty working garment. If we want to spin for gansey yarn, then, we don't need to literally make five plies; we need just enough plies to get the right end product. (Inland ganseys were sometimes made from the finer four-ply.) It seemed to have come down to the individual knitter's preference.

For hand spinners replicating gansey yarn, then, three or four plies are ideal. To choose the right fleece as raw material, we need to have a sense of what we're trying to achieve.

What Is Worsted?

In the US, worsted denotes a yarn weight and type, but in the UK, and in the world of hand spinning generally, it signifies a technique. In *Respect the Spindle*, Abby Franquemont defines worsted as yarn spun using a method where "twist only enters fibers after they have been drafted to the desired thickness" (p. 66). Abby goes on to say that "worsted methods such as short forward draw or 'inchworm' produce denser, smoother, drapier yarns." In *The Encyclopedia of Hand-Spinning*, Mabel Ross describes worsted-spun yarn as "a type of yarn spun from fibers of fair length which have been combed to remove any short fibers arranged to be as nearly parallel as possible and kept thus while spinning. This results in a clear, smooth, somewhat compact yarn, excellent for clarity" (p. 208).

3-PLY BLUE-FACED LEICESTER HANDSPUN GANSEY YARN. THIS YARN WAS PLIED IN THE TRADITIONAL WAY. CREDIT: NATHANIEL HUNT.

Machine-spun worsted can use much shorter fibres – down to 1½ inches or less. If you pull apart a modern millspun gansey yarn, you will see they are no longer made of really long fibres. The advantage of hand spinning is you can spin a true worsted with real, old-fashioned characteristics. The longer fibres that hand spinners can use will lead to a harder-wearing garment.

Worsted is also almost perfectly circular in cross section. This is important in a relief pattern where the garment's design is reliant on crisp, clear pattern definition. Two-ply yarn doesn't quite achieve this, but three-ply does. So the minimum number of plies you need for a gansey is three. You really don't need more though, as that's just making work for yourself!

The yarn is still spun Z twist and plied S. If you ply the same way as you spin, you end up with a cabled yarn, which may not be what you want. Be aware that when you ply, you undo some of the twist that you put into the singles when you

132—*River Ganseys*

SPINDLE SPINNING ON FILEY BEACH. A SOLID, WORSTED YARN FROM COMMERCIAL COMBED TOPS. RESIN SPINDLE AND HAND-DYED FIBER FROM KAREN TESSON AT WILDCRAFT, WILDCRAFT.CO.UK

originally spun them – though the untwisting effect is not as strong in a three-ply as it is in a two-ply. So spin your singles a bit tighter and with a steeper twist angle than you want them to have in the end product. A higher initial twist will yield a harder-wearing yarn – but avoid too much twist, or the yarn will be kinky (and not in a good way). You will also get a slightly fatter grist end product as you untwist the singles slightly by plying them. In other words, aim to spin a touch finer than you think you might need.

And sample yourself stupid. As a hand-spun gansey is a huge undertaking, sampling and taking detailed notes to record how you arrived at the sample's yarn is the only way to go.

If making a three-ply yarn, you have another decision to make: whether to Navajo ply or ply from three bobbins. Navajo plying will leave small, almost imperceptible bumps where you chained the singles. Some people can live with this; some can't. You get a more perfect yarn by three-plying from three bobbins. You can also replicate gansey yarn by six-plying (three pairs of singles) or four-plying (two pairs of singles). However many plies you go with, you will need to experiment and sample not only to find the right grist for your singles but to achieve a balanced, finished yarn.

Hand spinning for gansey yarn is not just about preserving the worsted nature of the yarn, but also about maximizing lustre. Some modern millspun gansey yarn lacks the typical lustre of the old Poppleton's yarn. This is to the detriment of gansey design, as a lustrous yarn makes for a pattern that pops more. As hand-spinners, we can claw this lustre back.

Under the microscope, wool fibres have overlapping scales. If you disrupt those scales to any extent, you reduce the lustre on your finished yarn. To maximize lustre in a gansey yarn:

Hand Spinning for Traditional Knitting —133

Soft, woollen-spun, 2-ply Ryeland, about the grist of a DK yarn. Motifs "pop" less with two plies and the ply twist angle is greater, making for a fuzzier yarn. Ganseys in Scotland were sometimes made from yarn like this. Credit: Nathaniel Hunt.

Wensleydale singles spun worsted on 1970s' (right) and 1990s' Timbertops flyers. This yarn was spun on a Timbertops Lonsdale and a Timbertops Chair Wheel (flyers interchangeable). Credit: Nathaniel Hunt.

1. Choose a lustrous wool type.
2. Spin fairly high-twist singles. (Spin fairly tightly, with a fast, high-speed flyer: use smaller whorls with a higher ratio.)
3. Spin from the tip, consistently. (If you break off a section of roving to make pencil roving, then eyeball the fibre to check that it is oriented correctly, so you are only ever spinning from the tips, not the shorn end of the locks.)

There is no reason you can't worsted spin a lustrous longwool with a hand-spindle. It will be longer by the day, shorter by the week to do this. Spindle spinning is no longer the poor relation of wheel spinning. There are some jaw-droppingly gorgeous, well-engineered spindles on the market. *Respect The Spindle* teaches the spinner how to get up to fierce speeds.

Breeds of Fleece Suitable for Hand Spinning a Gansey

A gansey worsted requires a true longwool. Again, I should point out there is nothing authentic about spinning an entire garment from one breed of sheep's wool. In the Yorkshire wool industry, there was no such thing as a breed-specific yarn. That is a very modern construct. Farmers' clips from all over the county were mixed at wool sorting warehouses. What they were looking for was a broadly uniform finished product – fibres of over a given staple – above 6 inches staple length in the case of worsted production. So the wool from hundreds of farms and many kinds of long wool sheep were mixed together. This was true from medieval times onward in the United Kingdom. Farmers would have some of their clip spun on site sometimes by servants and family members. In *The Old Hand-Knitters of the Dales*, one interviewee recalled her family using their Swaledale wool to hand spin. But the gansey was an industrial product and would rarely, in England, have been made from a single breed's fleece when it was made from millspun.

Long wools have crimpy (wavy) wool with staple lengths roughly 5–12 inches. Some can be longer. What we're looking for isn't just length of staple but lustre and fibre diameter. Most longwool breeds happen to be lustrous fibres anyway. But some of the longwools are among the older, unimproved, or less improved sheep breeds. Cotswold is thought to be Roman in origin, for example. It makes great bunting (tape) and carpets and might, on paper, look a strong candidate for ganseys. In reality, it's too coarse. The clue is in the age of the breed. In the Agricultural Revolution during the mid-eighteenth century, most British sheep breeds were improved in terms of fibre – that is, they were refined to produce more, longer, or finer fibre. The coarser wools tended to come from upland sheep (often longwools) and older breeds. That made them fair game for gansey yarn in theory, but, in reality, a coarser fibre might produce yarn when spun and plied, with a clumsy kind of drape more suitable for upholstery than clothing.

I find the old Bradford Yarn Count a useful guide (see the next section), as it really is a handy shortcut to what item you can make with which wool. I wouldn't want to spend more than 100 hours painstakingly hand spinning something and end up with the gansey equivalent of the silk purse from a sow's ear. The truth is, those old Bradfordians knew a thing or two. Might as well heed their guidelines and avoid anything with a Bradford count in the twenties or thirties. Wools today are measured in microns, but many hand spinners are still more familiar with the Bradford Count, and, as this is a book about the history of knitting in Yorkshire, I think we should stick with it.

The Bradford Count

In medieval and Tudor times, Yorkshire was known more for its woollens than worsteds. But by the eighteenth century the city of Bradford in the West Riding of Yorkshire had become the centre of the worsted industry, and it was decided that it

MASHAM SHEEP FAIR, IN THE DALES. THE FAIR IS AN ANNUAL EVENT WITH A FLEECE SALE AND LOTS OF WOOL "ON THE HOOF." SUCH EVENTS ARE THE BEST WAY TO LEARN ABOUT DIFFERENT WOOLS!
CREDIT: NATHANIEL HUNT.

would be commercially wise to know how much yarn was yielded by a given quantity of fibre. The Bradford Count was developed as a standard scale to measure how many hanks, at 560 yards long each, could be spun from one pound of any fleece. The higher the count, the finer the fibres. If a wool was classed as a 64, for example, that meant that 64 hanks of yarn 560 yards long could be spun from one pound of that wool. The Bradford Count was always something of an approximation. As Mabel Ross remarked, "Yarn is almost never spun to the maximum count" (Ross, *Encyclopedia of Handspinning*, p. 32).

Our little York charity school children would have been made familiar with the Bradford Count, just as workers in the Bradford and Halifax manufactories would have been conversant with it. Catharine Cappe said the spinning mistress had to account for every pound of spun yarn, "to see that it reaches the proper counts; that every pound is marked with the girl's name who spun it; that it is reeled right; that the mistress keeps her spinning closet in order, and spinning book with accuracy, to correspond with the manufacturer; keep all the accounts; receive the money earned by spinning; and to see every pound of yarn weighed before it is returned to the manufacturer" (Cappe, *Account of Two Charity Schools*). The system was standardized, and wool could be graded for a more predictable end result. Carpet and braid wool could have a count as low as 28. The best merino might get up into the 100s. By the mid-nineteenth century, one of the most common breeds used for knitting yarn was the semi-lustrous Blue-faced Leicester with counts ranging from

56 to 60. For our intents and purposes, we're mainly interested in fleeces with counts in the high 40s to 60s, as these will give us some drape, have less stiffness, but not be too short-fibred.

Fibres' grist is now measured in microns (a millionth of a meter). I still use the old Bradford Count. You can use either, of course, but as we're going all Yorkshire here, I'll stick with Bradford. In some cases, Bradford Count should only be seen as a rough guide, as I have seen some fine, strong, and excellent Wensleydale that would easily be up to making nice gansey yarn. Let your eyes and common sense guide you.

With these caveats in mind, we can survey some of the possible wools. You will have others available locally. When choosing a wool, think of the grist, staple length, lustre, and, if you think it hits our criteria, sample, sample, sample!

As a guideline, here are some of the most common long wools (as described in the *Fleece and Fiber Sourcebook*). I have bolded the Yorkshire breeds:

Blue-faced Leicester (46s to 50s)	Lincoln (36s to 40s)	**Teeswater** (40s to 48s)
Leicester (40s to 46s)	**Masham** (46s to 50s)	Texel (50s to 56s)
Cotswold (44s to 48s)	Perendale (48s to 56s)	**Wensleydale** (44s to 48s)
Gotland (48s to 52)	Romney (48s to 54s)	
	Swaledale (28s to 40s)	

For the adventurous, or those living in a less temperate climate, try plying wool together with another fibre of your choice. It's wise to experiment on a small scale with samples before you embark on a whole gansey, though. Don't say I didn't tell you so! Silk blended with wool, or even pure silk, would work well. De-gummed filament silk gives the longest fibres so would be best for stitch definition. I have seen ganseys with simple motifs or straightforward all-over patterns knitted with softer, fuzzier, woolly yarn, and certainly angora rabbit fur spun from the tip end, from premium, long fibre, and plied with wool would give a lofty, super-warm yarn with halo. Although you could say goodbye to stitches popping, you would have a very cosy and attractive garment. A cashmere/wool blend is another possibility.

Wheel or Spindle?

You can spin worsted on either a wheel or a hand spindle. Plying three yarns together, rather than spinning the singles, is probably the most challenging part of spindle spinning a gansey yarn. Worsted lends itself to the beginner spinner, as you can use the park-and-draft technique and inch along as slowly as you like.

For singles, grist a 25g, 1 oz., or thereabouts, spindle should do the trick. People talk about spinning and plying spindles, but in the past people tended to use only one spindle for both. I have a big collection of old lead, bone, soapstone spindle whirls from the United Kingdom that date from Roman to medieval times, and when we weighed them, the average spindle whirl weight was around the 27g mark. There were almost no whirls double that weight. In other words, if you can spin on it, you can ply with it.

MEDIEVAL SPINDLE WHORLS IN THE AUTHOR'S COLLECTION.

If using a wheel, select a smaller whorl to give a higher ratio to get you more twist. Some entry-level wheels may need some adjustment/work-arounds to make it easier for you to spin fine. You can master the technique of spinning a true (or true-enough) worsted, and slowly, automatically, you will go thinner as time goes on. Debate rages about double drive or scotch tension wheels. Scotch tension is a twentieth-century invention, so rest assured you can spin anything with double drive as folk did in the past. I find scotch tension more useful for spinning woollen than worsted yarns, but I haven't used the scotch tension option on my wheel for years, now, as double drive is so versatile.

When he built my wheel, I asked the inestimable Jim Williamson if he could give me a scotch tension option as well as double drive. He did it reluctantly saying, "You know, once you have this wheel and use double drive, you'll never need scotch tension." Mr. Williamson was correct. That said, if you're set up for scotch tension, and don't have a conversion kit, you will be able to spin this type of yarn perfectly well, albeit a little more slowly. No worries. All spinners and most fibres have their default setting in terms of yarn thickness, etc. Periodically check your yarn to make sure that you are not slipping into default mode. After nearly thirty years of hand spinning, I find that my default spinning is pretty much the same whatever the fibre or technique.

Spinning Gansey Worsted

Yarn Characteristics
1. Spin using worsted technique.
2. Spin to maintain lustre.
3. Ply at least three singles together to give a circular cross-section.
4. Spin for smoothness.
5. Spin from the tip.
6. Control your drafting zone, drafting towards the wheel (forward draw).

7. Deal with slubs as you go to make the yarn as smooth as possible. In reality, plying will take out a fair bit of inconsistency.

To make gansey patterns pop, spin your fibre using a short-draw, worsted technique. In recent years this has come to be known as the inchworm technique, and that's a good description. Inch along, maintaining control like a dominatrix. That should do it. I would be brutal about eliminating any vast slubs or inconsistencies at the singles stage. But plying does cover a multitude of sins.

Fibre Prep

For your finished yarn to be smooth and show off relief motifs, you need to spin with your fibres tidy and parallel. The easiest way to achieve this by far is to buy ready-prepared rovings. You can check which end of the commercial roving is the tip end; then, maintaining the integrity of the fibres' direction (tips all pointing one way, shorn ends the other), gently pull the roving into pencil-sized rovings and spin from these. The beauty of this method is that not only does it cut your prep time down to almost zero, but also with commercial rovings you have almost no wastage. All the wastage happened before you bought the fibre.

Another advantage to this method is that you can weigh out the roving and split it fairly accurately into three even piles before you start – one for each bobbin/ply. This ensures still less wastage in the end. Also, machine-roved wool is uniform and consistent. You'd have to be a very expert wool comber to comb from raw fibre to this level of perfection. Teaching the combing of wool is beyond the scope of our little book here, but should you want to learn it the original and definitive source is Peter Teal's book, *Hand Wool Combing and Spinning: A Guide to Worsteds from the Spinning-wheel*.

Spinning

To spin worsted, you control the fibre's drafting zone and attenuate fibre out, keeping that drafting zone under utter control until you're ready to let the twist invade it. So it's a case of draft (toward the wheel), attenuate, allow twist into the attenuated zone but only that zone. Constantly work toward the wheel, controlling everything. I find it best to work with a sample of the yarn that I am trying to emulate tied around a wheel post. Constantly stop and check your spun fibre against the sample yarn until you have it right. Then play around for a while spinning and knitting small samples until you get the effect you want.

Bear in mind the size needles you plan on using. Commercial gansey yarn dictates 2.5mm or 2.75mm needles (US sizes 1 to 2) for most knitters. But you are not making commercial yarn, so if you like the look and feel of knitting with 3mm (US size 2) needles, sample your yarn accordingly.

Alternatives to Wool

For those allergic to wool or living in warmer climes, there are alternative fibres that will still suit gansey knitting. I have already mentioned silk, angora, and

NATURALLY DYED WOOLLEN SPUN BUMP. SPUN FROM "FAUXLAGS" (COMMERCIAL TOPS TORN INTO STRIPS AND ROLLED AROUND A PENCIL). IT'S DENSER THAN TRUE ENGLISH LONGDRAW WOOLLEN BUT ALSO HARDER WEARING.
CREDIT: NATHANIEL HUNT.

cashmere. But also, how about soy, flax, cotton, or bamboo fibres? Look for combed tops where the individual fibres are fairly long – again, what you need is lustre.

Spinning Other Historic Yarn Types: Woollen Bump Yarn

One of Marie Hartley's interviewees, the son of a former mill owner, recalled the miners' wives rushing out of their cottages to buy bump yarn: "I remember … that when we got to Low Row the women came running out like mice for it" (Hartley and Ingilby, *Old Hand-Knitters of the Dales*, p. 45). An article in the November 1956 issue of *The Dalesman* noted, "Mrs. Bell recalls seeing her grandmother knitting long, grey sea-boot stockings of bump. This was thicker than worsted, and very greasy. Any bump left over was washed, dyed purple with logwood chips, and knit into children's socks." In an interview in *The Dalesman* in August 1970, Marie Hartley discussed the writing of her book that so many knitters have come to know and love, and how Dales' life was already changing. "Even then we were told 'Oh, what a change! What a change!' by Mr William Gill, aged 89, when we talked to him. His father and his two brothers had the woollen mill, Low Mill, at Askrigg, and they used to take the rove yarn (white wool) to Hurst and Marrick in Swaledale."

Spinning woollen bump provided an important part of the income for mining families in this region. In an earlier chapter, we met my great, great grandad, William Stephenson, the elderly Westmorland man who brought up my great grandma Emily. William Stephenson's ancestors included the Bellas family. My sixth great grandfather, John Bellas, died at Knock, Westmorland, in 1750, leaving £4/10s worth of wool and £49/6s worth of sheep in his inventoried goods. John's son, Joseph Bellas, who lived at Milburn Grange, combined sheep farming on the uplands with being a lead miner. When he died, his widow was described as "spinner."

In *Life and Tradition in the Lake District*, William Rollinson described mining in the area.

COCHINEAL-DYED ROLAGS OF A MEDIUM SHORTWOOL, READY FOR SPINNING. CREDIT: NATHANIEL HUNT.

> Working conditions in Lakeland mines were harsh and dangerous; in the days before gunpowder, "levels" were cut by hand using picks, hammers, and "stope and feather" wedges. Although the wages paid to miners were somewhat higher than those of agricultural workers, the arduous conditions and heavy manual work endured by these men brought premature old age and sometimes appalling injuries for which the extra financial reward was no compensation (pp. 164–165).

No doubt William's grandmother, Elizabeth Bellas, did the same knitting as the lead miners' wives described in *The Old Hand-Knitters of the Dales* – knitting with the "groove" yarn (bump).

Bump yarn can clearly be seen in the photo of Dales knitter, Mally Gibson, from the Beamish Museum. It is two-plied and thick almost as rope. There is another photo in the Dales Countryside Museum at Hawes which also clearly shows bump. (For both photos, see the following two pages.) I'm mindful of the 1950s Dales knitter who said the stockings they knit from bump were called "elephant stockings" (Hartley and Ingilby, *Old Hand-Knitters of the Dales*, p. 45).

FACING PAGE: DALES KNITTER OF BUMP YARN, MALLY GIBSON.
IMAGE COURTESY DALES COUNTRYSIDE MUSEUM.

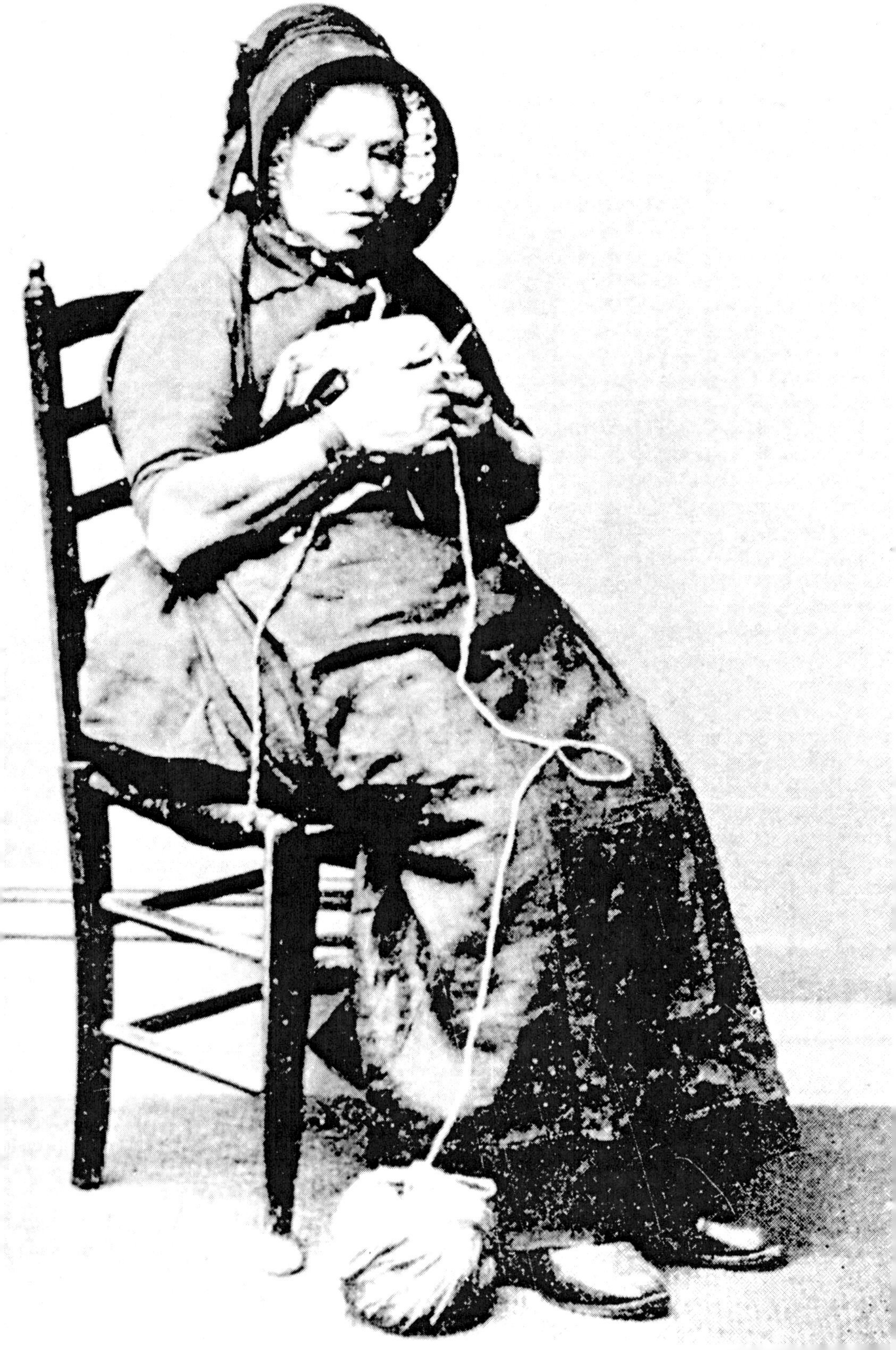

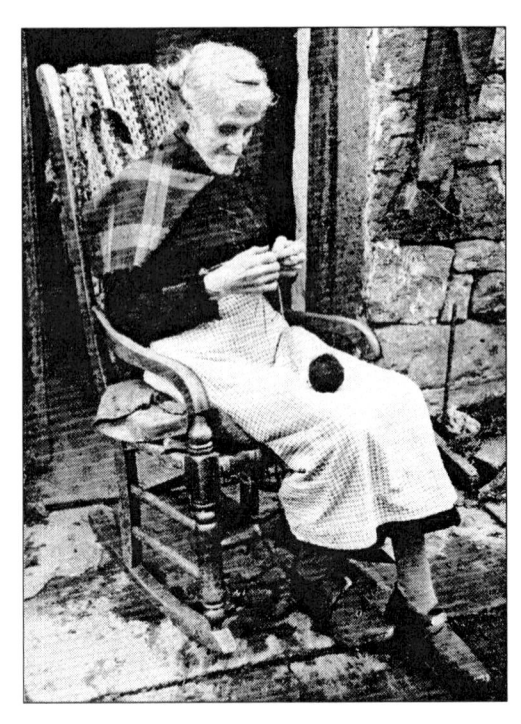

MARTHA DINSDALE, DALES KNITTER. "SHE USED TO KNIT SAILORS' JERSEYS WITH LONG SLEEVES, SOME HIGH-NECKED AND SOME OPEN-NECKED, FOR WHICH SHE WAS PAID 6-/ (30P) FOR SIX." [INTERVIEWED BY HARTLEY & INGILBY IN *THE OLD HAND-KNITTERS OF THE DALES*]. IMAGE COURTESY DALES COUNTRYSIDE MUSEUM.

Spinning Bump Yarn

Here we're aiming for almost the opposite of the worsted singles for gansey yarn. We're shooting for fat but with some loft.

Bump Characteristics
1. 5–6 wpi or less when plied
2. Some loft; an airy yarn
3. Spin using woollen technique

Bump seems to have been dyed after it was spun or left a natural creamy white. I found one reference to dyeing bump with logwood, a bark which produces a spectacular, deep purple. Jill Goodwin's *A Dyer's Manual* covers all traditional dyeing techniques and is foolproof. Although be warned: Logwood can bleed like a stuck pig if you're not careful.

Some Suitable Sheep Breeds for Woollen Spun Yarn

Down-type wools with shorter staples are suitable for spinning into bump or groove yarn and soft DK yarn for a non-gansey project. Look for a shorter staple length of 2½–3½ inches and a spongy texture, usually a finer grist (higher Bradford Count), but also maybe less lustre than the longwools we needed for gansey yarn.

Buying Raw Fleece

In the United Kingdom we are lucky enough to be able to buy many different breeds of fleece ready-processed. It is cheaper to go down the raw fleece route, so here are a few tips to help the tyro wool-buyer get started.

As a general rule, the crimpier (wavier) the wool fibres are, the better quality they are likely to be. If using a whole fleece, ruthlessly discard the lower-quality fibre, and carefully blend the higher quality fibres. Within a single fleece there can be much variation. I tend to buy raw wool at places like the Masham Sheep Fair or events like Woolfest, where the fleeces are laid out on a table so that you can look at, compare, and handle fleece before buying. If I had to buy sight unseen then, from the following list, the ones I'd be more likely to go for would be Shetland, Cheviot, and Ryeland, as I have had far more uniformly good fleeces of these breeds over the years than some of the others. Jacobs are notoriously variable and you buy one of their fleeces sight unseen at your peril.

Again, the list isn't exhaustive; just some useful pointers from various British breeds.

Black Welsh Mountain (46s to 56s)	Hampshire Down (46s to 60s)	Ryeland (56s to 58s)
Cheviot (46s to 58s)	Jacob's (44s to 56s)	Shetland (36s to 50s)
Clun Forest (56s to 58s)	Kerry Hill (54s to 56s)	Suffolk (46s to 58s)
Dorset Horn (48s to 58s)	Norfolk Horn (54s to 56s)	Whitefaced Woodland (46s to 54s)
	Portland (50s to 56s)	

Spinning Woollen

The following guidelines apply to spinning woollen-style yarn generally. Whether fat old bump yarn or regular double knit, the technique is the same.

Fibre Prep

Here, you're aiming at lofty and airy, and the prep comes into play. If working from raw fleece, you can sort, pick, and card using either hand carders or a drum carder. The more air you trap in your rolags, the loftier the final result. You can also work from commercially produced batts as they are becoming increasingly easy to source. They just need rolling into rolags. Failing that, you can even use commercial tops/roving. Pull off small amounts of fibre, and with the fibres at 90-degree angles (crosswise), hand roll into a little cigar/sausage, like a rolag. I find it's neater and traps the air better. I roll the rolags on a pencil. If using combed tops or batts, you have no need for carders.

Many spinners now just buy tops and while they're a wonderful thing, you can end up spending your entire life spinning worsted or worsted-ish if you don't make your own rolags to spin woollen style. It's a shame to miss out on this, as true woollen-spun yarn is a joy to use and much faster to spin than worsted or worsted-type. You can find excellent, free tutorials online that demonstrate how to card for woollen

CHEVIOT SPUN WOOLLEN.
CREDIT: NATHANIEL HUNT.

spinning. I also have found it very informative to search out footage from the 1940s and earlier of women in the Shetland and Hebridean Islands carding and spinning.

Spinning

Let the twist enter the fibres as you draft. The trick to spinning woollen is to be less of a control freak than you need to be when spinning worsted.

Long-draw

Again, you can use a spindle or a wheel and get the same result. My weapon of choice for spinning woollen is the great wheel: an Indian charka would work just the same. However, not many people are lucky enough to have a great wheel. Great wheels just survived into the nineteenth century as they spun a superior woollen yarn, or semi-worsted spun from the fold, which weavers preferred to millspun, for warp. They survived in the United States longer because they were easier to make and fix in remote places without a wheelwright or expert turner to hand as you'd need to repair a treadle wheel. But I have found a photo of an elderly man, in Haworth on the Yorkshire Moors, using a great wheel well into Victorian times. And in some outlying uplands, in Wales, the north of England, and in Scotland, they survived. Long-draw requires cojones, in the sense that the bolder you are with the technique, the easier it gets. I thought I had the long-draw for years, until I saw Mabel Ross's video *Advanced Hand-spinning Techniques* and realized I wasn't doing long-draw at all.

That said, you can use a sort of halfway-house, drafting semi-long draw, and still achieve a lovely woollen yarn. We want this yarn to have some loft (known in the business as spring). So you want the wheel to drag it onto the bobbin fast before you can insert too much twist – or conversely treadle slowly. Adjust your wheel. Use a larger circumference bobbin whirl, and again, keep testing the wraps-per-inch of your singles until you have found the grist you need. For bump yarn, singles (if you're planning on using singles, not plied) or plied finished yarn needs to be 5 to 6 wpi or even less. For a DK-equivalent yarn, you're looking for around 11 wpi in the finished yarn.

Spinning 4-Ply or DK for Popped 'Uns

Yarn for ganseys is best spun worsted or worsted-style. But there were other types of Yorkshire knitted jumpers, such as the stripey "popped uns" described by Marie Hartley and Joan Ingilby in *The Old Hand-Knitters of the Dales*. For these jumpers, a woollen-style fibre preparation and spinning techniques would be more useful.

The National Galleries of Scotland have a rare photo, from 1843, showing a Mr. Laing or Laine playing tennis. He is wearing a stripy sweater, almost precisely like those described in *The Old Hand-Knitters of the Dales*. A mariner wearing a striped sweater can be seen in naive art, at Hull Maritime Museum. In the *York Herald*, January 8, 1848, I found an account of a "FEROCIOUS STABBING IN HULL," describing the perpetrator, who had "the appearance of a sailor, dressed in a striped Guernsey frock."

In Yorkshire, we find the origin of the stereotype of "Burglar Bill" – the man with the swag bag, mask, and, yes, stripy sweater really did exist in reality before he became a cliché in the popular imagination. An 1840 news story in *The Standard* tells of a robbery at Thirsk:

> DARING BURGULARY [sic]
> It appears that the house was forcibly entered by three men, armed with pistols and long pointed knives; one of the men was very broad set, dressed in a Guernsey frock, with stripes across the body. The other two were similarly dressed.

The *York Herald*, July 18, 1840, similarly described the robbery and assault of toll bar keeper near Ripley. "The men had on tan or flesh coloured masks, striped jackets, and woollen caps that came on to the top of their masks." Witness George Bradfield described them: "They were dressed in short, striped frocks." In fact, I found numerous mentions of poachers wearing ganseys, as in a chase it gave them an advantage over the cumbersomely dressed police. It would seem the striped gansey was the provenance of the matelot but also, more surprisingly, of the career criminal, the gypsy desperado we encountered in an earlier chapter, and the sporting hero. Mr. Laing's is the only known extant close-up photo, at least for such an early date.

We can reproduce this yarn as either a four-ply or as a thicker DK. The pattern for Mr. Laing's Popped 'Un (see page 198) uses DK because when I reverse-engineered the garment, I found to my surprise that it was more likely knit with a DK than a four-ply.

To spin airy woollen yarn, follow the same techniques as for bump above, and spin two-ply yarn to a grist of roughly 11 wpi in the finished yarn. If you have a favourite commercial four-ply or DK that you'd like to replicate by hand-spinning, tie a length to the post of your wheel (or keep it by you if spindling) for reference. And again: sample your proverbial socks off!

Stripes could be worked in two contrasting, natural fleece colours. For example, you might choose moorit (brown) Shetland and creamy white Shetland or sort a good quality Jacob's fleece for colours as well as fibre quality. Then alternate the dark and the light yarns. In the nineteenth century, stripy sweaters seem to have alternated natural cream yarn with another colour: most commonly red, dark blue, or grey.

Keep eyeballing and checking as you spin so that your dark yarn is the same wpi as your light, as consistency is vital. The technique is the same for either bump or DK. You may find bump harder to do as it is a universally acknowledged fact that the more experienced you get at spinning, the harder it is to spin thick. But let's face it, even on an off-day, you are far less likely to find some of your wrong yarn pinned to the shoulder of your bed gown, like those poor charity school pupils of the 1780s.

⌘

Having prepared our own handspun yarns for gansey knitting, let me leave you with the words of William Wordsworth, written in 1812, to mourn the fate of the cottage spinning wheels, falling silent all over the north of England. Wordsworth recalled the old Westmorland superstition that wool spins easier by night when the sheep are asleep. May the flocks who gave your wool stay dozy and your wheel keep turning.

Song for the Spinning Wheel

Swiftly turn the murmuring wheel!
Night has brought the welcome hour,
When the weary fingers feel
Help, as if from faery power;
Dewy night o'ershades the ground;
Turn the swift wheel round and round!

Now, beneath the starry sky,
Couch the widely-scattered sheep;–
Ply the pleasant labour, ply!
For the spindle, while they sleep,
Runs with speed more smooth and fine,
Gathering up a trustier line.

Short-lived likings may be bred
By a glance from fickle eyes;
But true love is like the thread
Which the kindly wool supplies,
When the flocks are all at rest
Sleeping on the mountain's breast.

*Spinning Wheel from
Aysgarth
(Bolton Castle Museum)*

MARIE HARTLEY'S ENGRAVING OF A GREAT WHEEL
FROM *OLD HAND-KNITTERS OF THE DALES*.

GANSEY PATTERNS

Phoebe Carr

This pattern is taken is taken from a gansey knitted by Mrs. Phoebe Carr of Thorne. Mrs. Carr was one of the last knitters of keelmen's ganseys, and was well known for the quality of her work. This pattern was given to us by the Keel and Sloop Preservation Society, and we reproduce it with their kind permission.

Mrs Carr's idiosyncrasies include an ingenious two-purl seam stitch (so when you start the gusset, it arises very naturally between these two stitches) and paired decreases inside the gusset, but not along the rest of the sleeve seam. (Not mirroring decreases or cables was the 'traditional' way for many knitters.) The shoulder was bound off on the outside of the work, to give a decorative ridge. Mrs Carr also carried a purl stitch down the centre of the gusset – it was only when figuring out her pattern that I realized that feature wasn't just ornamental, but served the practical function of signalling the start of rounds on the sleeve.

Finished Measurements

Chest: 30 (34, 38, 42 46) inches; shown in size 38; designed to be worn with 0–2 inches of positive ease
Length: 27 (28, 29, 30, 31) inches
Sleeve length: 16½ (17, 18, 19, 19½) inches

NB: *For different length ganseys, you may find yourself with incomplete pattern repeats, vertically. You can always complete a repeat – but bear in mind this will lengthen the gansey slightly.*

Materials

Frangipani 5 ply Guernsey: 1(2, 2, 2, 2) cone(s); 100% wool; 1240 yds/500g shown in Falmouth Navy colorway

US#1/2.25mm circular needle
US 2/2.75mm circular needle, or size needed to obtain gauge

Stitch holders or waste yarn
Stitch markers

Gauge

28 sts and 36 rnds = 4 inches square in stockinette

Pattern Notes

The charts show how to work motifs when knitting in the round. When you reach the gussets and are knitting flat, read charts from right to left for odd rows and from left to right for even rows.

Pattern

Body

Using smaller needles and yarn held double, use Channel Island cast on to CO 208 (240, 256, 280, 320) sts. Continue with 1 strand of yarn unless otherwise stated.

Rnd 1: P1, [k2, p2] to last st, p1, placing markers before the first and 105th (121st, 129th, 141st, 161st) st. The markers denote the 2 purl sts that form

your faux seam on either side of the body of sweater.
Rep Rnd 1 until welt measures 2 (2½, 2½, 3, 3) inches.

Change to larger needles.
Rnd 1:
» Size 30 & 34: [P1, m1, k26 (30), m1, k50 (58), m1, k26 (30), m1, p1] twice – 216 (248) sts.
» Size 38: [P1, (k14, m1) 8 times, k14, p1] twice – 272 sts.
» Size 42: [P1, (k15, m1) 3 times, (k16, m1) 3 times, (k15, m1) twice, k15, p1] twice – 296 sts.
» Size 46: [P1, k15, (m1, k16) 8 times, m1, k15, p1] twice – 338 sts.

Rnd 2: [P1, knit to 1 st before marker, p1] twice.
Rep Rnd 2 until work measures 6½ (7, 8, 8½, 9½) inches total.

Ridge section
Rnd 1: Purl.
Rnds 2–7: [P1, knit to 1 st before marker, p1] twice.
Rnds 8–14: Rep Rnds 1–7.
Rnd 15: Purl.
Rnd 16: [P1, k1, m1, k57 (61, 66, 73, 83) m1, k57 (61, 66, 73, 84) m1, k1, p1] twice – 222 (254, 278, 302, 344) sts.

Beg with Rnd 1 of all charts, est your patt as follows:
» Size 30: [P1, work Chart B, C, B, D, B, C, B, p1] twice.
» Size 34: [P1, work Chart A over 8 sts, B, C, B, D, B, C, B, A over 8 sts, p1] twice.
» Size 38:
  » Rnds 1 & 2: [P1, work Chart A over 12 sts, p2, B, C, B, D, B, C, B, A over 12 sts, p3] twice.
  » Rnds 3 & 4: [P1, work Chart A over 12 sts, k2, B, C, B, D, B, C, B, A over 12 sts, k2, p1] twice.
» Size 42: [P1, work Chart A over 20 sts, B, C, B, D, B, C, B, A over 20 sts, p1] twice.
» Size 46: [P2, work Chart A over 8 sts, B, A over 12 sts, B, C, B, D, B, C, B, A over 12 sts, B, A over 8 sts, p1] twice.

Work the faux seams and motifs as est until the gansey measures 18½ (19, 18½, 18½, 19) inches total.

Underarm gusset
Continuing the charts along the front and back of the gansey as est, work the gussets (the 2 purl sts of the side seams) as follows. If you would prefer to use one of the underarm gusset charts for your size, work Rnds 64–66 below, then begin at Rnd 3 of that chart.

Rnd 64: P1, m1, p1.
Rnd 65: P1, k1, p1.
Rnd 66: P1, k1, p1.
Rnd 67: P1, m1L, p1, m1R, p1 (5 sts in gusset – p, k, p, k, p).
Rnd 68: P1, k1, p1, k1, p1.
Rnd 69: P1, k1, p1, k1, p1.
Rnd 70: P1, m1L, k1, p1, k1, m1R, p1.
Rnd 71: P1, k2, p1, k2, p1.
Rnd 72: As Row 71.
Rnd 73: P1, m1L, knit to central st, p1, knit to last st, m1R, p1.
Rnd 74: P1, knit to central st, p1, knit to last st, p1.
Rnd 75: As Rnd 74.
Rep Rnds 73–75 until you have 15 (15, 21, 23, 23) sts between first and last purl st.

Back
Work across next rnd in est patt until you reach the first purl st of the gusset. Turn, and put seam st, gussets, and front of gansey on waste yarn or stitch holders.

On rem 109 (125, 137, 149, 170) sts, continue working motifs as est until armhole measures 6½ (7, 7½, 8, 8½) inches

Note that you are now working flat, so the charts should be read right to left for RS rows and left to right for WS rows.

Neck edge

Row 1: Purl.
Row 2: Knit.
Row 3: P37 (44, 49, 53, 60), sl next 35 (37, 39, 43, 50) sts onto waste yarn, p37 (44, 49, 53, 60).
Row 4: Knit.
Rows 5 & 7: Knit.
Rows 6 & 8: Purl.

Slip sts onto waste yarn, then work the other shoulder in the same way.

Front

Place the faux seam and gusset sts onto waste yarn – 17 (17, 23, 23, 25, 25) sts each.

Continue working on rem 109 (125, 137, 149, 170) sts until front is the same length as back. Work neck edge in the same manner as on the back.

Shoulder seams

Using 3-needle bind off, and with wrong sides together, BO the shoulder seams forming a ridge on the right side of the gansey.

Neckband

Using larger needles, with RS facing, and beg at back sts, pick up and knit 35 (37, 39, 43, 50) sts across back, 19 (19, 19, 19, 20) sts across shoulder saddle, 35 (37, 39, 43, 50) across front and 19 (19, 19, 19, 20) sts across rem shoulder saddle – 108(112, 116, 124, 140) sts total.

Rnd 1: [K2, p2] to end of rnd.
Rep Rnd 1 for 2½ inches.
With yarn held double, BO loosely in patt.

Sleeves (both alike)

Pick up and work one set of gusset sts, placing a stitch marker before the central purl (this denotes the new beg of a rnd), pick up and knit 108 (112, 116, 124, 138) sts around armhole and work gusset sts to marker.

Rnd 1: P1, knit to 2 sts before next purl st, k2tog, est sleeve patt as follows: p3(7, 11, 0, 3), [chart E] 3(3, 3, 4, 4) times, p3(7, 11, 0, 3), p1, k2tog, k to end

Maintaining continuity of sleeve chart as est, dec on either side of the outside purl sts of the gusset every 3rd rnd until 3 purl sts remain, then p3tog.

Continue in patt as est until 2 complete reps of chart have been completed.

Rnd 65: Purl.
Rnd 66: P1, ssk, knit to last 2 sts, k2tog.

Mrs Carr favored knitting 2 together immediately on either side of the purled seam stitch. Many contemporary knitters use mirrored decs (k2tog, ssk) on either side of purled seam st. Use which you prefer.

Continue in stockinette, decreasing 1 st either side of the purl st every 5th rnd until 64 (68, 72, 76, 80) sts rem. Work even until sleeve measures 14½ (15, 16, 17, 17) inches.

Switch to smaller needles and work in [k2, p2] rib for 2 (2, 2, 2, 2½) inches. Holding yarn double, BO loosely in patt.

Finishing

Blocking tames the savage gansey – evens out stitches and shapes the entire garment, so you can make it conform to how you want it to look. It also sets the stitches and size. And sometimes you can use a bit of judicious blocking to fudge a problem. See page 127 for blocking instructions.

Chart A

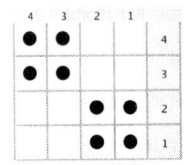

Chart B

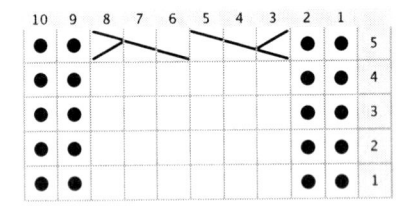

Phoebe Carr—155

Chart C

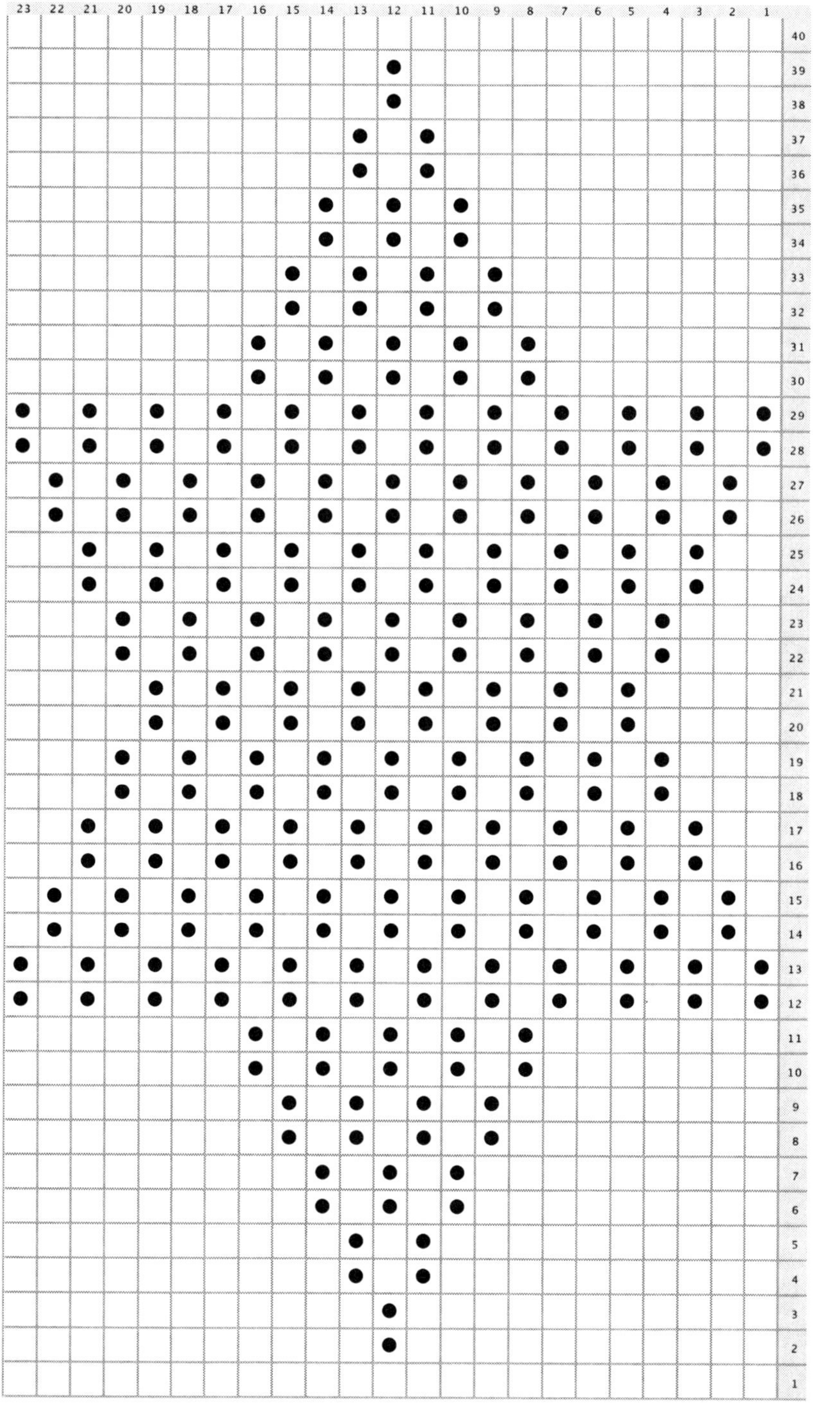

156—*River Ganseys*

Chart D

Phoebe Carr—157

Chart E

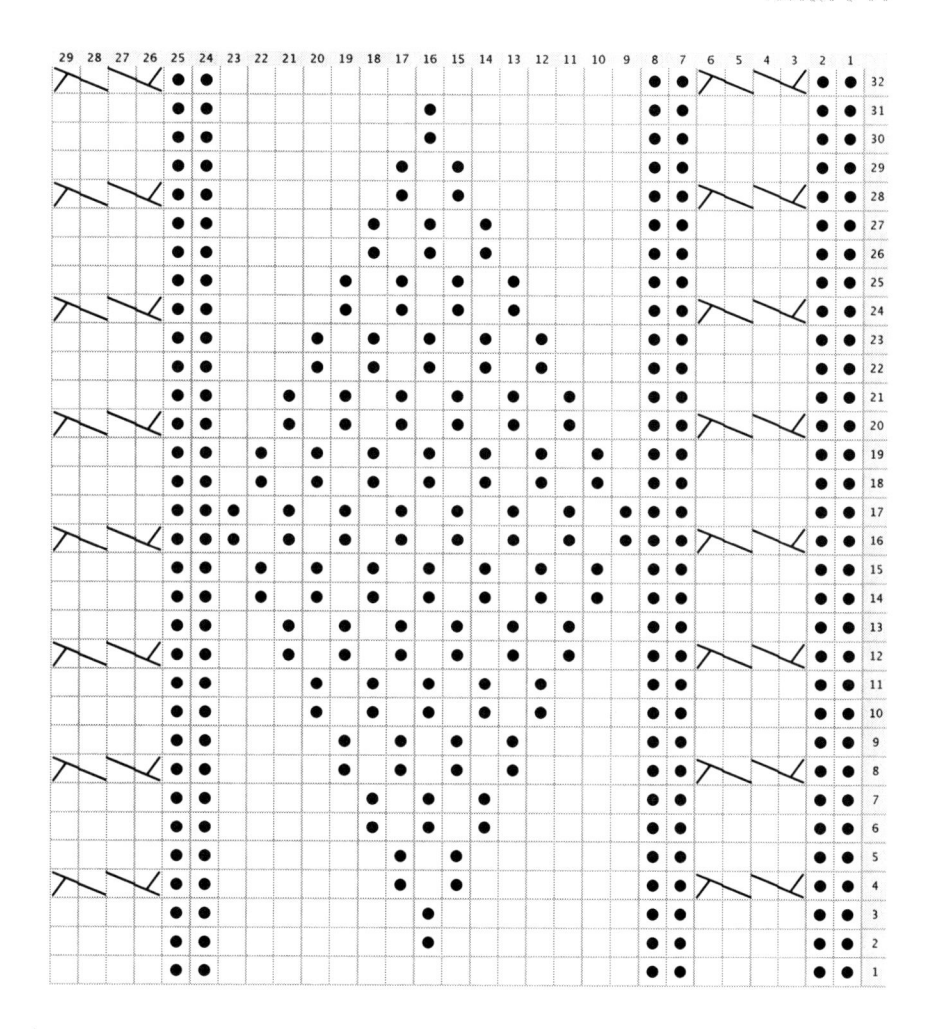

Ebiezzer

Ebiezzer was a vessel on the Ouse, co-owned by my ancestor, Isaac Moses, and his son, William. When Isaac Sr. died in 1820, he left his shares to pay for the education of his grandchildren, and said it could be run by his feckless son William, on condition William paid all port dues and settled bills on time. William's own son, Isaac Mosey, born in York in 1819, was to become Master Mariner, working vessels on the river Trent down in the Midlands, and died at sea in 1862. I originally designed this for Isaac Sr's great-great-great-great-great grandsons to wear.

Finished Measurements

Chest: 26 (28, 30, 32, 34) inches; shown in size 32; designed to be worn with 0 inches of positive ease
Length: 22 (24, 26, 27, 28) inches from neck to welt
Sleeve length: 13 (14, 15, 16, 16½) inches

Materials

Frangipani 5 ply Guernsey: 1 (1, 1, 1, 2) cone(s); 100% wool; 1240 yds/500g shown in Denim colorway

US #1/2.5mm circular needle
US #2/2.75mm circular needle, or size needed to obtain gauge
Set of US #2/2.75mm double-pointed needles (for working shoulder saddle)
Size G/4mm crochet hook for provisional cast on

Waste yarn in a similar weight to project yarn
Stitch holders
2 row/round counters
2 stitch markers

Gauge

28 sts and 36 rnds = 4 inches square in stockinette on larger needles

Pattern Notes

Ebiezzer was designed for kids to wear, but it works fine for adults, too! You can lengthen the sleeves (stop decreasing at the same point, just knit stockinette down to the cuff) or, as we did here, keep it the original length for a ¾-length sleeve.

The traditional approach to ganseys is to use k2tog and p2tog for decs and m1 for incs, unless otherwise stated. You may substitute mirrored incs and decs if you prefer.

For some sizes, motif repeats will be complete but for others; incomplete. When you are close to the neck edge, you need to decide whether to have a partial repeat of the motif, or switch to a plain stockinette block after the final complete repeat.

Pattern

Using smaller needles and Channel Island method, CO 188 (202, 218, 230, 242) sts. You can CO and work the first 3 rnds in either the main yarn or a contrasting color.

Join in the round and, being careful not to twist, work [k1, p1] rib for 3 inches.

Change to larger needles.

Rnd 1: [M1p, k94 (101, 109, 115, 121)] twice – 190 (204, 220, 232, 244) sts. The 2 purl sts you just made will be your faux seam sts, and will run the whole way up the gansey's body.

Rnd 2: [Pm, p1, k95 (102, 110, 116, 122)] twice.
Rnd 3: [P1, k95 (102, 110, 116, 122)] twice.
Work 3 rnds in stockinette, maintaining faux seam sts.

Work initials

The next section is a traditional aspect of ganseys. Initials were placed on many sweaters. Choose one of the alphabet charts on page 208 and pick three letters. Use the blank chart provided on page 208 to transpose your initials and work from that chart in this section. The initials section is worked over the 15 rnds for alphabet 1 or 14 rnds for alphabet 2; work your initials wherever looks good to you. (I prefer front left, about 10 sts after seam st.) Wherever you decide to place initials, place a marker before first st of initials chart.

When initials are complete, work 3 rounds in stockinette, maintaining faux seam sts throughout.

Work transitional pattern

Rnd 1: [P1, k2 (1, 4, 3, 1), work Chart A 9 (10, 10, 10, 11) times, k2 (0, 4, 2, 0)] twice.
Maintaining continuity of motifs as est, work all 16 rnds of Chart A.
Rnds 17 & 18: [P1, k95 (102, 110, 116, 122)] twice.

Work main pattern

- Size 26: [P1, k1, p1, work Charts C, D, E, D, C, p1, k1] twice.
- Size 28: [P1, k1, p2, work Charts C, D, E, D, C, p2, k1] twice.
- Size 30: [P1, k1, work Charts B, C, D, E, D, C, B, k1] twice.
- Size 32: [P1, k1, p2, k1, work Charts B, C, D, E, C, B, k1, p2, k1] twice.
- Size 34: [P1, k1, work Charts B, B, C, D, E, D, C, B, B, k1] twice.

Maintain continuity of motifs and sts as est until gansey measures 13½ (15, 15, 16½, 16½, 17) inches from cast on.

Underarm gusset

Rnd 1: [Work Rnd 1 of Chart F over faux seam st, work main motifs as est] twice.

Before first faux seam stitch, m1p, knit the purled seam stitch, m1p. This will form the base of your diamond-shaped gusset.

Continue incs for underarm gusset (Chart F) and working the body motifs as est until you reach Rnd 30(30, 30, 33, 33). From this point, you will work the back and front of your gansey separately and flat, so read your charts from right-to-left for odd (RS) rows and left-to-right for even (WS) rows.

Back

Place gusset sts and front of gansey on separate pieces of waste yarn or stitch holders, and continue working on back 95 (102, 110, 116, 122) sts.

** Maintaining continuity of motifs as est, work flat until back measures 19 (21, 23, 24, 25) inches. **

Maintaining continuity of Charts B and D, work rem sts in stockinette for 2 inches, ending with a WS row.

Place next 30 (31, 35, 37, 38) sts onto waste yarn (shoulder), 35 (40, 40, 42, 46) sts onto waste yarn (neck), and rem 30

(31, 35, 37, 38) sts onto waste yarn (other shoulder).

Front

Work as for Back from ** to **, then divide for neck as follows:
Rows 1 & 3 (RS): K30 (31, 35, 37, 38), turn.
Rows 2 & 4: Purl.

Break yarn and slip these sts onto waste yarn (shoulder).

With RS facing, slip next 35 (40, 40, 42, 46) sts to waste yarn (neck), then rep Rows 1–4 above on rem 30(31, 35, 37, 38) sts. Slip sts onto waste yarn.
Working on one shoulder at a time, place Front and Back sts onto separate dpns or straight needles, with the point facing the neck edge.

Shoulder strap

Using crochet provisional cast on (to keep sts live), CO 14 sts.

Row 1 (WS): Purl.
Row 2 (RS): Work 13 sts of Chart G, graft the last st with the first st of the back neck edge – 14 sts in saddle.
Row 3: Work Chart G across first 13 sts, graft the last st of saddle with first st of front neck edge – 14 sts in saddle.

Continue in this manner, and at the end of every row, purl or knit together your 14th (last) st with corresponding 1st st from back or front shoulder needle, so you're incorporating the live sts from back and front of gansey, as you knit down from the neck towards the arm.

When all back and front live sts are consumed, you will have reached the top of the arm. Keep the 14 sts live.

Sleeves

Rnd 1: With RS facing, work the next row of Chart G, pick up 40 (43, 46, 49, 52) sts down back of armhole, work next row of Chart F, pick up 40 (43, 46, 49, 52) sts up front of gansey armhole.

You will once again be working in the round, so all charts should now be read from right to left.

Rnd 2: Work Chart G over 14 saddle sts, work Chart J 6 (7, 7, 8, 8) times, work Chart F once, k4 (1, 4, 1, 4), work Chart H 6 (7, 7, 8, 8) times.

Maintain continuity of charts as est until 1 st rem in Chart F (underarm gusset).

Rnds 1–3: Work charts as est, purling rem gusset st on every rnd to form a faux seam.
Rnd 4: Work to 2 sts before faux seam, k2tog, p1, ssk, work rem of rnd as est.
Rep Rnds 1–4 until 40 (42, 42, 46, 48) sts rem. Work as est until sleeve measures 11 (12, 13, 13, 14) inches from midpoint of gusset.

Change to smaller needles and work in [k1, p1] rib until sleeve measures 13 (14, 15, 16, 16½) inches. BO all sts.

Work second saddle and sleeve in the same manner.

Finishing

See page 127 for blocking instructions.

162—*River Ganseys*

Chart A

Chart B

Chart D

Chart C

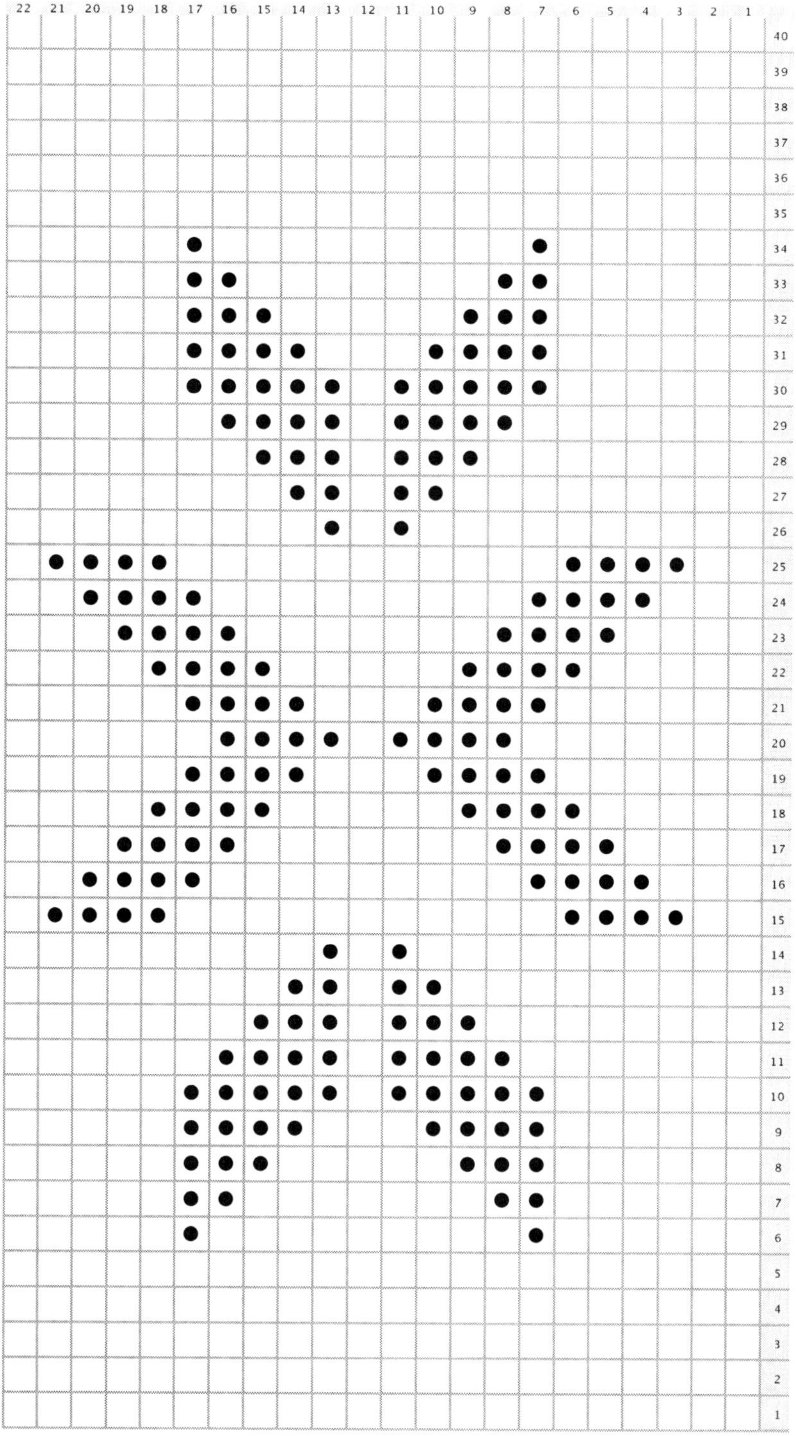
22 21 20 19 18 17 16 15 14 13 12 11 10 9 8 7 6 5 4 3 2 1
40 39 38 37 36 35 34 33 32 31 30 29 28 27 26 25 24 23 22 21 20 19 18 17 16 15 14 13 12 11 10 9 8 7 6 5 4 3 2 1

164—River Ganseys

Chart E

Ebiezzer—165

Chart F

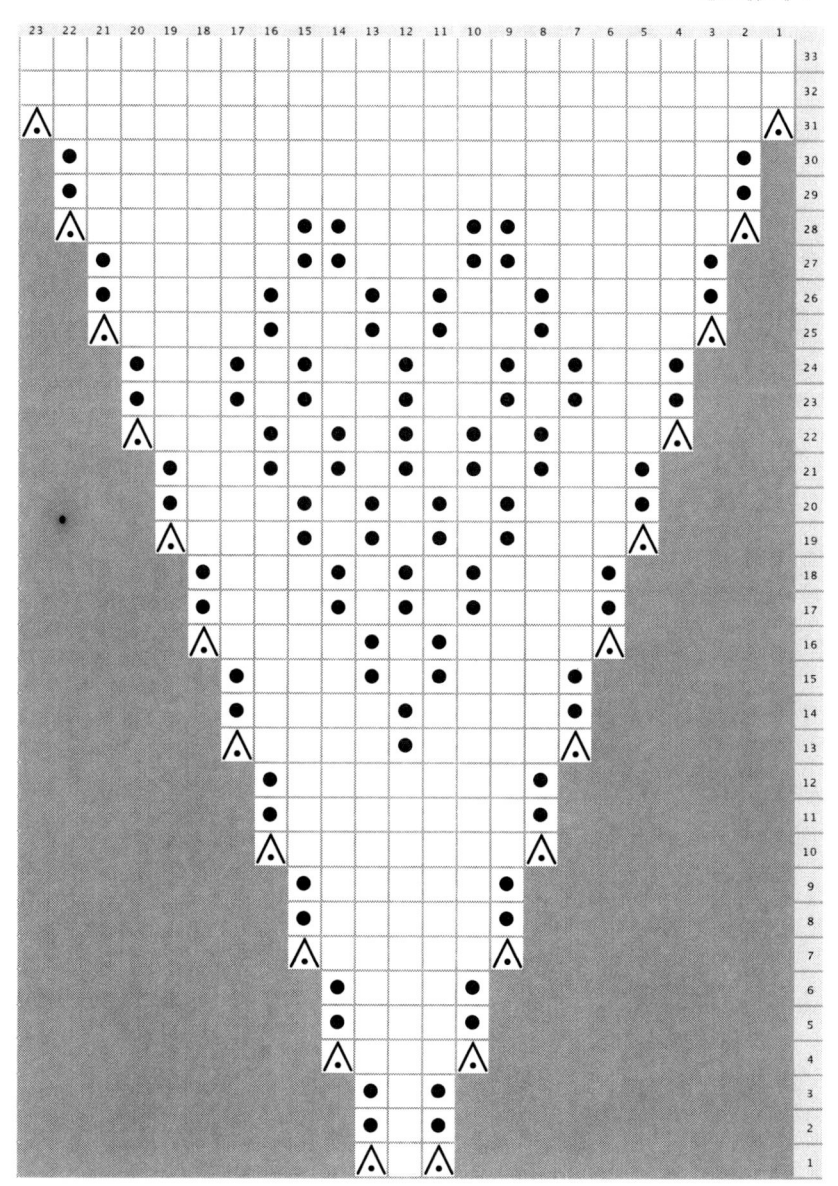

166—River Ganseys

Chart G

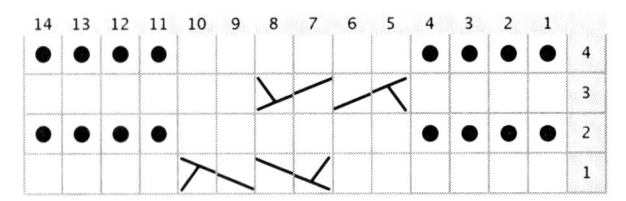

Chart J

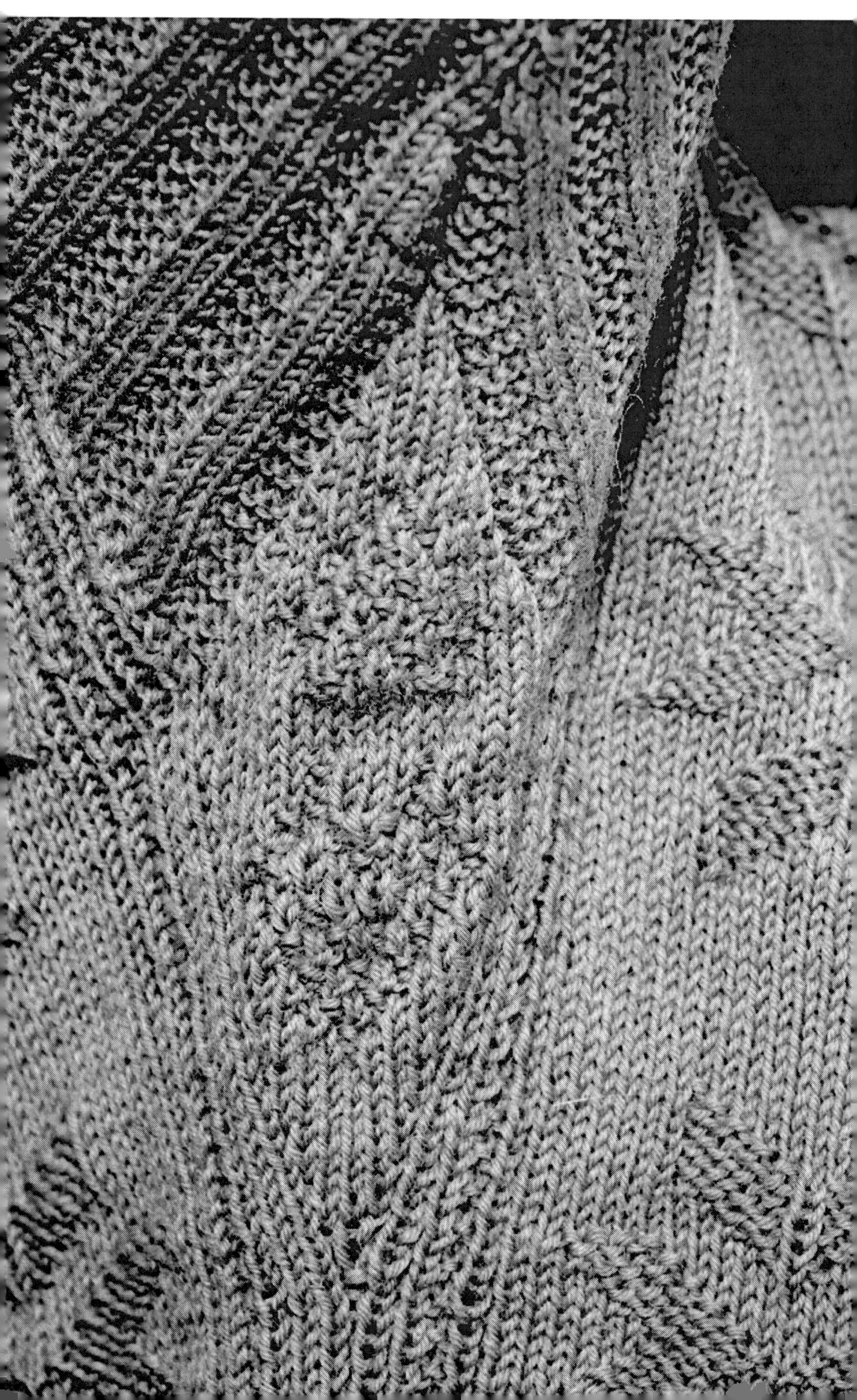

Whitby Wyrms

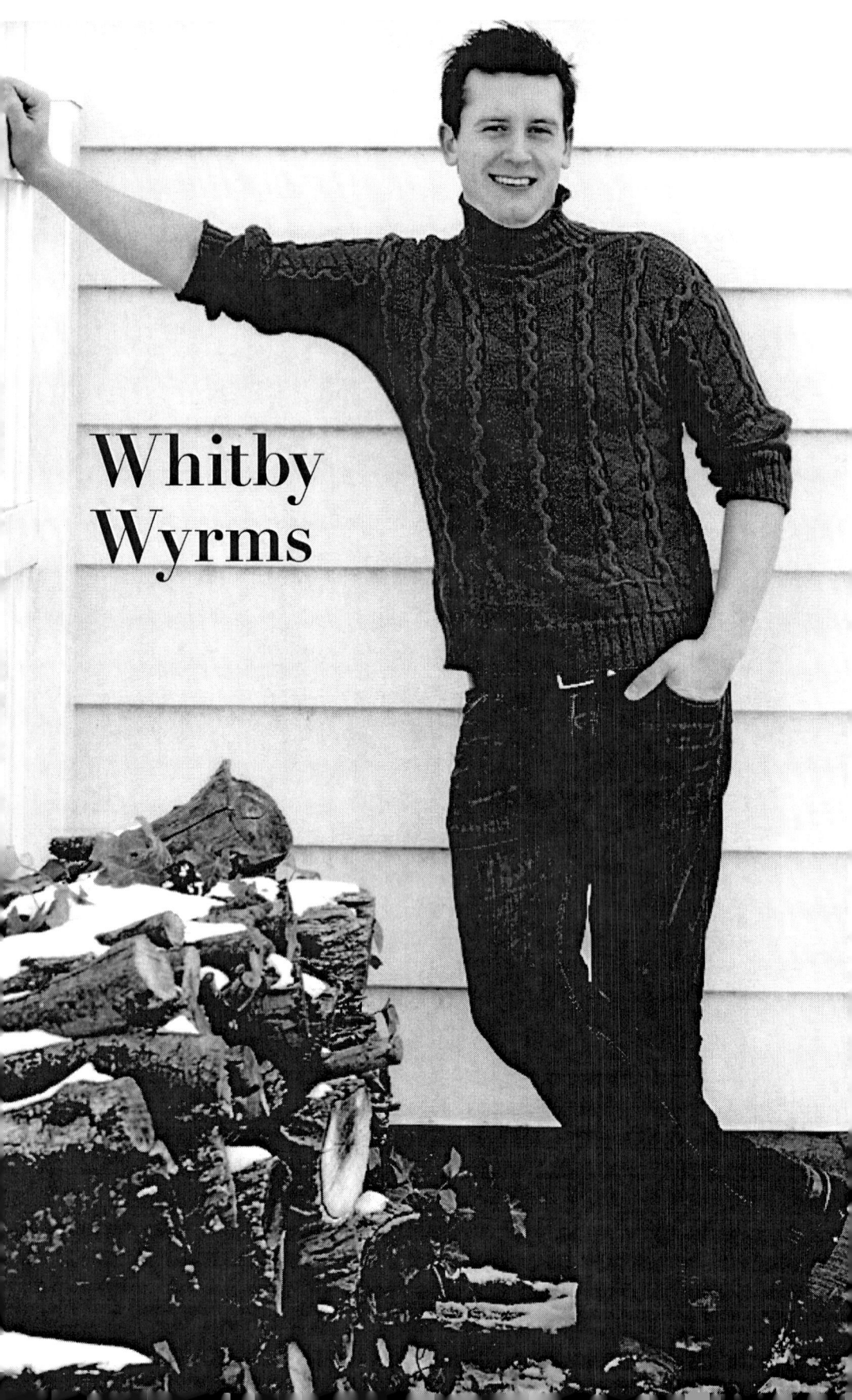

The Whitby Wyrm was a dragonlike serpent that lived in Whitby, according to folklore. Another local legend tells of Saint Hilda turning a plague of snakes into stone.

For this gansey, I did the time-honoured gansey thing and "borrowed" a nice zigzag motif from a sock pattern by Cookie A. Gansey knitters have always borrowed motifs from other knitters. It's tradition. In fact, it is how motifs became so universal across the British Isles. My other inspiration and starting point was the gansey of Robert Harland which used traveling stitches to create a zigzag design. This zigzag is simpler but more contemporary – it makes a change from the old pattern Marriage Lines that you can see in Parthenope (page 174).

Finished Measurements

Chest 34 (36, 38, 40, 42) inches; shown in size 38; designed to be worn with 0 inches of positive ease
Length: 28½ (29, 29½, 30, 30½) inches
Sleeve length: 17 (17, 17, 17½, 17½) inches

Materials

Frangipani 5 ply Guernsey: 2 cones; 100% wool; 1240 yds/500g shown in Red colorway

US #2/2.75mm circular needle, or size needed to obtain gauge
US #1/2.5mm circular needle

Cable needle
2 row/round counters
Stitch markers
Stitch holders or waste yarn

Gauge

28 sts and 36 rnds = 4 inches square in stockinette using larger needles

Pattern Notes

The traditional approach to ganseys is to use k2tog and p2tog for decs and m1 for incs, unless otherwise stated. You may substitute mirrored incs and decs if you prefer.

The charts show how to work motifs when knitting in the round. When you reach the gussets and are knitting flat, read charts from right to left for odd rows and from left to right for even rows.

Pattern

Body

Using smaller needles and using Channel Island method, CO 252 (264, 280, 296, 308) sts.
Being careful not to twist, join in the round and work [k2, p2] rib for 2½ (2½, 3, 3, 3½) inches.
Sizes 34 & 36 only: Inc 2 sts on final rnd of rib – 254 (266) sts.

All sizes: Changing to larger needles, establish faux seams as follows:
Rnd 1: [Pm, p1, k126 (132, 139, 147, 153)] twice.

You will purl these 2 faux side seam sts on every rnd of the body. They are not charted; just remember to p1 after each marker.

Work 2 rnds in stockinette.

The next section is a traditional aspect of ganseys. Initials were placed on many sweaters. Choose one of the alphabet charts on page 208 and pick three letters. Use the blank chart provided on page 208 to transpose your initials and work from that chart in this section. The initials section is worked over the 15 rnds for alphabet 1 or 14 rnds for alphabet 2; work your initials wherever looks good to you. (I prefer front left, about 10 sts after seam st.) Wherever you decide to place initials, place a marker before first st of initials chart.

When initials are complete, work 3 rounds in stockinette, maintaining faux seam sts throughout.

Establish motifs as follows:
- *Size 34:* [P1, (work Chart B then Chart C) 6 times] twice.
- *Size 36:* [P1, work Chart A over 3 sts, (work Chart B then Chart C) 6 times, work Chart A over 3 sts] twice.
- *Size 38:* [P1, work Chart A over 6 sts, (work Chart B then Chart C) 6 times, work Chart A over 7 sts] twice.
- *Size 40:* [P1, (work Chart B then Chart C) 7 times] twice.
- *Size 42:* [P1, work Chart A over 3 sts, (work Chart B then Chart C) 7 times, work Chart A over 4 sts] twice.

Maintaining charts and sts as est, work until piece measures 19¼ (19½, 18¾, 19¼, 19) inches from cast on.

Underarm gusset

You can work this diamond-shaped gusset in stockinette, or follow a gusset chart for a fancy pattern.

Maintaining continuity of charts as est, work gussets as follows:
Rnd 1: Use purled seam st as tip of gusset. When you reach the st before the seam st, m1p, knit the purled seam st, m1p. Do the same when you reach the second purled seam st.
Rnds 2 & 3: Work gusset sts as they appear without shaping.
Rep Rnds 1–3 until you have 15 (15, 21, 21, 21) sts between the 2 purls in each gusset.

Divide for front and back

You will now be working flat. Place the gusset sts and the purls on either side each on their own length of waste yarn, and the front of the gansey on a separate length of waste yarn.

Back

Continue working in patt as est until work measures 27½ (28, 28½, 29, 29½) inches.

With RS facing, work the next 41 (43, 46, 48, 50) sts in patt for 1 inch, then slip them onto waste yarn (right side of back). Slip next 43 (45, 46, 50, 52) sts onto waste yarn (neck) and then work rem 41 (43, 46, 48, 50) sts in same manner as right back for 1 inch, finally slipping them onto waste yarn (left side of back).

Front

Work as for back, leaving last 41 (43, 46, 48, 50) sts on your needle.

Place corresponding sts from back onto a needle, and holding both needles together, with wrong sides together, work a 3-needle bind off.

Work the other shoulder in the same manner.

Sleeves (both alike)

With RS facing, pick up 128 (132, 150, 150, 160) sts around armhole; work the 17 (17, 23, 23, 23) gusset sts, pm after the last purl st of the gusset – 145 (149, 173, 173, 183) sts.

At first, your decreases will be confined to the inside of the underarm gusset.

For gusset: Dec 2 sts just inside purls every 3rd rnd; one either side. Once you've decreased the gusset away, having purled the final 3 sts tog to make a new seam st, you should have your original 128 (132, 150, 150, 160) sts plus 1 purl st – 129 (133, 151, 151, 161) sts total. Maintain the purl as a seam st the whole way down the arm.

Dec 1 st on either side of seam st every 6th rnd until 68 (72, 72, 76, 76) sts rem. Work even until sleeve measures 3½ inches less than required length of arm.

Work [k2, p2] rib for 3½ inches, then BO loosely with yarn held double.

Neck

Using smaller needles, and with back facing, [pick up 43 (45, 46, 50, 52) sts, and 11 (11, 12, 12, 12) sts along shoulder] twice – 108 (112, 116, 124, 128) sts total.

Join into the round.
Rnds 1 & 3: Knit.
Rnds 2 & 4: Purl.
Work 2½ (3, 3, 3½, 3½) inches in [k2, p2] rib.
BO all sts loosely in patt.

Finishing

See page 127 for blocking instructions.

172—*River Ganseys*

Chart A

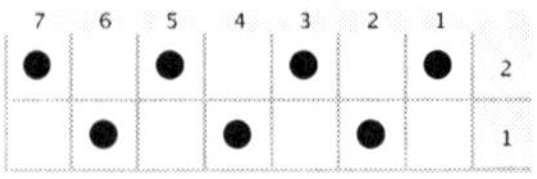

Chart B

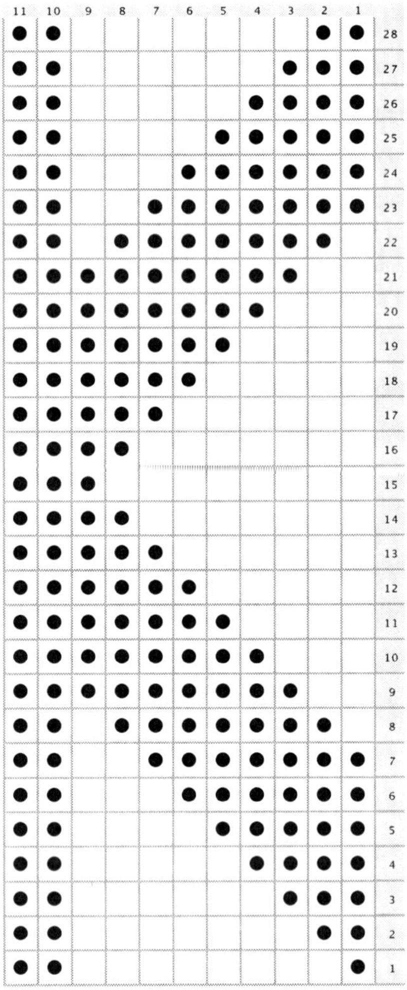

Chart C

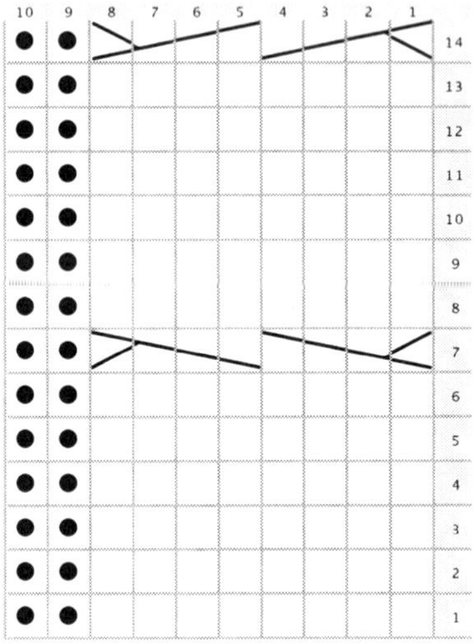

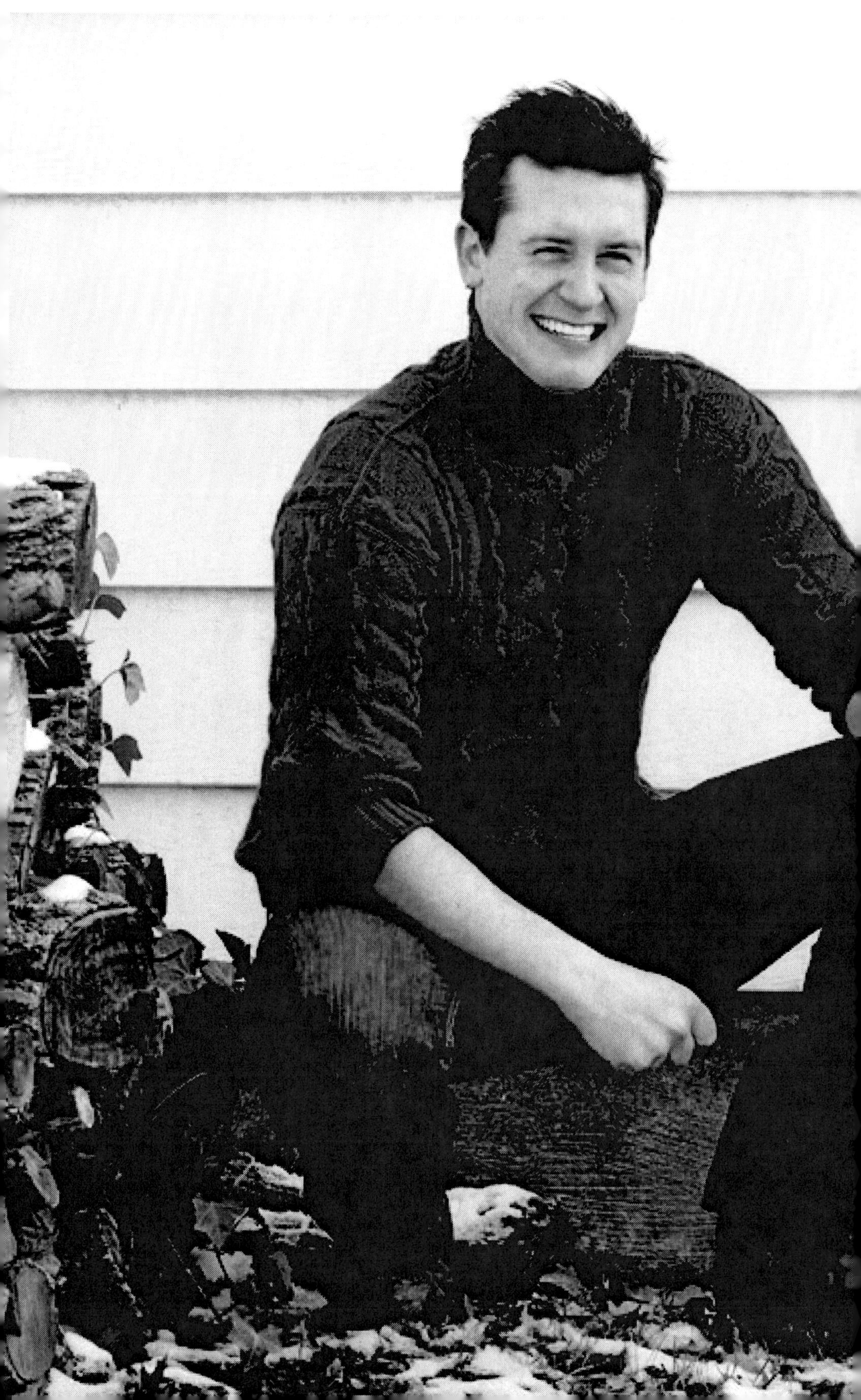

Parthenope

Parthenope *was a ketch (two-masted ship) built on the river at Howdendyke in 1885. She was owned by John Holmes who lived on Neptune Street in Hull. The ship was named after one of the sirens of Greek myth. The gansey that this ship inspired has the hearts pattern commonly found on the rivers between Howden and Hull.*

Finished Measurements

Chest: 34 (36, 38, 40, 42) inches, shown in size 40
Length: 28½ (29, 29½, 30, 30½) inches
Sleeve length: 17 (17, 17, 17½, 17½) inches

Materials

Frangipani 5 ply Guernsey: 2 cones; 100% wool; 1240 yds/500g shown in Claret colorway

US #1½/2.5mm circular needles or needles needed to obtain gauge
2 sets of US #2/2.75mm circular needles

Cable needle
Waste yarn or stitch holder
Stitch markers

Gauge

28 sts and 36 rnds = 4 inches square in stockinette using smaller needles

Pattern Notes

The traditional approach to ganseys is to use k2tog and p2tog for decs and m1 for incs, unless otherwise stated. You may substitute mirrored incs and decs if you prefer.

Pattern

Lower body

Using smaller needles, yarn held double, and the Channel Island method, CO 216 (240, 260, 288, 312) sts.

Continuing with yarn held double:
Rnd 1: P1, [k2, p2] to last st, p1.
Rep Rnd 1 for 2 (2½, 2½, 3, 3½) inches.

Increase Rnd:
» Size 30: K20, [m1, k54] 3 times, m1, knit to end – 220 sts.
» Size 34: K30, [m1, k60] 3 times, m1, knit to end – 244 sts.
» Size 38: K8, [m1, k21] 12 times – 272 sts.
» Size 42: K12, [m1, k24] 12 times, knit to end – 288 sts.
» Size 46: K8, [m1, k19] 16 times – 328 sts.

Change to working with a single strand of yarn. Next rnd to est faux seams: [Pm, p1, k109 (121, 135, 149, 163)] twice.

You will be purling these 2 sts the entire way up the body in order to create fake side seams. They will not be charted, just remember to p1 after stitch markers.

Work 2 rnds in stockinette (maintaining faux seam sts).

The next section is a traditional aspect of ganseys. Initials were placed on many sweaters. Two alphabet charts are

provided; choose whichever one you prefer, and pick three letters to knit.

Use the blank chart provided to transpose your initials and work from that chart in this section. The initials section is worked over the 15 rnds for alphabet 1 or 14 rnds for alphabet 2. Work initials wherever they look good to you; I prefer front left, about 10 sts after seam st. Wherever you decide to place initials, pm before first st of initials chart.

When initials are complete, work 3 rnds in stockinette, maintaining faux seam sts as you go.

Commence stitch patt, as follows, maintaining seam sts on each rnd:
» Size 30: [P1, work Charts B, C, B, D, B, E, B, F, B, C, B] twice.
» Size 34: [P1, work Charts H, B, C, B, D, B, E, B, F, B, C, B, H] twice.
» Size 38: [P1, work Charts A, B, C, B, D, B, E, B, F, B, C, B, G] twice.
» Size 42: [P1, k3, work Charts B, A, B, C, B, D, B, E, B, F, B, C, B, G, B, k3] twice.
» Size 46: [P1, work Charts H, B, A, B, C, B, D, B, E, B, F, B, C, B, G, B, H] twice.

Maintaining continuity of charts as est, continue working in patt until gansey measures 17½ (15, 14¾, 14¾, 14¾) inches.

Underarm gusset

Working charts as est, work the gusset chart – or a plain gusset if you prefer – at the purled seam st on both sides of the gansey, until you have 15 (15, 21, 21, 21) sts on either side of your side seam sts.

Divide for front and back

Place gusset sts, the outer purls surrounding them, and front sts onto separate pieces of waste yarn.

Back

Now you are knitting flat; work charts from right to left on odd rows and from left to right on even rows.

Continue working your patt as set until Back measures 24 (25, 26, 27, 28) inches from start.

Leave all sts on waste yarn.

Front

Place sts back onto your needles and work the Front as for the Back.

Divide for neck (for both the Front and the Back)

Work the first 36 (40, 45, 49, 54) sts in patt, slip the next 37 (41, 45, 51, 55) sts onto waste yarn, and the following 36 (40, 45, 49, 54) sts onto a separate piece of waste yarn.

Using larger needles, place front and back right shoulders onto needles, with pointy ends at neck side.

Right shoulder

With a second set of US#2/2.75mm needles, provisionally CO 40 sts.

Row 1: Work 39 sts across chart (saddle), k2tog incorporating your final st of the shoulder saddle together with the first live st of the shoulder.

Row 2: Work 39 sts across chart (saddle) p2tog, incorporating your final st of the shoulder saddle together with the first live st of the other shoulder.

When you have used up all the Front and Back live sts, you are ready to work down the arm. Leave your 40 sts live.

Left shoulder

Work to match the Right Shoulder.

Sleeves

With RS of a sleeve facing you, pick up the 17 (17, 23, 23, 23) gusset sts, 38 (42, 36, 47, 50) sts up the armhole to the saddle, 40 saddle sts, and 38 (42, 36, 47, 50) sts down the other side of the armhole back to the gusset – 133 (141, 135, 157, 163) sts total.

Note: All your decreases at first will be confined to within the gusset diamond. Once these sts are consumed, you can then continue to decrease down the arm.

Rnd 1: Est sleeve pattern as follows:
- » *Size 30:* Work gusset, k2, work sleeve chart, k2.
- » *Size 34:* Work gusset, work sleeve chart 2, sleeve chart, sleeve chart 2.
- » *Size 38:* Work gusset, work sleeve chart.
- » *Size 42:* Work gusset, p1, k1, p1, work sleeve chart 2, p1, k1, sleeve chart, k1, p1, sleeve chart 2, p1, k1, p1.
- » *Size 46:* Work gusset, [work sleeve chart 2, p1] twice, sleeve chart, [p1, sleeve chart 2] twice.

For a fully patterned sleeve:
Continue working sleeve patt as set. AT THE SAME TIME, work decreases in your gusset patt as set in the chart you're using until you work a final p3tog and create a seam st, which will be purled every rnd.
After the gusset has been decreased, work a dec either side of the purled seam st every 4 rnds until you have 68 (72, 72, 76, 80) sts, then work without shaping until sleeve is either 14 (14, 13½, 14, 14) inches from start or 3 (3, 3½, 3½, 3½) inches shorter than desired length.

Work a [k2, p2] rib for 3 (3, 3½, 3½, 3½) inches, then bind off loosely.

Skip to instructions for neck treatment.

For a half-patterned, half-plain sleeve:
Work sleeve as set until it is 8 inches long, then switch to sleeve chart 3. Work 15 rnds (3 reps) of this chart, then continue in stockinette, keeping continuity of decs until you have 68 (72, 72, 76, 80) sts, then work without shaping until sleeve is either 14 (14, 13½, 14, 14) inches from start or 3 (3, 3½, 3½, 3½) inches shorter than desired length.

Work a [k2, p2] rib for 3 (3, 3½, 3½, 3½) inches, then bind off loosely.

Neck treatment

With smaller needles, and starting at the beg of a shoulder saddle, pick up and knit [40 saddle sts, 37 (41, 45, 51, 55) body sts] twice – 154 (162, 170, 182, 190) sts total.

For a [k2, p2] ribbed neck:
Work [k2, p2] rib, increasing 2 sts for sizes 30 (34, 42, 46) only. Work in rib for 4 inches. BO very loosely in pattern, fold the neckband under, and whip stitch to make a crew neck.

Skip to finishing section.

For a neckband that continues the shoulder saddle pattern:
- » *Sizes 30 (34, 38, 46):* [Work continuing row of shoulder saddle chart, m1, k1, (p2, k2) to end of body section] twice - 156 (164, 172, 192) sts.

» *Size 42 only:* [Work continuing row of shoulder saddle chart, k2tog, k1, (p2, k2) to end of body section] twice – 180 sts.

Continue working saddle stitch charts and [k2, p2] rib (without shaping) for 4 inches.

BO very loosely in patt, fold the neckband under and whip stitch to form a crew neck.

Finishing

See page 127 for blocking instructions.

Parthenope—179

Chart A

Chart B

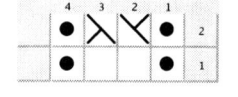

180—*River Ganseys*

Chart C

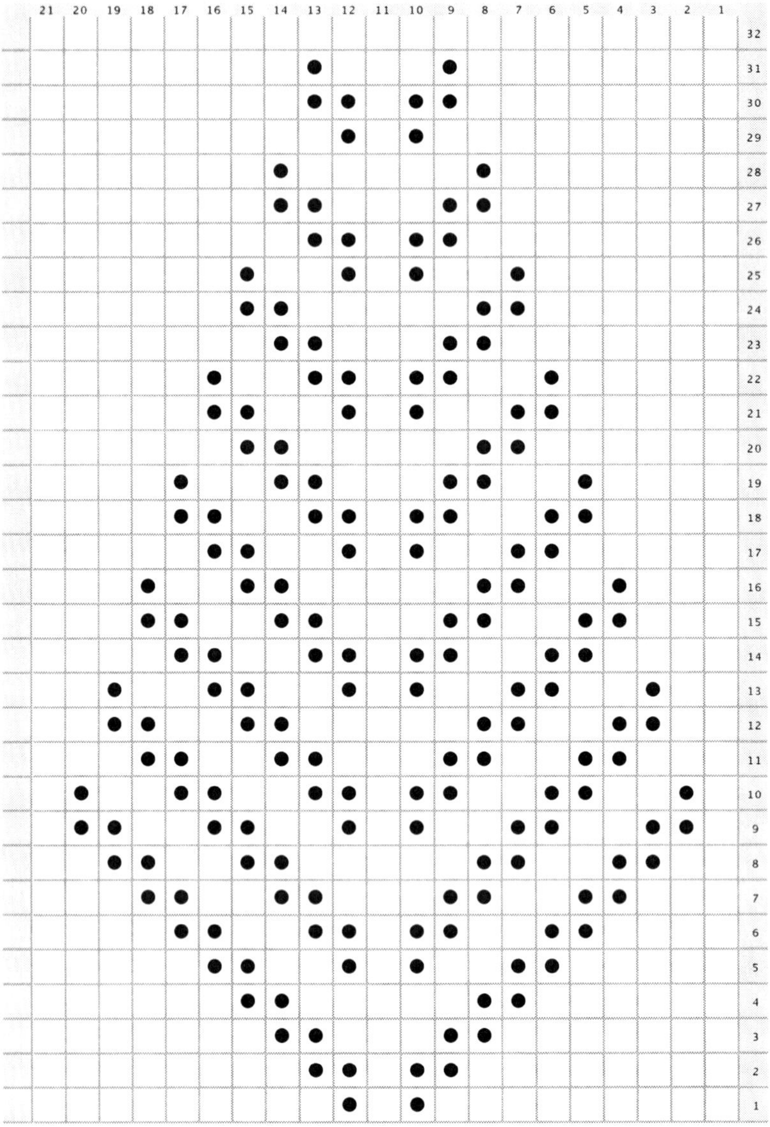

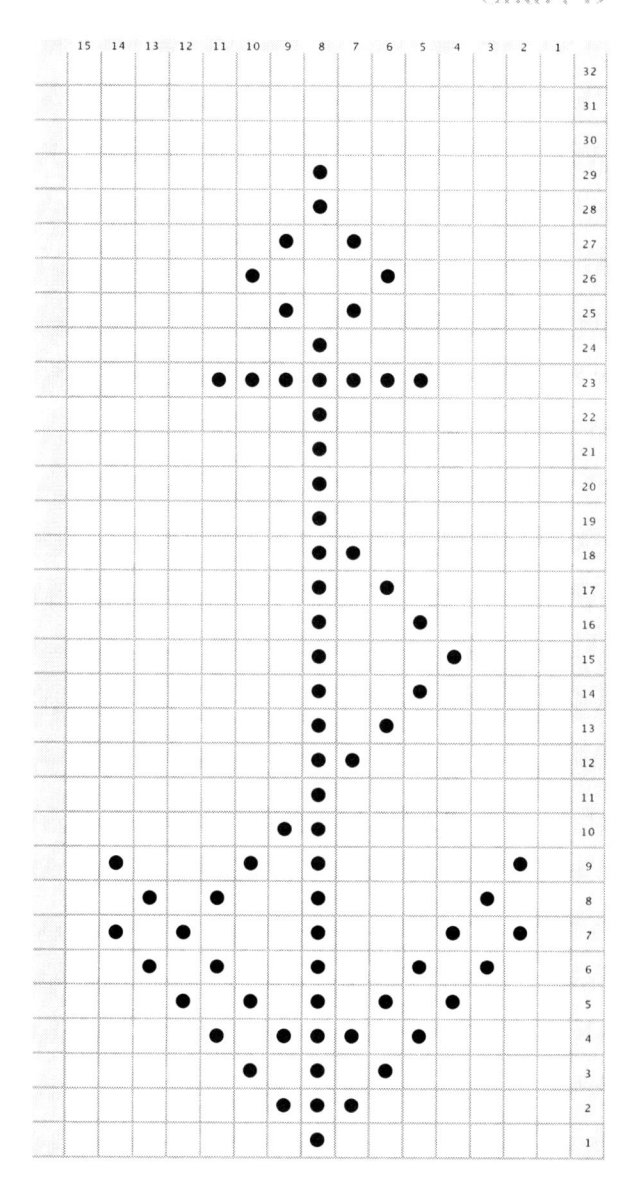

Parthenope—181

Chart D

Chart E

Parthenope—183

Chart F

184—*River Ganseys*

Chart G

Chart H

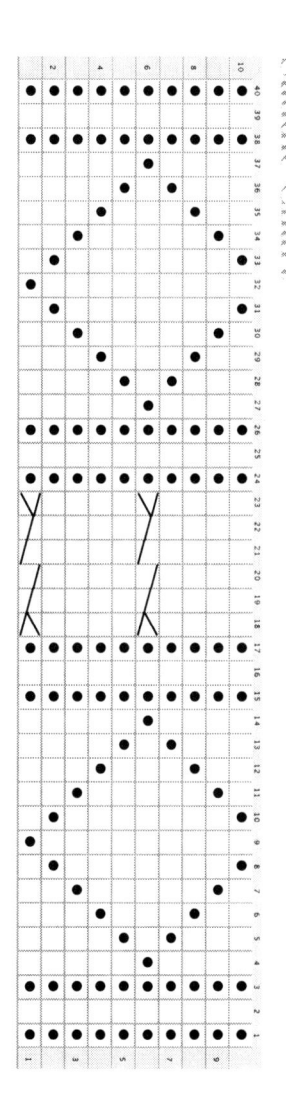

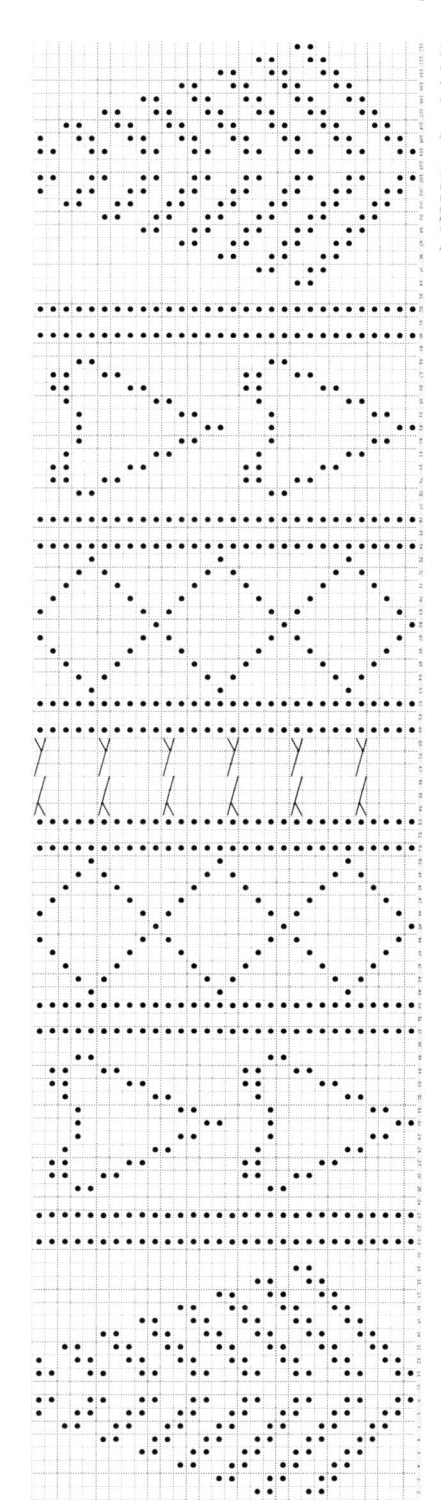

Parthenope—185

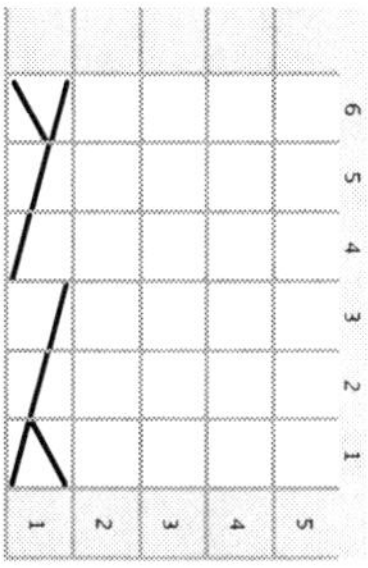

186—*River Ganseys*

Gusset Chart

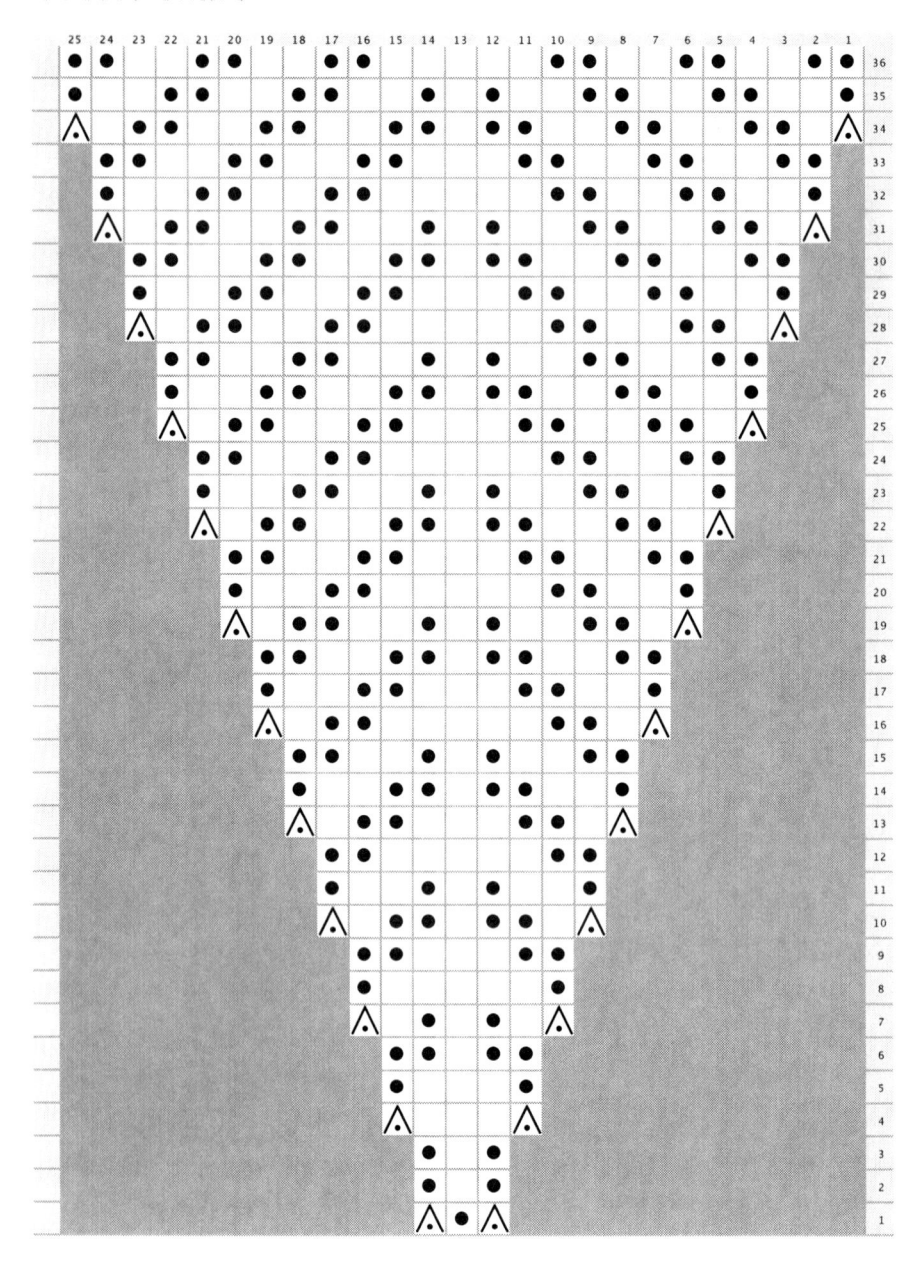

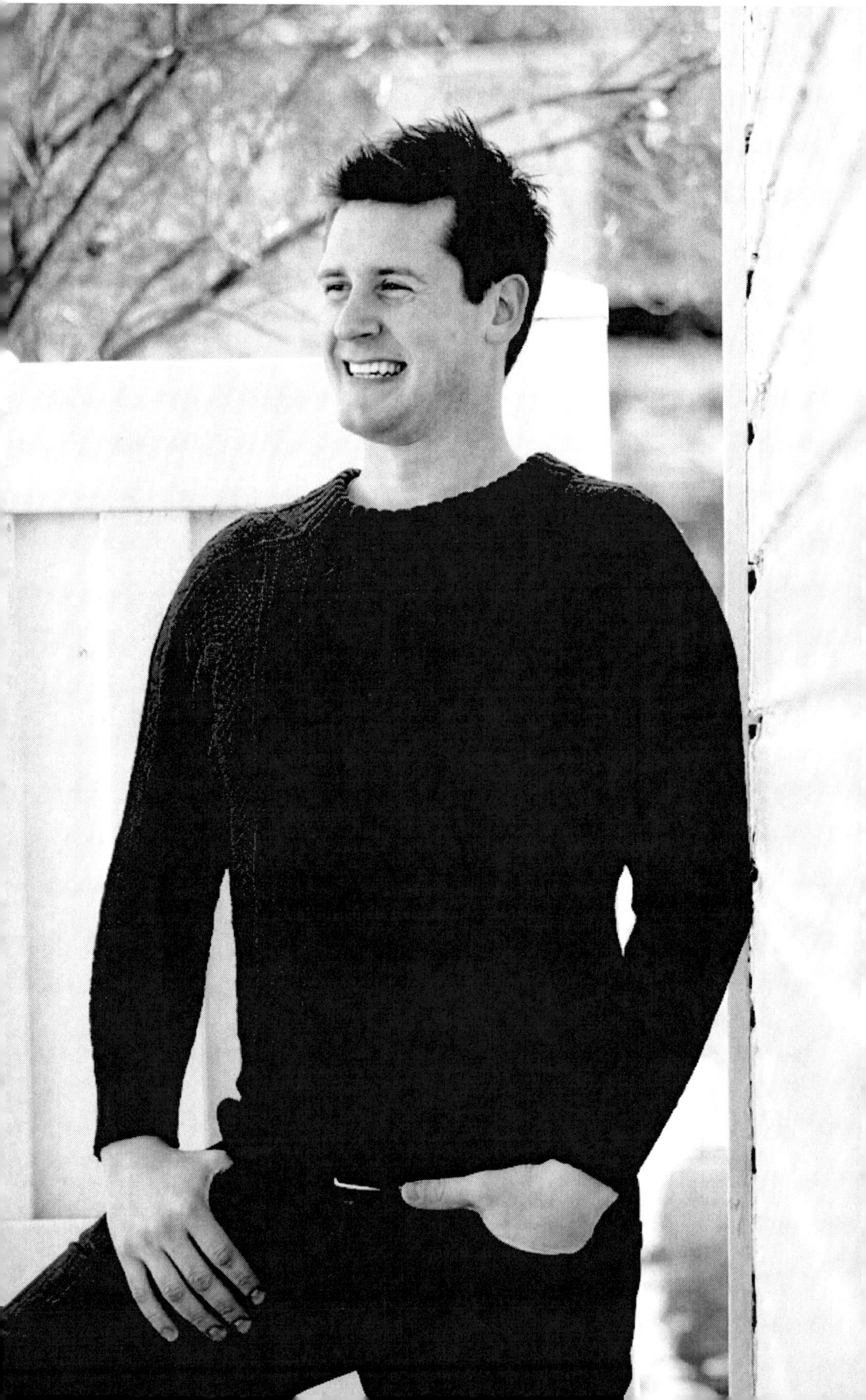

Lizzie Lee

This gansey is named after the Lizzie Lee, *a brigantine built in Suffolk in 1856 that worked out of Knottingley, Yorkshire, on the river Aire.*

The gent pictured second left, front row in the 1914 photo of the Stainforth Aquatic Sports Committee (see page 74) has a central hearts motif. Due to the poor photo quality, that's about all I could make out, so, for the rest of this gansey, I used the Walter Fisher photograph of an anonymous girl in Filey (see page 27) in the 1860s or 70s as the girl in this photo has a gansey with lots of cables and masks (diamonds) – precisely the same as many, many inland ganseys. In the Fisher photo, the central panel is not legible but the Stainforth hearts fitted it perfectly.

Brigantines were large, two-masted ships that only worked the larger inland waterways and the coastal trade. So the gansey's name reflects the fact that these motifs were found on coastal and inland waters, like the brigantines and the motifs on Lizzie Lee are all very common inland ones.

Finished Measurements

Chest: 32 (36, 40, 44, 48) inches; shown in size 40, designed to be worn with 0 of positive ease
Length: 28½ (29, 29½, 30, 30½) inches
Sleeve length: 16½ (17, 17, 18, 18) inches

Materials

Frangipani 5 ply Guernsey: 1 (2, 2, 2, 2) cone(s); 100% wool; 1240 yds/500g shown in Clover.

US #1½/2.5mm circular needles, or needles required to attain gauge
US #2/2.75mm circular needles

2 row/round counters
Stitch markers
Stitch holders or waste yarn

Gauge

28 sts and 36 rnds = 4 inches square worked in stockinette on larger needles

Pattern Notes

To maintain C6F every 6th rnd the entire way up the gansey: after your first repeat of Chart A, you will find the cables go out of sync with the motifs. One solution is to keep a second row counter, so you have one row counter for the gansey as a whole, and another for the cables.

Pattern

Using smaller needles and Channel Island method, CO 224 (244, 272, 304, 336) sts.

Work [k2, p2] rib for 2½ (2½, 3, 3, 3½) inches.

Switch to larger circular needle. Next rnd (est faux seams): [Pm, p1, k111 (121, 135, 151, 167)] twice. You will be purling these 2 sts as faux side seams the entire way up the body. They will not be charted; just remember to p1 after each marker.

Work 3 rnds in stockinette.

The next section is a traditional aspect of ganseys. Initials were placed on many sweaters. Two alphabet charts are provided (see page 208); choose whichever one you prefer, and pick three letters to knit.

Use the blank chart provided to transpose your initials and work from that chart in this section. The initials section is worked over the 15 rnds for alphabet 1 or 14 rnds for alphabet 2. Work initials wherever looks good to you. (I prefer front left, about 10 sts after seam st.) Wherever you decide to place initials, pm before first st of initials chart.

When initials are complete, work 3 rnds in stockinette.

Commence patt as follows:
- » *Size 32:* [P1, work Chart A, B, C, p1, D, p1, E, p1, F, p1, E, p1, D, p1, C, B, A] twice.
- » *Size 36:* [P1, work Chart A, p1, k1, B, k1, C, k1, p1, k1, D, k1, p1, E, p1, F, p1, E, p1, k1, D, k1, p1, k1, C, k1, B, k1, p1, A] twice.
- » *Size 40:* [P1, work Chart A, p1, k3, B, k2, C, k2, p1, k2, D, k2, p1, E, p1, F, p1, E, p1, k2, D, k2, p1, k2, C, k2, B, k3, p1, A] twice.
- » *Size 44:* [P1, k3, work Chart E, k2, p1, A, p1, k3, B, k2, C, k2, p1, k2, D, k2, p1, E, p1, F, p1, E, p1, k2, D, k2, p1, k2, C, k2, B, k3, p1, A, p1, k2, E, k3] twice.
- » *Size 48:* [P1, work Chart F, p1, A, p1, k3, B, k2, C, k2, p1, k2, D, k2, p1, E, p1, F, p1, E, p1, k2, D, k2, p1, k2, C, k2, B, k3, p1, A, p1, F] twice.

Continue in patt as est, maintaining seam sts on each rnd, until work measures 13 (13¾, 12¾, 13½, 13¾) inches from cast on.

Underarm gusset

Maintaining continuity of stitch patt as est, work either a plain gusset chart or the fancy Lizzie Lee gusset chart, until you have 17 (17, 23, 23, 23) total sts in each gusset.

Divide for front and back

Place gusset sts (including the purl sts) onto waste yarn, 111 (121, 135, 151, 167) front sts onto a separate piece of waste yarn, and following gusset sts onto a third piece of waste yarn.

Back

Continue working in patt as set, until work measures 25 (26, 27, 28, 29) inches.

The charts show how to work motifs when knitting in the round. When you reach the gussets and are knitting flat, read charts right to left for odd rows and left to right for even rows.

Divide for neck

Row 1: K37 (40, 45, 50, 55). Slip next 37 (41, 45, 51, 57) sts onto waste yarn for neck and rem 37 (40, 45, 50, 55) sts for left shoulder onto a second piece of waste yarn.
Row 2: Purl.

Rows 3–5: Knit.
Row 6: Purl.
Rep Rows 3–6 until back measures 27 (28, 29, 30, 31) inches. Place sts on waste yarn.

Work left shoulder in same way.

Front

Work exactly the same as the Back.

Now match up front and back shoulders and BO shoulders on the outside of work (grafting them tog) with RS facing; binding off 1 st from back over 1 st from front, all the way across. This will give a decorative ridge on the outside of the work. I prefer to start grafting from the neck side, finishing at the arm side, just in case I make a small mistake – it's easier to fudge at the arm side!

Sleeves

Gansey sleeves are usually worked in the round, from the top down.

Starting at beg of gusset, work next rnd of gusset, pick up and knit 66 (69, 75, 77, 82) sts to top of shoulder and 66 (69, 75, 77, 82) sts down armhole back to gusset – 149 (155, 173, 177, 187) sts total.

Rnd 1: Work next rnd of gusset chart, k0 (3, 9, 0, 5) sts, work Chart G 6 (6, 6, 7, 7) times, k0 (3, 9, 0, 5).

Continue as set, until you have done your final gusset dec, which leaves you with 1 purl st – 133 (139, 151, 155, 165) sts total.

Once you've decreased the gusset away, purling the final 3 sts tog to make a new seam st, you should have your original 110 sts plus 1 purl [111]. Maintain the purl as a seam st the whole way down the arm.

Dec 1 st on either side of seam st every 6th rnd, maintaining patt in Chart G, and the p1 faux seam as set until 61 (65, 69, 73, 77) sts rem. Work even until sleeve measures 14 (14½, 14, 15, 14½) inches, beginning last rnd with a p2tog – 60 (64, 68, 72, 76) sts.

Work in [k2, p2] rib for 2½ (2½, 3, 3, 3½) inches. BO loosely.

Complete 2nd sleeve to match.

Neck

Bear with me whilst we work a few short rows before we join in the round for the neck, as this builds up the back of the gansey.

Place 37 (40, 45, 50, 55) sts from the back of the sweater onto needles.

Row 1: Starting from back right, work in [k2, p2] rib across to the last stitch. Knit the last stitch together with the first stitch of the bound off edge. Turn.

It's OK to end with a k1, k2, or p1 as you increase your stitch count – just be sure to keep the continuity of the pattern columns as set in this first round.

Following 5 rows: Slip first st, continue in [k2, p2] rib as set to the last stitch and knit or purl the last stitch together with the next bound off stitch of the neck edge.

Sizes 32, 40, 48 only:
Rnd 7 (now working in the round): Work across the back sts, pick up 10 sts across left shoulder, m1, 6 sts across neck shaping, 37 (45, 55) sts across front, 6 sts across next neck shaping, m1, pick up 10 sts across right shoulder – 108 (124, 144) sts.

Sizes 36 & 44 only:
Rnd 7 (now working in the round): Work across the back sts, pick up 10 sts across left shoulder, 6 sts across neck shaping, 40 (50) across front neck, 6 sts across next shoulder shaping and 10 sts across right shoulder – 112 (132) sts.

All sizes:
Work [k2, p2] rib for 2 (2.5, 3, 3, 3.5) inches. Work 4 rnds garter sts (knit 1 rnd, p1 rnd). Bind off loosely.

Pick up the Back 45 sts. Starting from back right, [k2, p2] rib across 45 sts. Incorporate 1 st at the end. [46sts]. Turn. Slip all 1st sts; continue in [k2, p2] rib to end, again incorporating 1st at the end, by purling or knitting last st together with shoulder edge, st closest to where you land at end row. Turn. Do this for 6 rows. Pick up 10 sts from across each shoulder, and the 45 Front neck sts. (Neck = 116 sts).

Continue in [k2, p2] rib for 3 inches. Work 4 rows garter st (knit each row). BO loosely.

Finishing

See page 127 for blocking instructions.

Lizzie Lee—193

Chart A

194—*River Ganseys*

Chart B

Chart D

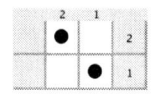

Lizzie Lee—195

Chart E
Chart F
Chart C

Chart G

Lizzie Lee—197

Fancy Gusset Chart

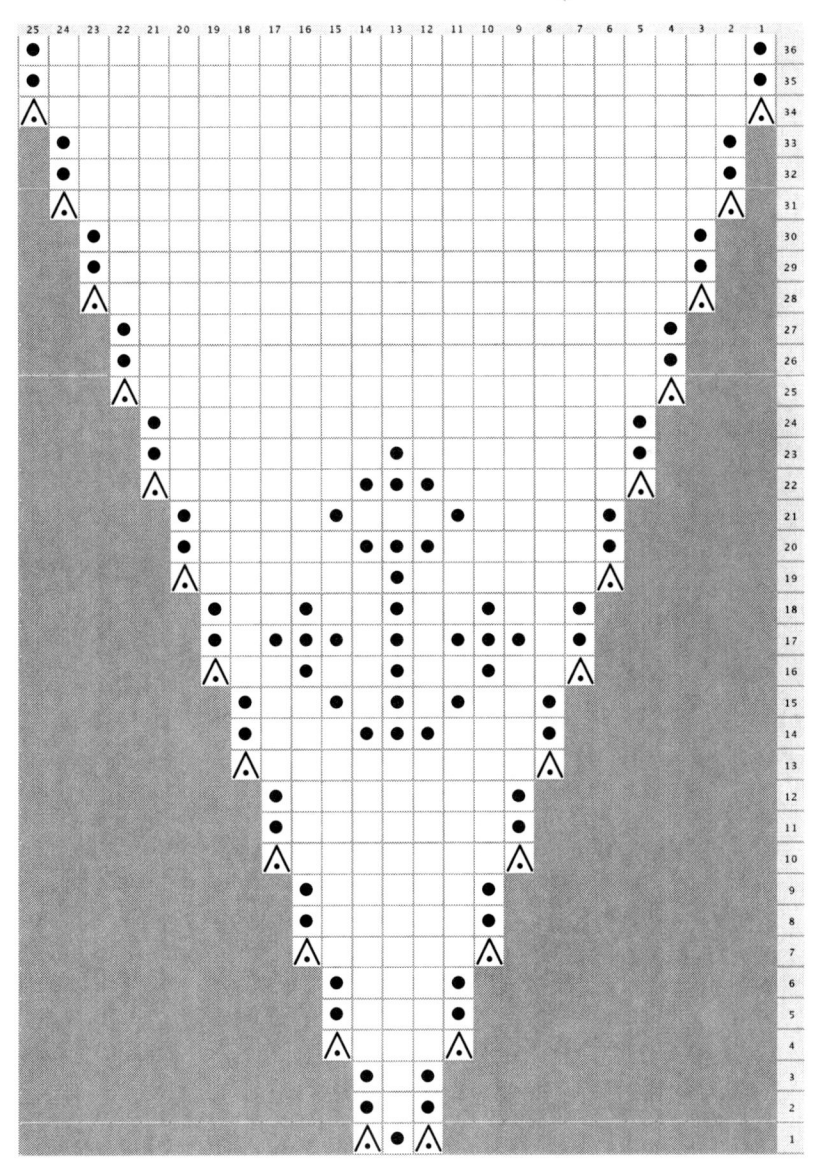

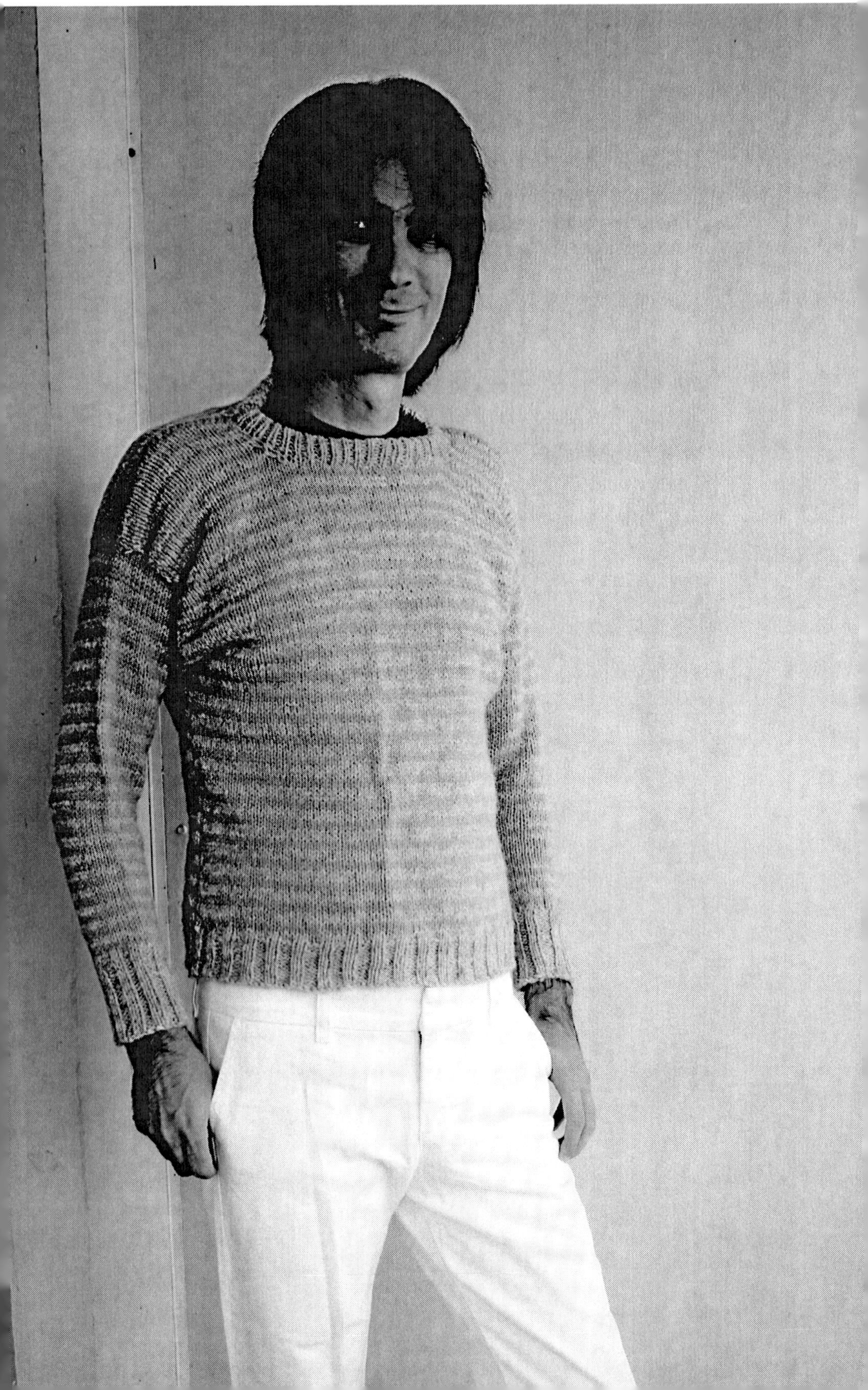

This simple, instant-gratification jumper is an interpretation of a "lost" type of nineteenth-century knitting. This Popped Un is a great way to work a fast knit that will teach you all the techniques you need for a gansey, like underarm gussets, knitting in the round, seam stitches, and working sleeves from the top down. But it is way faster than knitting a traditional gansey, or one of the "plain-vanilla" gansey recipes often found in books – they may indeed be simple, but are worked at knitted gansey gauge, so they can become rather boring, with no motifs or patterns to encourage you onwards.

These simple jumpers with bands of red or blue worked on a natural-colored background, were a common sight in the Dales. Yet there were no known extant examples of "Popped Uns," despite their being knitted in their thousands, for decades.

As I was researching for Cooperative Press's new edition of the classic Old Hand-Knitters of the Dales, I stumbled on an 1843 photograph in the collection of the National Galleries of Scotland, by the famous Edinburgh photographers, Hill and Adamson. I think this may be the only sighting of a Popped Un in the wild.

Finished Measurements

Chest: 30 (34, 38, 42, 46, 50) inches; shown in size 38; intended to be worn with 0 inches positive ease
Length: 27 (28, 29 30, 31, 32) inches
Sleeve length: 16½ (17, 17, 18, 18) inches

Materials

Blacker Yarns British Classic DK: 100% wool; 119 yds/109m per 50g ball
» [MC] Undyed Grey Blue-Faced Leicester 4 (5, 5, 6, 7, 8) balls
» [CC] True Blue Blue-Faced Leicester 4 (5, 5, 6, 7, 8) balls

US#6/4mm circular needle, or size needed to obtain gauge
US #3/3.25mm circular needle

Stitch holder or waste yarn

Gauge

18 sts and 24 rnds = 4 inches in stockinette on larger needles

Pattern Notes

Popped Uns, like most early Victorian stripey knitting, used blue or red on a natural background. Experiment with your own color combinations and motifs!

Stripe pattern

Rnds 1–3: Knit with MC.
Rnds 4–6: Knit with CC.

Pattern

Using MC and provisional cast on method, CO 132 (150, 168, 186, 204, 220) sts. Join into the round, taking care not to twist.

Rnd 1: [P1, k65 (74, 83, 92, 101, 109)] twice.

Work in stripe patt (see Pattern Notes) until sweater measures 10 inches (approx 12 CC stripes completed).

You may choose to make this slightly longer or shorter to accommodate a complete stripe pattern – the choice is yours.

Underarm gussets

Keep continuity of stripe pattern throughout.

Rnd 1: Before purled seam st, [m1p, knit the purled st, m1p, k65 (74, 83, 92, 101, 109)] twice – 136 (154, 172, 190, 208, 224) sts.

From now on, purl these 4 purl sts on every rnd.

Rnd 2: Work in patt as est.
Rnd 3: [P1, m1, k1, m1, p1, k65 (74, 83, 92, 101, 104)] twice – 136 (154, 172, 190, 208, 224) sts.

Continue to work in patt as est, maintaining the purl sts outlining your underarm gussets and making incs every 3rd rnd, placing those m1 incs as in Rnd 3 above – 4 sts added on each inc rnd – until you have 5 (7, 9, 11, 13, 15) sts between the 2 purls.

Work 2 rnds even.

Place armhole gussets each on a separate piece of waste yarn. Place 65 (74, 83, 92, 101, 109) front sts on a third length of waste yarn.

Back

Work flat in stockinette, maintaining stripe patt as est, until back measures 20½ (21, 22, 22½, 23, 24) inches (approx 28 CC stripes completed).

On next right facing row, place first 22 (26, 29, 32, 35, 37) sts on waste yarn, place central 21 (22, 25, 28, 31, 35) sts on stitch holder. You're going to work on the final 22 (26, 29, 32, 35, 37) sts.

Right Shoulder
Slip first st of every row, either knit- or purlwise.

With WS facing, and using CC:
Row 1: Purl.
Row 2: K1, sl1, k1, psso, work to end of row.

Maintaining stripe patt, rep these 2 rows 2(2, 3, 4, 4, 5) more times – 19 (23, 25, 27, 30, 31) sts.

Still maintaining patt, complete shoulder with no further shaping, working back and forth until work measures 24 (25, 26, 27, 28, 29) inches from cast on edge. Leave last row of sts on waste yarn or stitch holder.

You may choose to complete a half or full stripe for symmetry.

Left Shoulder
Place rem 22 (26, 29, 32, 35, 37) sts from left side onto needles. With RS facing, and keeping continuity of stripe patt:
Row 1: Knit.
Row 2: Sl1, p2tog, work to end of row.

Maintaining stripe patt, rep these 2 rows 2(2, 3, 4, 4, 5) more times – 19(23, 25, 27, 30, 31) sts. If you have completed a full or half stripe on the right shoulder, repeat this on the left.

Front

Place front sts on needles and work as for back until length is 21½ (21, 22, 22½, 23, 24) inches.

Shape Neck

On next RS row, place first 22 (26, 29, 32, 35, 37) sts on waste yarn, place central 21 (22, 25, 28, 31, 35) sts on stitch holder. You're going to work on the final 22 (26, 29, 32, 35, 37) sts.

Right Shoulder
Work as for Back Right Shoulder.

Left Shoulder
Work as for Back Left Shoulder.

Shoulder Treatment

Turn sweater inside out. We're going to bind off on the inside of the work.

Place on larger needle the 22 (26, 29, 32, 35, 37) sts from Front. Place on needle the first 25 sts from Back. Using yarn that corresponds with last stripe knitted, knit first st from back needle, knit first st from front needle, pass first st over second.

Continue to BO first a back, then a front st, until you have bound off all the sts. Weave in end.

Sleeve

With RS facing, and starting at the gusset, with the correct yarn to keep the continuity of the gusset stripes in place, pick up and knit the 5 (7, 9, 11, 13, 15) sts across the gusset, 42 (44, 48, 50, 53, 56) sts up the front, 42 (44, 48, 50, 53, 56) sts down the back of the armhole – 89 (95, 105, 111, 119, 127) sts total.

Maintaining stripe patt:
Rnd 1: Dec 1 stitch either side of the purl sts inside the gusset, knit to end of rnd – 85 (91, 101, 106, 115, 123) sts.
Rnd 2: Knit.

Rep these 2 rnds until you are left with a p, k, p within your gusset.

Next rnd: P3tog, knit to end. The remaining purl is now your faux seam and should be purled on every round.– 89 (95, 105, 111, 119, 127) sts.

From this point, dec 1 st either side of the purl, every other rnd, until 39 (41, 43, 49, 53, 57) sts rem.

Dec 1 st on next rnd – 38 (40, 42, 48, 52, 54, 56) sts rem.

Knit without further decs, until you are 2½ (3, 3, 3½, 3½, 3½) inches shy of desired length of sleeve.

With smaller mm needles and MC, work in 1×1 ribbing for 2½ (3, 3, 3½, 3½, 3½) inches. Bind off.

Knit second sleeve to match.

Welt

Using MC, pick up your live cast-on edge – 132 (150, 168, 186, 204, 220) sts. Work in 1×1 ribbing for 3 inches or desired length. Bind off.

Neckband

Using MC, pick up 3 (3, 4, 5, 5, 6) shoulder sts, 21 (22, 25, 26, 31, 35) front sts, 3 (3, 4, 5, 5, 6) shoulder sts, and 21 (22, 25, 26, 31, 35) back sts – 48 (50, 58, 66, 72, 82) sts total.

Work in 1×1 ribbing for 3 inches. Bind off loosely. Fold over and whip st down on the inside.

Finishing

See page 127 for blocking instructions.

Sunk Island

This child's gansey artfully uses every gansey technique you'll ever need to know. The patterns include waves, Humber Star, ropes, and ladder pattern with "hit and miss it" – moss stitch to you and me!

Finished Measurements

Chest: 24 (26, 28, 30, 32) inches; shown in size 28; intended to be worn 0 inches positive ease
Length: 15 (16, 18, 20, 22) inches

Materials

Frangipani 5 ply Guernsey: 1 (1, 1, 1, 2) cone(s); 100% wool; 1240 yds/500g shown in Ocean Deep colorway

US #1½/2.5mm circular needle
24-inch US #2/2.75mm circular needle, or size needed to obtain gauge
US #2/2.75mm needles: dpns, two circulars, or one long circular for magic loop (your choice)

Stitch markers
Waste yarn
Yarn needle

Gauge

27 sts and 36 rnds = 4 inches square in stockinette on larger needles

Pattern

Lower body

Using smaller needle, yarn held double, and Channel Island method, CO 154, (166, 180, 194, 208) sts. Join into the round, taking care not to twist the sts.

Continue with yarn doubled and work in garter st for 4 rnds. Break off one yarn and continue with yarn held single, weaving in ends as you go, working in [k2, p2] rib for 2 inches.

Next rnd: [Pm, m1p, k78 (84, 91, 98, 105)] twice – 156, (168, 182, 196, 210) sts.
The 2 purl sts you just made will be your faux seam sts, and will run the whole way up the gansey's body.

Next rnd: Work in patt as est, increasing evenly by 4 (8, 6, 8, 6) sts – 160 (176, 188, 204, 216) sts.

Change to larger needle. Work in stockinette (maintaining faux seam sts) until body measures 3 (4, 7, 8, 10) inches.
Purl 1 rnd.
Keep markers in place and for rest of body, continue to purl the seam sts after markers.

Establish transitional pattern

Work Chart A across front and back, maintaining 2 faux seam sts as you go, until body measures 5½ (6½, 8, 10, 11) inches.

Underarm gusset

Begin underarm gusset, keeping Chart A patt as set between the seam sts.

At seam st: M1p, knit original purled seam st, m1p. This knit stitch will be the lower tip of the underarm gusset (diamond shape). Continue to purl the 2 sts on either side of it as you progress, working the gusset in stockinette between the 2 purl sts. Work 79 (87, 91, 101, 107) sts in patt as set; when you reach the second marker, again m1p, knit your existing purl st, m1p.

Continue in patt as set, using 2 purl sts either side of gusset as outline. Inc 2 sts at beg and end of gusset, (after 1st purl st, before last) every 4 rnds until you have 11 (13, 13, 13, 15) sts between the 2 purls, then place gusset sts and the 2 purl seam sts on waste yarn.

Setup rnd for Main Pattern: *K7 (11, 14, 18, 21), pm; k20, pm; k25, pm; k20 pm; k7, (11,14, 18, 21), pm; work gusset sts as set, rep from *.

Main pattern body

At end of Chart A, work Chart B. Establish main patt. If it helps, use markers to signal beg of each section of patt, until patt is established.

Continue working gussets inc every 4 rnds. Cable 6 every 6th rnd. Cable 6 by slipping 3 st to cable needle, hold at front, k3, k3 from cable needle.

When you have 11 (13, 13, 13, 15) sts on the gusset, work 3 more rnds in patt; then divide for armhole. Place Front Body sts and both gussets and gusset purl sts on waste yarn.

Back body

Work Back of gansey, cabling the rope patterns every 6th rnd, and continuing Chart B. When you have completed all rows of Chart B, rep once more from beginning and including Rnd 1 of Main Patt, so you have 2 Humber stars, one above the other.

At end of Chart B, place Back sts on waste yarn. To save time later, place first third of your sts on one length of waste yarn for shoulder, place central

Variations

Part of the fun of ganseys is that no two need be the same. Experiment, and try out variations if you feel like it.

- » Work your cast-on row in a contrasting gansey yarn.
- » Knit initials above the welt, before pattern starts. There are plenty of knitters' alphabet charts online, in books, or make up your own! I use a chart from a seventeenth-century embroiderers' handbook, *The Scholehouse for the Needle* for my lettering!
- » Knit sleeves plain from top of arm. Or, use hit and miss it (moss stitch) on either side of the cable for a heavily textured and warmer sleeve, maintaining cable down arm. Some ganseys break the pattern at the elbow, some continue down to the cuff. You could place the garter ladders down the sleeves, or maybe do the wave pattern followed by a cables divided by the garter ladders the whole way round the sleeves.
- » For larger sizes, add to hit and miss it either side of central pattern panel. For smaller, decrease number of sts cast on, taking from hit and miss it.
- » You can make a more decorative seam stitch by making a 2- or 3-stitch wide band of hit and miss it, on either side of the purl. This will affect the fit of the gansey but not enough to write home about!

third on another piece of waste yarn for neck, and final third on a third length waste yarn, for other shoulder. If you have an odd number of sts when dividing into thirds, add the extra sts into the central (neck) section.

Front body

Work Front as Back, continuing in patt and cabling 3F each 6th rnd. At the end of chart B – approx 15 (16, 18, 20, 22) inches – divide live sts into thirds, same as you did for the back. Place the final third for shoulder onto larger needle, with needle's tip pointing inwards towards the neck. (I find this easier to do with straight needles not dpns or circs). Place the corresponding Back shoulder sts onto other side of the larger needle.

Shoulder saddle

On lefthand side of your work, provisionally CO 12 sts. (I use crochet provisional cast on – but use provisional cast on of your choice!)

Follow Chart C. At end of each row of 12 shoulder saddle sts, incorporate 1 st from front or back, by knitting or purling together with last st of the 12 shoulder saddle sts. (Knit or purl according to chart C). Work back and forth, working cable between garter st ridges down from neck towards top of armhole, consuming 1 st from Front body or Back body shoulder at end each row until all live Front and Back sts are consumed. Continue to cable 3F every 6th row as you go. Keep going until you reach top armhole, and have just the 12 shoulder saddle sts on your needles.

Sleeves (both alike)

Slip 12 live shoulder saddle sleeves onto larger needle. On same needle, pick up 30 (30, 30, 30, 35) sts along Front body, place 11 (13, 13, 13, 15) live underarm gusset sts onto needle, knit across them, purl the 2 purl sts; pick up 30 (30, 30, 30, 35) sts along Back body; pm.

Set the patt: continue Chart C down the central 12 sts from shoulder saddle. Dec 2 sts within the gusset diamond every 2 rnds, until only seam sts and 1 knit st remain, then p3tog. This purl st will be your underarm seam st. Now, continue dec 1 sts either side of seam st every 2nd (4th, 4th, 4th, 4th) rnd, maintaining cable every 6th rnd.

Either continue cable right down to wrist, or knit cuff completely in 2×2 rib. Dec until 50 (52, 52, 52, 56) sts rem. Knit until sleeve is 2 inches short of desired length.

Change to smaller needles and knit cuff in 2×2 rib for 2 inches or to desired length. BO loosely.

Neckband

With larger needles and RS facing, pick up central third of sts front, make 4 sts by picking up between the existing live sts, knit across 12 live shoulder saddle sts (maintaining ladder and cable patt), make 4 sts by picking up between live sts, pick up back sts, make 4, knit across 12 live shoulder sts, make 4. Work in 2×2 rib until neckband is 4 inches or depth you prefer. BO loosely. Maintain the two ropes and ladders either side of them, in pattern, up into the neckband. Fold down and sew in place. These are the only sewn stitches on a gansey!

Finishing

See page 127 for blocking instructions.

206—*River Ganseys*

Chart A

Chart C

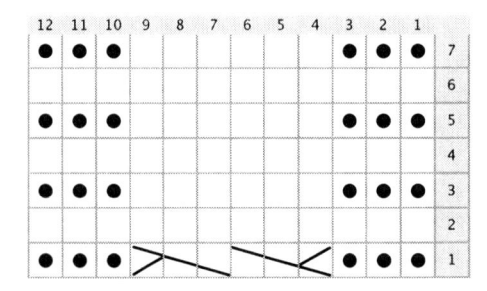

Sunk Island—207

Chart B

Alphabets for All Ganseys

Blank Chart

Use the blank at right to chart out the three initials you will use in your project.

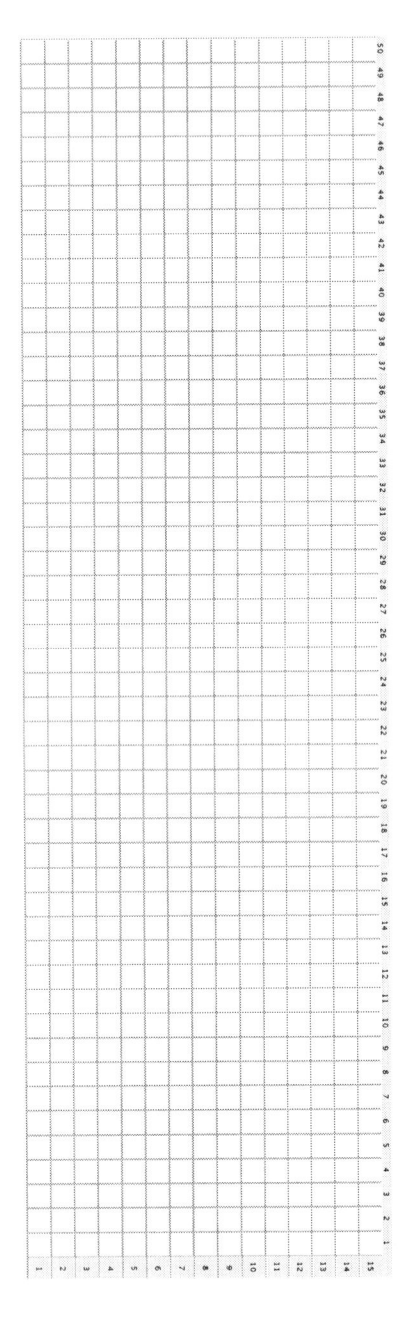

Alphabets for All Ganseys—209

Alphabet 1

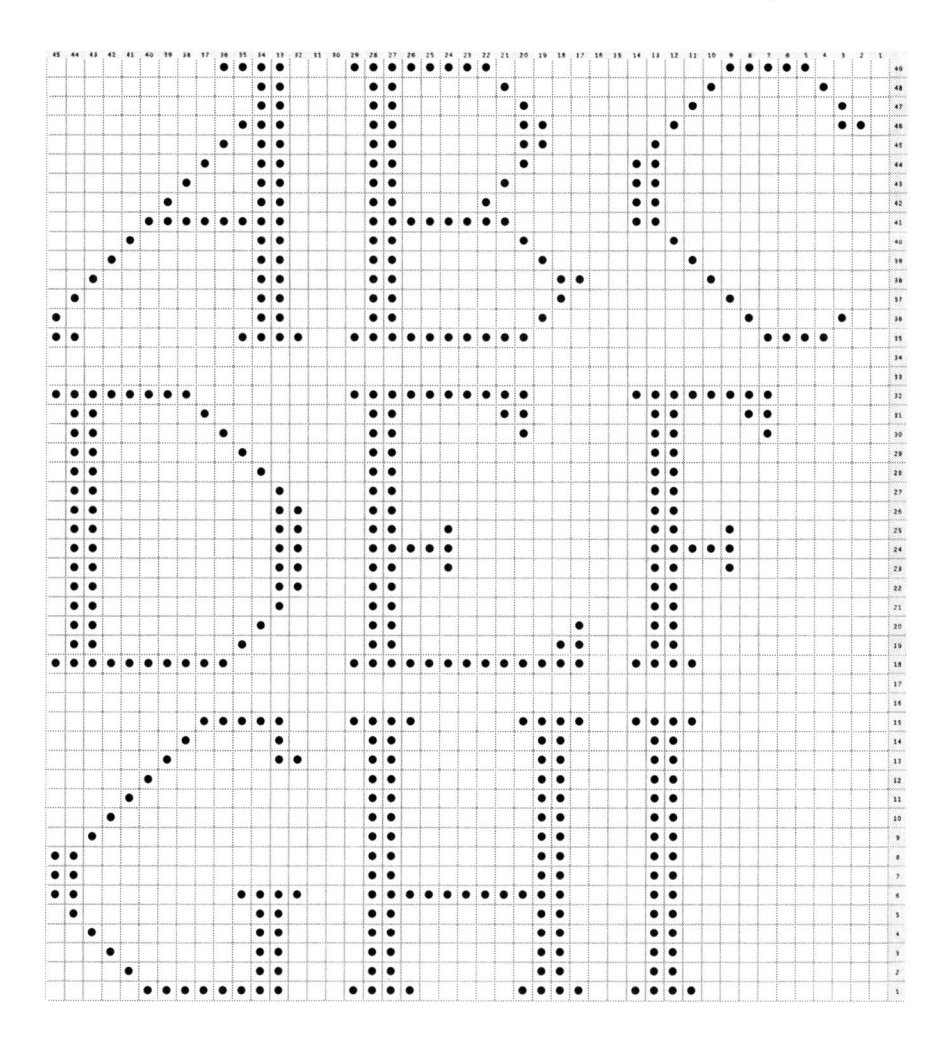

210—*River Ganseys*

Alphabets for All Ganseys—211

Alphabet 2

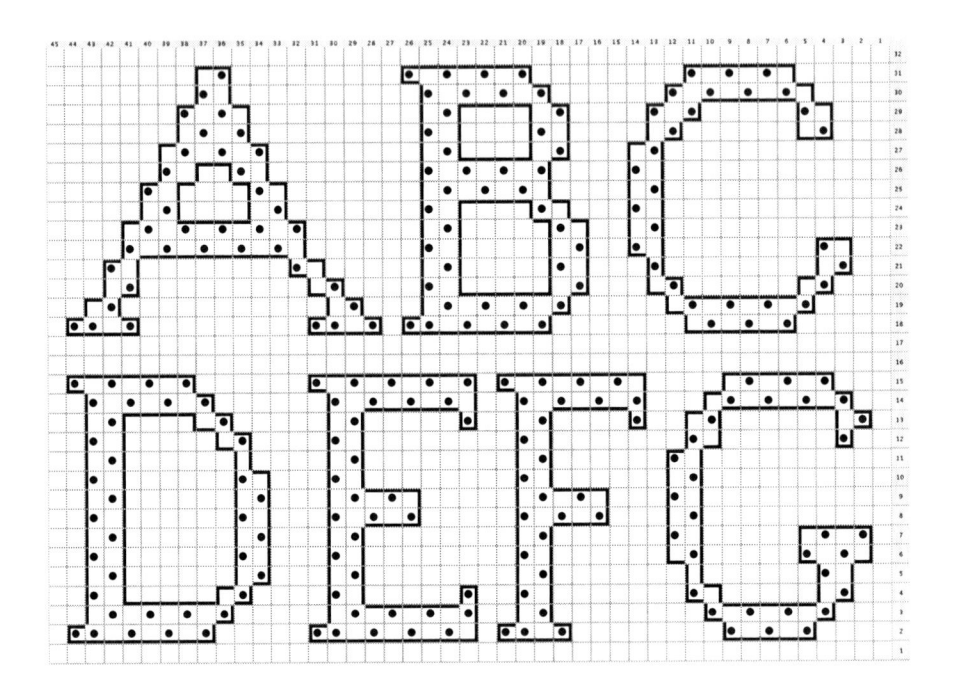

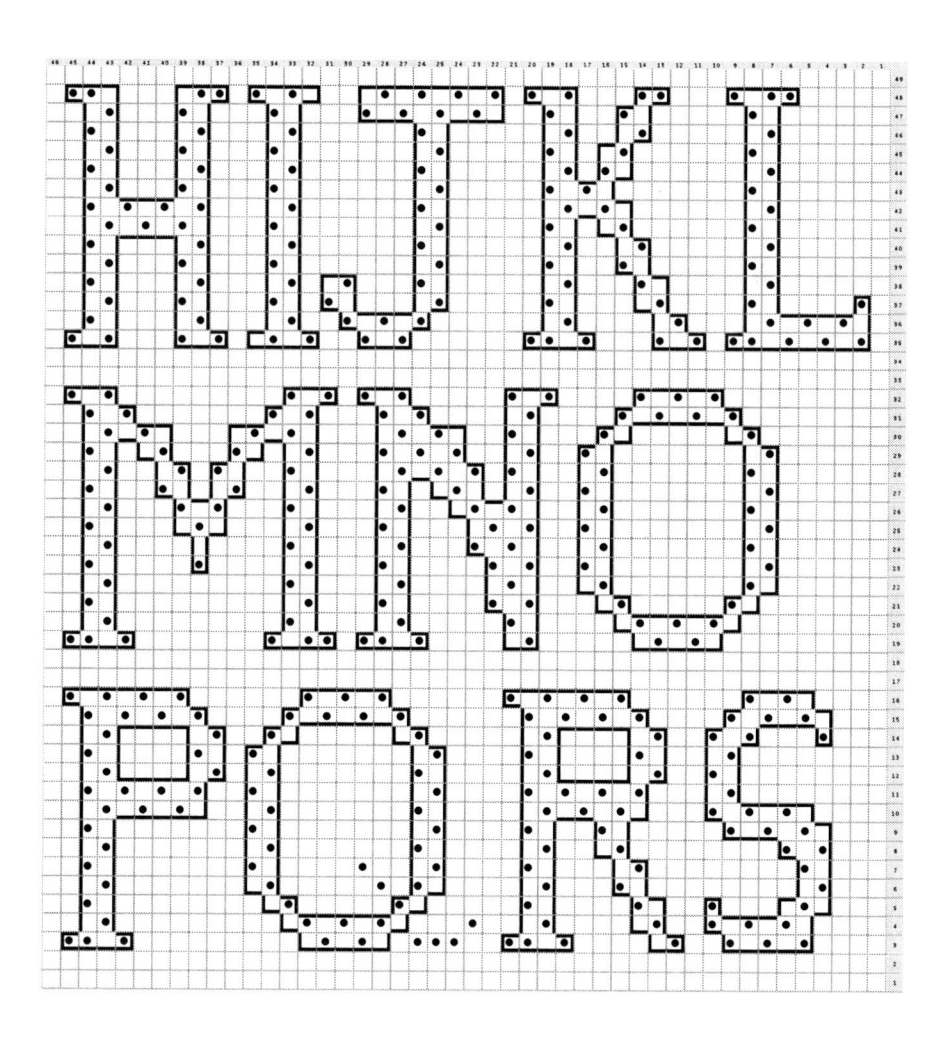

Alphabets for All Ganseys—213

214—*River Ganseys*

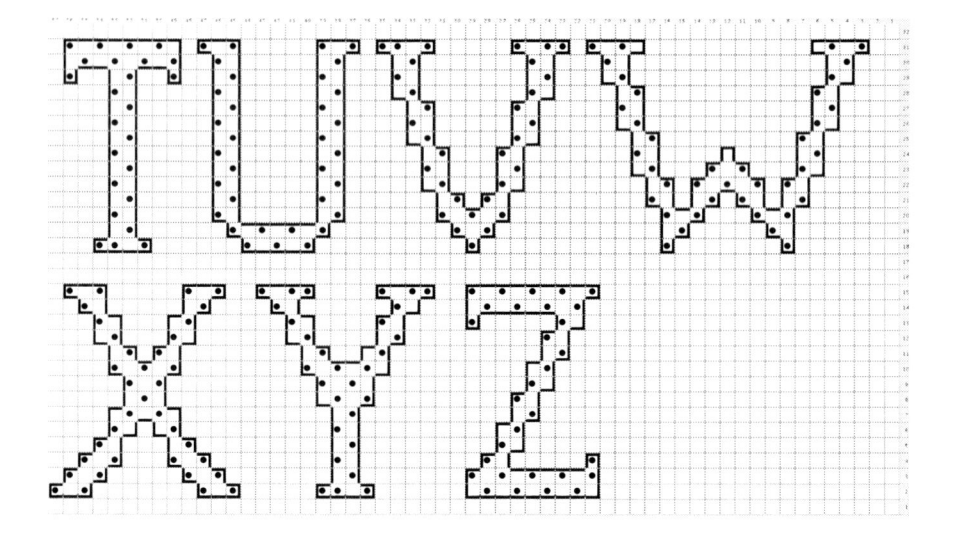

Abbreviations

approx	approximately
beg	beginning
BO	bind off
CC	contrasting color
CO	cast on
dec(s)	decrease(s)
dpn(s)	double-pointed needle(s)
est	established
inc(s)	increase(s)
k	knit
k2tog	right-leaning decrease: knit 2 sts together
m1	make one (increase)
m1L	use tip of left needle to lift strand between sts from front to back; knit loop through the back loop (increase)
m1p	use tip of left needle to lift strand between sts from back to front; purl loop (increase)
m1R	use tip of left needle to lift strand between sts from back to front; knit loop (increase)
MC	main color
p	purl
p2tog	purl 2 sts together
p3tog	purl 3 sts together
patt	pattern
pm	place marker
rem	remain(ing)
rep	repeat
rnd(s)	round(s)
RS	right side
sl	slip
ssk	left-leaning decrease: slip 2 sts knitwise one at a time, then knit them together through the back loop
st(s)	stitches
WS	wrong side

Techniques & Symbols

Cast on tutorials

» Channel Island cast on:
  bit.ly/17B3FJT
» Crochet provisional cast on:
  stitchdiva.com/tutorials/knitting/provisional-cast-on

Master Chart Key

Symbol	Name	Description
	No Stitch	Placeholder - no stitch made
	Knit	Knit stitch
	Purl	Purl stitch
	M1P	Lift bar between next two sts, and purl it
	c2 over 2 left	Sl 2 to CN, hold in front, k2, k2 from CN
	c2 over 2 right	Sl 2 to CN, hold in back, k2, k2 from CN
	c3 over 3 left	Sl3 to CN, hold in front, k3, k3 from CN
	c4 over 4 left	Sl 4 to CN, hold in front, k4, k4 from CN

Bibliography

Knitting

Brown-Reinsel, Beth. *Knitting Ganseys*. Interweave Press, 1993.

Colbeck, Maurice. "Gran Taught Her To Knit at the Age of Three." *The Dalesman*, Vol. 57, January 1996.

Compton, Rae. *The Complete Book of Traditional Guernsey and Jersey Knitting*. Batsford Books, 1995.

Douglas-Kay, Freda M. "These Daleswomen Still Use Knitting Sticks." *The Dalesman*, Vol. 18, November 1956.

Elliot Scrivenor, M. Collection of Knitting and Crochet Receipts, 1903.

Fletcher, Terry. "Traditional Purls of Wisdom." *The Dalesman*, Vol. 57, June 1995, pp. 58-60.

Hartley, Marie, and Joan Ingilby. *The Old Hand-Knitters of the Dales*. (Originally published Dalesman, 1951.) New edition, ed. Pen Lister Hemingway. Cooperative Press, 2013.

Hartley, Marie, and Joan Ingilby. "Quest for the Hand-Knitters." *The Dalesman*, August 1970, pp. 424-426.

Kinder, Kathleen. "Knitting in the Dales Way." *The Dalesman*, Vol. 42, February 1981, p. 908.

Macdonald, Anne L. *No Idle Hands: The Social History of American Knitting*. Ballantine Books, 1988.

Norbury, James. *Knit with Norbury*. Odhams Press, [n.d., 1950s?].

Norbury, James. *Traditional Knitting Patterns*. Dover, 1962.

Pearson, Michael. *Traditional Knitting*. Collins, 1984.

Rutt, Richard. *A History of Hand Knitting*. Batsford, 1987.

Simon, Helen. "Love Tokens for Knitters." *Yorkshire Life*, Vol. 39, No 7, Feb 1985.

Starmore, Alice, and Anne Matheson. *Knitting from the British Islands*. Bell & Hyman, 1983.

Thompson, Gladys. *Patterns for Guernseys, Jerseys and Arans*. Dover, 1979.

Thompson, G. "When Did the Dales Knitters Begin to Knit." *The Dalesman*, Vol. 47, Nov 1985, p.650.

Van der Klift-Tellegen, Henriette. *Knitting from the Netherlands*. Dryad, 1987.

Vogue Knitting: The Ultimate Knitting Book. Sixth & Spring Books, 2008.

Zimmermann, Elizabeth. *Knitting Without Tears.* Simon & Schuster, 1971.

Spinning and Textile History

Amos, Alden. *The Alden Amos Big Book of Handspinning.* Interweave Press, 2001.

Barker, Malcolm. "Wonders of Yorkshire: The Life and Works of Marie Hartley and Joan Ingilby." *The Yorkshire Journal*, Spring 1996, p. 86ff.

Brears, Peter C.D. "The York Spinning Wheel Makers." *Furniture History*, Vol. XIV, 1978, 19–24.

Crowder, Etta May Lacey. "Pioneer Memoirs from Palo Alto County." *Iowa Journal of History and Politics*, Vol. 46, Issue 2, April 1948.

Franquemont, Abby. *Respect The Spindle.* Interweave Press, 2009.

Gibson-Roberts, Priscilla A. *High Whorling.* Nomad Press, 1998.

Goodwin, Jill. *A Dyer's Manual.* Pelham Books, 1982.

Heaton, Herbert. *The Yorkshire Woollen and Worsted Industries.* Oxford Clarendon Press, 1965.

Lowry, Priscilla. *The Secrets of Silk: From the Myths and Legends to the Middle Ages.* St. John's Press, 2003.

Lowry, Priscilla. *The Secrets of Silk: From Textiles to Fashion.* St. John's Press, 2004.

Robson, Deborah, and Carol Ekarius. *The Fleece and Fiber Sourcebook.* Storey Publishing, 2009.

Ross, Mabel. *Encyclopedia of Handspinning.* Batsford, 1988.

Maritime and Yorkshire History

Anonymous. "Sir J. Franklin and the Arctic Crews." *The Morning Post* (London), January 1, 1852.

Anonymous. *Souvenir of the Bi-Centenary of the York Blue-Coat Boys' and the Grey-Coat Girls' Schools.* York, 1945.

Butlers, Susan, and Ken Powls. *Howden, an East Riding Market Town.* Gilberdyke Local History Society, 1995.

Cappe, Catharine. *An Account of Two Charity Schools For the Education of Girls; and of a Female Friendly Society in York; Interspersed with reflections on Charity Schools and Friendly Societies in General.* William Blanchard, 1800.

Cappe, Catharaine. *Observations on Charity Schools, Female Friendly Societies and Other Subjects Connected with the views of the Ladies Committee.* Blanchard, 1805.

Carr, Marion. *Call of the Running Tide: Girl Aloft in the Days of Trade.* Maldon, 1983.

Clarke, Mike. *The Aire & Calder Navigation.* Tempus, 1999.

Credland, Arthur G. *Humber Shipping*. Hull Maritime Museum, 1991.

Day, Nicholas J., comp. and ed. *Humber Keels by John Frank and the Sloop Men of South Ferriby*. River & John Frank Enterprises, 1996.

Day, Nicholas J., ed. *Sloopmen of South Ferriby: Memoirs of Fred Harness, Cyril Harrison and T.H. Birkill*. The Humber Keel and Sloop Preservation Society, 1996.

Duckham, Baron F. *The Yorkshire Ouse*. David & Charles, 1967.

Duckham, Baron F. *The Inland Waterways of East Yorkshire 1700-1900*. East Yorkshire Local History Society, 1973.

Fletcher, Harry. *A Life on the Humber: Keeling to Shipbuilding*. Faber & Faber, 1975.

Frank, Peter. *Yorkshire Fisherfolk*. Phillimore, 2002.

Gill, Alec. *Superstitions and Folk Magic in Hull's Fishing Community*. Hutton Press, 1993.

Gill, Alec. *Good Old Hessle Road*. Hutton Press, 1991.

Gosney, Ron, and Rosemary Bowyer. *The Sailing Ships and Mariners of Knottingley*. Ron Gosney & Sons, [n.d.].

Hartley, Marie, and Joan Ingilby. *The Yorkshire Dales*. Aldine, 1963.

Hartley, Marie, and Joan Ingilby. *Fifty Years in the Yorkshire Dales*. Smith Settle, 1995.

Jones, Pat. *Navigation on the Yorkshire Derwent*. The Oakwood Press, 2000.

Morgan-Rees, David. "Heritage of Patience." *Yorkshire Life*, Vol. 37, February 1983.

Morgan-Rees, David. "Marie Hartley: A Distinguished Yorkshire Artist-Writer in a New Light." *The Dalesman*, Vol. 54., November 1992.

Ogden, John. *Yorkshire's River Aire*. Terence Dalton Ltd, Suffolk, 1976.

Pearson, F. H. *The Early History of Hull Steam Shipping*. 1896.

Schofield, Fred, and Terence Dalton. *Humber Keels and Keelmen*. Suffolk, 1988.

Strang, Nelle. *Prairie Smoke*. Unpublished MS.

Ulyatt, Michael. *Flying Sail: Humber Keels and Sloops*. Mag Pye Books, 1995.

Miscellaneous

Masterson, Bat. "Ben Thompson and Other Noted Gunmen." *Human Life* (Boston), 1907–1908. Republished in W. B. (Bat) Masterson. *Famous Gunfighters of the Western Frontier: Wyatt Earp, Doc Holliday, Luke Short and Others*. Dover Publications, 2009.

About Penelope Lister Hemingway

PENELOPE LISTER HEMINGWAY WRITES FOR VARIOUS GENEALOGY and knitting magazines in the UK and US, and edited a new edition of *Old Hand-Knitters of the Dales* for Cooperative Press (2014).

She has a degree and PGCE from The University of Birmingham, where she specialized in Old Norse and Old English, as well as eighteenth-century literature and also studied at the University of Northern Colorado. She was born in the West Riding of Yorkshire; and descends from a long line of wool weavers, and pioneers of aniline dyeing, as well as Dales knitters, farmers, and inland mariners. She has five sons, and when she is not reverse engineering nineteenth-century knitting, or in an archive researching the history of knitting, can be found spinning and dyeing.

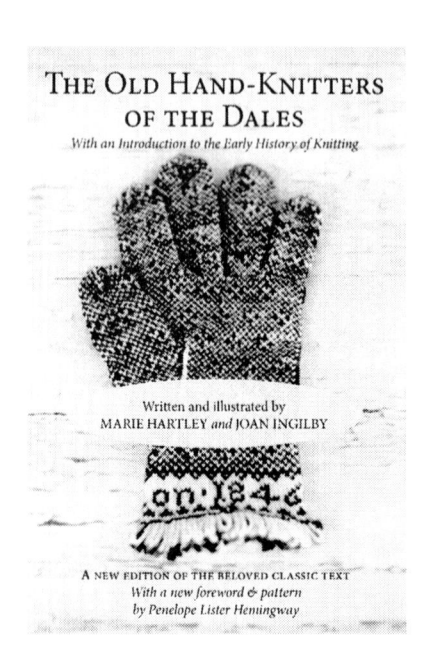

More fascinating reading on the history of knitting can be found in Old Hand-Knitters of the Dales, *brought back into print under the expert editing of Penelope Lister Hemingway and published by Cooperative Press.*

Acknowledgments

The author wishes to thank the following individuals and institutions:

Jeff Cowton, MBE., Curator, the Wordsworth Trust, Grasmere, Cumbria,
Dr Alec Gill, MBE
Elizabeth Green Musselman, editing beyond the call of duty
Fiona Jenkinson, Beverley Curator, East Riding Museums
Carol Kocian, for her expertise on the *General Carleton* knitted artefacts
Shannon Okey, long-suffering publisher
Brian Peeps, Humber Keel and Sloop Preservation Society
Andi Smith, designer, tech editor and Yorkshirewoman extraordinaire
Janet Tierney, Goole Museum
Elżbieta Wróblewska, The Polish Maritime Museum, Gdansk

❧

Beamish Museum
The Dales Countryside Museum
Filey Museum
Goole Museum
Hull Maritime Museum
The Humber Keel and Sloop Preservation Society
The Leeds & Liverpool Canal Society
Polperro Heritage Press
The Scarborough Maritime Heritage Centre
The Wordsworth Trust, Dove Cottage, Grasmere, Cumbria
York Art Gallery & Museums Trust
Yorkshire Archaeological Society, Leeds
Yorkshire Inland Waterways Museum. Goole Long Preston Heritage Group

About Cooperative Press

partners in publishing

Cooperative Press (formerly anezka media) was founded in 2007 by Shannon Okey, a voracious reader as well as writer and editor, who had been doing freelance acquisitions work, introducing authors with projects she believed in to editors at various publishers.

Although working with traditional publishers can be very rewarding, there are some books that fly under their radar. They're too avant–garde, or the marketing department doesn't know how to sell them, or they don't think they'll sell 50,000 copies in a year.

5,000 or 50,000. Does the book *matter* to that 5,000? Then it should be published.

In 2009, Cooperative Press changed its named to reflect the relationships we have developed with authors working on books. We work together to put out the best quality books we can and share in the proceeds accordingly.

Thank you for supporting independent publishers and authors.

cooperativepress.com